FREEDOM
IN THE
FIGHT

FREEDOM
IN THE
FIGHT

**DAILY REFLECTIONS FOR
RECOVERY**

SCOTT ABRAMS, M.D.

TRISTAN PUBLISHING
MINNEAPOLIS

Library of Congress Cataloging-in-Publication Data
Names: Abrams, Scott, 1973-author.
Title: Freedom in the Fight / written by Scott Abrams.
Description: Golden Valley, MN : TRISTAN Publishing, [2020]
Identifiers: LCCN 2018036137 | ISBN 9781939881199 (pbk.)
Subjects: LCSH: Bible—Meditations.
Classification: LCC BS491.5 .A27 2019 | DDC 242/.5—dc23
LC record available at https://lccn.loc.gov/2018036137

TRISTAN Publishing, Inc.
2355 Louisiana Avenue North
Golden Valley, MN 55427

Text copyright © 2020, Scott Abrams
ISBN 978-1-939881-19-9
Printed in Canada
First Printing

To learn more about all of our books with a message,
visit us at **www.TRISTANpublishing.com**

To my loving family—Barb, Jake,
and Maggie—who have been there
through the good times and the bad.
Though I love you dearly, I can't
promise perfection. I can promise,
however, that today, I'll fight the good
fight. Tomorrow, I'll do the same.
~ Scott

INTRODUCTION

In 2014 I found myself in an epic disaster of my own making. As my addiction to pain medications became something I could no longer hide, my marriage fell apart and I had to leave my job as an ER physician. With my career evaporating and my family life in shambles, I was on my way to chemical dependency treatment—and I was lost.

How could a Christian act this way? I grew up believing in God. I was more than familiar with the Bible. I knew I was supposed to be a new creation in Christ, but I didn't feel like a new creation. I was hopelessly enslaved to my destructive appetites. I had been here before and had once claimed deliverance from my addiction. *How could it come back? What did that mean for my faith? Where was God?*

While abusing drugs, I prayed again and again for God to take my addiction from me. I begged Him to make me want good, while I enjoyed bad. When He did not do this, I became bitter and disillusioned. *Did God abandon me? Is He even real?* Eventually, I came to understand that my prayers went unanswered because I had been unwilling to do anything to obey. I just wanted God's magical fix. Embracing this fanciful view of faith, I remained unwilling to do anything; and I discovered that if nothing changes, nothing changes.

In treatment, I asked God what I must do to change. This was the beginning of transformation for me: to go to God, asking what I must do to obey. He insisted that I must daily do whatever it takes to deny myself and follow Him. So, I started.

This devotional was born out of that painful encounter. I do not do it perfectly; but now I daily pick up my Bible, read, pray, meditate, and journal about God's Word and what it means to my life. This devotional is a chronicle of my own daily walk with God. It is not a declaration that I have it all figured out. It is, however, an (imperfect) example of something we are all meant to do daily. The Christian life is a battle that is not won by participating only for an hour on Sunday morning.

You will still fail. I will too. We won't be made flawless in this life, but if we want to change and if we want to know God, this is how we do it. We must daily do whatever it takes, no matter how painful or radical, to turn our gaze from self to God, following Him. Growth and change are rarely instantaneous. This is a life-long process that will not be completed in this life. God, however, is always faithful to draw near to us when we draw near to Him. Despite our struggles, in daily following Christ, we can experience freedom in the fight.

Day 1

BORN OF SCANDAL

*Now the birth of Jesus Christ took place in this way. When his
mother Mary had been betrothed to Joseph, before they came
together she was found to be with child from the Holy Spirit.*

MATTHEW 1:18

I find it telling that God began Jesus' time on earth in what seemed to
us like disgrace and humility. I cannot miss the reality that He was born
in circumstances that we would consider shameful. I am also quite sure
that this did not escape God. It was his purpose to allow Jesus' earthly
arrival to be underwhelming. He chose everything about Jesus' origins to
be the exact opposite of what everyone would expect.

This should not be surprising, based on the many flawed people God
chose to use throughout the Bible. It seems that God is pleased to use
people and situations that many of us would look down upon today. David
killed a man to cover up an affair with his wife. Peter denied Christ. Paul
killed Christians.

With that, suddenly, I do not feel quite so disqualified by my own
defects. God is not afraid of the weak and the needy. It is the poor and
humble who need God and thus, inherit his kingdom. The defective seem
to be God's kind of people. I am happy to count myself as one of His. I
have been there, at the bottom, when life seemed hopeless. My thoughts
were lower than low. *I am done. I have killed everything good in life, and I
have destroyed any chance I ever had to be what I wanted to be. God cannot
do anything with this.*

Jesus, however, came looking for the sick and needy. To me, He says,
*"Just watch what I can do with your mess. You think you have screwed up
beyond repair? Ha! Do not think for a moment that I cannot redeem your
life and make something out of your disaster. You may feel that life is over. It
will be one day; but now, rise up from your ashes. Abandon yourself and
follow me. Just watch what I can do . . ."*

Day 2

THE WEIGHT OF PRIDE

*And her husband Joseph, being a just man and unwilling
to put her to shame, resolved to divorce her quietly.*

MATTHEW 1:19

When Joseph found out Mary was pregnant, he made the dignified decision to quietly end things with her. He could have publicly embarrassed her to avoid his own disgrace, but he decided to leave quietly. To this, God said no and commanded Joseph to marry Mary. God was apparently more concerned with His plan than He was with Joseph's dignity.

Like Joseph, I have preferred to hide my shame. The last thing I want to do is talk about my failures. It's precisely through my failures, however, that God works in me and in the lives of those around me. It is through my humility and my need that I find God—and that God finds me. I must learn not to sweep pain away, but rather allow God to work through my failures.

If I want to try to maintain my pride and dignity, God allows this. To my dignity, God says, *"Go ahead. Carry your vain attempt at pride. I will not carry it for you. When you are ready to abandon pride, and give to me your disaster, I will bear that weight for you. Then your burden will be light. Or . . . keep your pride and be crushed by the weight of it."*

When I visit our local jail, it is not as a minister. It is as a fellow struggler who, like each inmate I meet, needs God. God uses my need and defect to speak into the lives of others who have need and defect too. I do not need a dramatic story. I just need to be honest about whatever defect I have. I may struggle with anxiety, anger, resentment, greed, pornography, or affirmation. Whatever my struggle is, the inmates have similar struggles. When I am honest and use my defect to turn me to God, He will always use it to help draw others toward Him.

Day 3

THE WISE MAN

> *Now after Jesus was born . . . wise men from the east came*
> *to Jerusalem, saying, "Where is he . . . ? For we saw his*
> *star when it rose and have come to worship him."*

MATTHEW 2:1–2

In Matthew's book, we read the only account of those whom he refers to as wise men. These learned men, Matthew reports, read of Christ's birth in the stars. Interpreting some truth about His divine origins, they traveled from afar, bearing lavish gifts and bowing down to Him. In short, they discovered a truth and responded appropriately. In theory—in my heart, I want to be wise like these men. In reality, I have more often been a fool.

There are those who believe that I am the sum of my knowledge: *"If you just know the truth, you will act accordingly."* I stand as evidence that this theory is not universally true. I don't think I've ever engaged in any pursuit of my flesh while thinking it a right behavior. Mine has never been a problem of *knowing* right, but rather, *behaving* right.

Knowing a route may be necessary to get somewhere; but knowledge of a route is not the same as traveling the route. Solomon insisted that *"The fear of the Lord is the beginning of wisdom"* (Proverbs 9:10). He described it as the *beginning* because *fear of God* is the right starting point, but it is not the end. Wisdom is when right knowledge leads to right action.

I have *known* right but just *wanted* wrong more. I have found destruction, not out of ignorance, but simply out of preference. Wisdom makes the sacrifice up front, reaping the rewards later. Foolishness wants pleasure now, not caring about the consequences.

The wise men bear witness that it is not enough just to know *of God*. If I really want to know God, I must follow Him. If I find God distant, despite all my knowledge, I must choose to obey Him. My knowledge is useless if it does not affect my behavior.

Day 4

THE CORRUPTION OF POWER

> *Then Herod, when he saw that he had been tricked by the*
> *wise men, became furious, and . . . killed all the male children*
> *in Bethlehem . . . who were two years old or under.*
>
> **MATTHEW 2:16**

As I read today's passage, I reacted in revulsion at Herod, the murderer of infants, but I could see no immediate lesson for myself. Then, I was struck with a particularly painful childhood memory.

When I was seven or eight, I was picked on for being overweight. Before you give me any sympathy, know that I, in turn, picked on one beneath me in the pecking order. I cruelly taunted this other boy, reducing him to tears. I vividly remember the horror of realizing what I had become. Even as a young child, I could see that I had become that which I despised.

It is easy to insist that *power corrupts.* Herod committed horrific atrocities because of it. That power did not *cause* Herod's evil though. It simply *exposed* it. I suspect the biggest difference between Herod and me is not the amount of evil in us but in the amount of power we have possessed.

Like Herod's, my flesh had and still has the capacity for tremendous evil. What horror would I commit if I knew I could get away with it? Unfortunately, I have seen what I am capable of when I believe myself to be immune.

Some insist that because I am a Christian, evil no longer resides in me. Denying that my flesh is evil though, does not make me immune to evil. It just blinds me. In denial, I succumb to my blinding pride.

Am I then destined for evil deeds? No, it is always my choice to follow my flesh life or my spirit life. It is only in daily choosing God that I can rise above the corruption of my flesh. I am not destined for evil, but the solution does not lie in denying my capacity for it. The solution is in turning to the One who can deliver me from myself.

Day 5

THE KINGDOM OF SELF

> *In those days John the Baptist came preaching in the wilderness of Judea, "Repent, for the kingdom of heaven is at hand."*
>
> **MATTHEW 3:1–2**

I am no prophet, but I am pretty good at seeing the destructive behavior in the lives of those around me. I am gifted at recognizing stupidity . . . when it is not mine. When it's my stupidity, well, that's different. I have justifications that no one else has, right? It's different when it is me.

As a Christian, I'm often tempted to think of the truth as something I need to apply to the disasters around me, but I tend to ignore its application in my own life. When John says, "Repent, for the kingdom of heaven is at hand," I think of the poor choices my neighbor is making. John's message, however, is for me. John insisted that the kingdom of heaven came to replace my own kingdom of self.

It is, after all, the kingdom of self that blinds me to God's kingdom. The two don't coexist well. I can't pursue the flesh life while pursuing the spirit life. That doesn't mean I don't try to do both at once. I often attempt to pursue God while justifying resentment, anger, lust, or pride. John's words remain though. I must evict the kingdom of self if I truly want to know the kingdom of heaven in me.

Though I have come to know God and have this eternal spirit life, I can have either a little or a lot of God's kingdom manifest in me. Repentance does not stop once I accept Christ. As Jesus said in Luke 9:23, I must daily deny self and follow Him.

When I feel that God is distant, John insists that I must turn from myself to follow God. I cannot pursue the kingdom of self and God at the same time. Daily, I must choose God.

Day 6
PRETEND SORRY

> When he [John the Baptist] saw many of the Pharisees and Sadducees
> coming . . . he said to them, "You brood of vipers! Who warned you to
> flee from the wrath to come? Bear fruit in keeping with repentance."
>
> **MATTHEW 3:7–8**

Have you ever apologized and then failed to change your behavior? I have. As the consequences of my addictive behaviors piled up, I felt a deep sense of sorrow. Over and over I promised I would never do it again . . . but in my actions I changed nothing. That, John says, is not repentance.

I may feel real pain, but if *sorry* is not accompanied by *change*, then it is not repentance. Without change, the destructive behavior that caused my sorrow will remain. The result? I will return to my destruction, and my next "I'm sorry" will ring hollow.

The problem hasn't been that I don't want my destructive behavior to go away. The problem is that I've been unwilling to do what it takes to get there. I've just promised myself that I would *never do it again*. This is not a plan. It is preparation for failure.

If I say I am going to stop a behavior that involves pornography, anger, greed, bitterness, alcohol, or pride—but I *do nothing* to change, then I am at worst a liar and at best, ignorant. Repentance is change in behavior, which is radically difficult. If I truly want repentance, it is not a switch I flip once. It is a daily battle to focus my thoughts and actions on God instead of on myself.

For example, if I'm an alcoholic and I work in a bar, I will need to leave that job. Repentance is a radical commitment to doing whatever it takes. God wants me to pursue Him, and He allows it to be hard work.

If I truly desire change, then "I'm sorry" must lead to action. "I promise I will never do it again" will always lead back to failure. No change in behavior leads to no change in behavior. If I truly want to repent, I must daily *do whatever it takes* to deny self and follow God.

Day 7

TEMPTING JESUS

*And after fasting forty days and forty nights, he was hungry.
And the tempter came and said to him, "If you are the Son of
God, command these stones to become loaves of bread."*

MATTHEW 4:2–3

Often, when I get home from work, I am starving, not literally, but still, I will eat until my stomach hurts. My appetite commands and I obey. My appetite reminds me that, at times, I am still under the influence of my flesh.

Jesus' temptation in the wilderness revealed that He, too, knew the temptations of the flesh. He knew hunger and fatigue. He knew the temptation of lust. It is not sin to know temptation. Christ never sinned, but He certainly shared in the temptations of the flesh.

Some will insist that when we come to Christ, our flesh nature disappears, but Christ's temptation revealed this not to be the case. As long as we are in this flesh, we will be tempted by its desires. Jesus showed us though, that we have a choice.

How did Jesus respond when Satan tempted his flesh? He didn't insist that He wasn't hungry. He turned His focus to that which He desired more than food. He looked away from His own will to His Father's will.

In denying self and following God, Jesus modeled how we combat the temptations of our flesh. He showed that true satisfaction comes not from the immediate gratification of the flesh, but rather in pleasing God. He did not deny that eating would have been pleasurable. He just knew the destruction that would follow, and He chose life instead of destruction.

It is not helpful to deny the existence of my flesh. I must acknowledge it and the destruction that comes with it. Likewise, I must know the life that comes from God. I must follow Christ's example and choose the life of denying self and following God.

Day 8

DO CHRISTIANS NEED SEAT BELTS?

> *Then the devil . . . said to him, "If you are the Son of God, throw yourself down, for it is written, " 'He will command his angels concerning you. . . .' " Jesus said to him, "Again it is written, 'You shall not put the Lord your God to the test.' "*

MATTHEW 4:5–7

I have often wondered if Christians need seat belts. *If God really is in complete control, then He knows the day of my death. I cannot affect it one way or the other, so why participate in vain efforts to prolong my life? If God is in control, I can drive with my knees while texting, right?* This seems ridiculous, but Satan's second temptation of Jesus reveals how I strike this attitude with God.

Having failed with food (yesterday's verse), Satan changed his strategy, taking Jesus to the top of the temple pinnacle, telling Him to prove it—as if to say, *"If you really are who you say you are, show your power."* Jesus' response exposed the defect in putting God to the test. God is no genie in a lamp.

As a child, I climbed a ladder up onto our roof and asked God to catch me if I jumped. It was stupid, but I still do something similar as an adult. I test God whenever I ask Him to deliver me from a temptation that I have created in the first place. I am like an alcoholic working in a bar, begging for God's help in sobriety.

It is usually less subtle than this, starting with small justifications. *No big deal. Just one taste. God will forgive me tomorrow.* I find myself balancing precariously on the temple pinnacle, preparing to jump. Then, as the ground rushes up, I beg God for deliverance, but He allows consequences.

I bear significant responsibility in my own walk with God. I must continually keep my eyes on Him. When I choose destruction, I am throwing myself off the proverbial pinnacle. Then, when I beg for deliverance, I will find only painful consequences. It is in my daily walk with God that He grows His life in me.

Day 9
A SMALL COMPROMISE

> *Again, the devil took him to a very high mountain and showed him*
> *all the kingdoms of the world and their glory. And he said to him,*
> *"All these I will give you, if you will fall down and worship me."*

MATTHEW 4:8–9

Having twice failed, Satan swung big for his third and final temptation. Who knows if he would have delivered . . . but to Jesus, he offered the world. *"You can have it all, if you will just do this one little thing for me."*

The temptation he used on Jesus echoed the one he had used on Eve—and the words he still uses on me. *"Just compromise a little and the rewards will be great. You can have it all: power, sex, fame, money, and popularity. Just this once. God will forgive you. He is just a giant fun killer anyway. He does not want you to follow your dreams."*

When temptation says that I can have it all, it is *always* a lie. When I give in once, the gates of my mind open up to invite that behavior again . . . and again. One compromise leads to another; and soon, I am addicted to the behavior. This is not just about drugs. This is about any destructive behavior, whether it involves pride, lust, food, bitterness, or anger.

When I am tempted, I often lie to myself. *No one knows. I'm not hurting anyone. Just this once. God will forgive.* My voice sounds eerily similar to Satan's. To this voice, Jesus supplied the answer: "Be gone, Satan! For it is written, "'You shall worship the Lord your God and him only shall you serve'" (Matthew 4:10).

Jesus' answer was to turn His gaze from self to God. He demanded that Satan leave Him, reminding Satan and Himself: *"I follow God alone."* Thus, I myself have only one right response to temptation: *I do not follow self or Satan. I follow God alone.*

Day 10

A HERO'S CALLING

> *While walking by the Sea of Galilee, he saw two*
> *brothers . . . casting a net into the sea, for they were fishermen.*
> *And he said to them, "Follow me, and I will make you fishers*
> *of men." Immediately they left their nets and followed him.*

MATTHEW 4:18–20

I often insert myself into heroic action movies, wondering if I would make the right but difficult choices as the hero would, or if—like a coward—I would choose the easy way out. Likewise, when I read of Jesus' call to the disciples, I wonder what my response would have been. The story is short on details, but basically, Jesus just showed up and told Peter and Andrew to drop what they were doing and follow him. "Immediately they left their nets and followed him." They did not stop to question or make excuses. They did not ask if maybe they could financially support Jesus' ministry. They dropped what they were doing, and they answered the call.

What would I do if God just walked into my workplace and asked me to abandon everything to follow Him? I imagine a fantastic day with some heroic opportunity to make the right choice. The reality, of course, is that this is the choice I face every day. Daily, Jesus calls me to deny self and follow him. I do not have to wait for some far-off day. This choice is today. This choice is every day. This choice is mine to make right now.

How often do I make excuses? *I am a little busy today, God. Perhaps there is some other way I could support your work . . . maybe giving financially. Someone has to do that, right? I've got important stuff to do . . .*

Every day, a hundred times a day, Jesus calls. *"Follow me. Leave your self-pursuits. Be my hands and feet. Love your neighbor. Take time to share your story. Tell others what I have done for you."*

Every day, I have this choice to follow God—or follow self. I would love to say that I always get it right, but I don't. Every day though, thankfully, I have a new opportunity to answer Jesus' call.

Day 11
I AM NO JESUS

> *And he went throughout all Galilee, teaching in their*
> *synagogues and proclaiming the gospel . . . healing every*
> *disease and every affliction among the people.*
> **MATTHEW 4:23**

I am full of excuses. When Jesus says I must follow him, I have plenty of reasons not to. *I am not you, Jesus. I can't heal. I can't teach like you. I've got bills to pay and a job to do. I'm not a rabbi. I'm just a doctor. I'm no Jesus . . .*

To this, God says, "*You do not need to heal miraculously to love your neighbor as I have loved you. I'm not asking you to save the world. I'm just asking you to share what I've done for you with those in need.*"

I do not need miraculous powers to listen, love, or share my story over a cup of coffee. I don't need to be a messiah to give my time and effort.

Here is what I do need to follow Jesus: obedience, selflessness, humility, and love. These are what I am actually telling God that I'm not willing to give when I refuse to follow Him. *I just don't want to love my neighbor. My time is for me. I don't want to visit drug offenders in jail or those in treatment. Those places are scary.*

I use the excuse that I'm not Jesus, but that's just a lie to hide the reality that I just don't want to obey. The truth is, I'd much rather spend my time, effort, and money on myself.

God allows me to pursue the desires of my own flesh . . . or to follow Him. He also reminds me where the pursuits of my flesh have taken me. He reminds me of what He did for me. "*As I have loved you, love your neighbor. I am not asking you to save the world. I am asking you to go to those who are in need. Love them and tell them what I have done for you. You do not have to be me. You just have to follow me.*"

Day 12

I NEED MY NEED

> *Blessed are the poor in spirit, for theirs is the kingdom of heaven. . . .*
> *Blessed are the meek, for they shall inherit the earth. Blessed are those*
> *who hunger and thirst for righteousness, for they shall be satisfied.*
>
> **MATTHEW 5:3, 5–6**

I never understood the opening verses of the Sermon on the Mount until I recognized how poor, meek, and needy I truly was. It was only in my self-inflicted disaster that I understood Jesus to say, *"Blessed are those who see their own need, for it is only the needy who seek God. It is only those who seek who also find."*

It was only in my hour of greatest need that I came to God with nothing left. This is how I should always approach Him: with my hands empty, clinging to nothing of myself. It is in my self-sufficiency that I come half-heartedly to God, wanting Him a little, but not really desperate for Him.

When I tell others what He has *sort-of done* for me, it rings hollow . . . as if it's not real for me. In my supposed success, I never really knew God— or what He could do for me. Worldly success is the opposite of what it takes to find God.

It is only in realizing my constant need that I truly rely on God. Blessed am I, when I see that my need is as great today as it was in my disaster. I need God as much now as I did in treatment, and I need God as much as the man sitting in prison needs Him.

The difference between the man who knows God and the one who does not, does not lie in how much each has. The difference is in *how much each one recognizes his need.* We all need God. Some see it but some are blinded by self-sufficiency. As I was. God draws near only to those who seek Him desperately.

If we want God, we must be honest about our perpetual poverty before Him. We must reject the lie of self-sufficiency. It is only in our need for God that we find Him.

Day 13
EDDIE'S BURRITO

> *Blessed are the merciful, for they shall receive mercy. . . . Blessed are the peacemakers, for they shall be called sons of God.*
> **MATTHEW 5:7, 9**

The guys in my Bible study at the local jail once relayed to me the following story. In their pod, a self-proclaimed white supremacist often used derogatory racial terms from behind the safety of his cell door. A *cell warrior*, they called him. One day, he used a particularly offensive term regarding Eddie, one of the black men attending our Bible study. This greatly agitated Eddie's friends, who threatened the cell warrior with great bodily harm.

Eddie didn't get mad though. Instead, he did what I couldn't have done. He took of his own limited resources, bought a burrito out of the vending machine, and slid it under the cell door of the agitator. In jail, a burrito is no small gift. It was, however, apparently a miracle burrito . . . the agitator later apologized. Eddie, who would have been justified in hating, chose instead to make peace.

Jesus, in today's passage, said that those who are merciful will receive mercy and those who make peace shall be called the sons of God. Frankly, it's much easier for me to harbor resentment and malice. When I'm wronged, I wrong in return. When I am offended, I desire to return the offense. What does this profit me? Do I satiate my appetite for justice with my petty revenge? No, indulgence in my natural but twisted sense of justice does not improve my position. Rather, it breeds bitterness, resentment, and anger within me. In my anger, I grow my own destruction.

I can though, like Eddie, choose to act in a manner completely contrary to my nature. Kindness and mercy may not guarantee perpetual peace; but when I choose kindness and mercy, I extinguish my role in conflict. When I choose to follow Jesus' commands, I grow His life in me and I do my part to maintain peace. Like Eddie, I must follow Christ's example, abandoning my right to be angry.

Day 14

THE ADDICTION OF APPROVAL

> *Blessed are you when others revile you and persecute you and utter all kinds of evil against you falsely on my account.*
>
> **MATTHEW 5:11**

Though we usually understand addiction in reference to drugs or alcohol, in our defectiveness, we have the capacity to be addicted to many things. In fact, most can better identify with an addiction to affirmation than to drugs.

We may not all understand the alcoholic, but most can understand the desire to be valued. This desire can become an addiction as sure as any chemical. When we pursue the affirmation of others, we surrender control to them just as the alcoholic surrenders control to the bottle. We feel terrible when put down. We feel good when praised. Relying on others for happiness, we become addicted to approval.

When news of my own addiction hit the local newspaper, it felt as if everyone was talking about it. I desired to control what others thought of me, and I hated feeling that others looked down on me. In treatment, when I felt God telling me to follow Him, my thoughts turned to what others would think. *I do not want to be seen as a religious nut.* In both circumstances, with the newspaper and with God, my focus was on what others would think of me. I was—in addition to being chemically addicted—addicted to the approval of others.

In today's passage, Jesus insisted that we must not be consumed with the world's opinion of us, but rather with its opinion of *God in us*. If others see God in us and do not like it, should that wreck our day? No, we are blessed, Jesus said, when we are rejected because of God. We must learn to find our value in God, not in the opinions of others.

My true meaning and approval come not from man but from God. As He sees me with the perfection of Christ, I do not ever need to feel *worthless* again. I am loved by the only one whose opinion matters. My value lies not in me, but in *God in me*.

Day 15

LICENSE TO BE A JERK

You are the salt of the earth. . . . You are the light of the world. . . .
Let your light shine before others, so that they may see your good
works and give glory to your Father who is in heaven.

MATTHEW 5:13–14, 16

Once, in a fit of what I—at that moment—called *righteous anger*, I walked into a pastor's office and cursed at him. I am not proud of this story; but at the time, I felt I was right. As God was on my side—or so I believed—I had cause to behave however I wanted. I was the salt of His earth and the salt in his wounds. *God wanted me to do it.*

In retrospect, I can see how wrong I was, and I have long since apologized. At the time though, no one could have convinced me otherwise—mine had been a just cause. My truth—my own truth, not God's—gave me license to be a jerk.

I have often used this verse to justify such behavior. I have told myself that as a Christian, I have a divine mandate to carry the truth. Truth has sometimes become the license to behave badly. *If I am on the side of right, I cannot act wrong.*

I was wrong though, to swear at the pastor, and I am wrong when I use truth to justify bad behavior. What do I do then? Do I abandon truth for love? I often see love and truth as mutually exclusive. In my defective thinking, I must choose one or the other.

Jesus did not teach that we must choose one or the other. He said that, as Christians, we must stand out in the world as something different. Through our good works, we are to display Christ's love *while* carrying the truth of the gospel.

Jesus' message will always offend some. Not everyone will embrace the idea that we need a Savior. I must carry the truth, whether anyone agrees with me or not. I must never, however, use the truth to justify my bad behavior. When I use the defective weapons of my own flesh nature, I am no longer on Christ's side. The truth is not a license to act like a jerk.

Day 16

LUST

> *You have heard that it was said, "You shall not commit adultery."*
> *But I say to you that everyone who looks at a woman with lustful*
> *intent has already committed adultery with her in his heart.*
>
> **MATTHEW 5:27–28**

When I was a teenager, a well-meaning youth leader at our church told us it was fine to fantasize about sex if it kept us from actual sex. He felt that whatever went on in the secrecy of the mind was harmless.

That would be great if it were true. Jesus insisted though, that what happens in my mind matters very much. While this concept may seem archaic to some, lust is a highly addictive defect of the flesh, causing destruction whether or not it ever leaves the confines of the mind.

The first problem with fantasy is that it is practice for real life. If I practice failure in my mind, I will fail when real temptation comes knocking.

The second problem is more insidious. Even if lust never leaves my mind, it decimates my spirit life. Sexual fantasies are not compatible with the daily pursuit of God. When I fill my mind with pornography, I cannot fill myself with Him. I cannot pursue the flesh and the Spirit at the same time. If I find that God feels absent in my life, I have but to examine that which I think is harmless and hidden.

Some of you will think I have gone too far. *"What a nut."* If I were the devil, though, I would think it profoundly successful to get an entire generation of young Christians secretly addicted to pornography. And if they didn't act out—all the better, as long as it paralyzed them from the pursuit of God. If I could cripple all the men in the church and convince them that it was no big deal . . . well, my job would be done.

What goes on in your mind—it matters. If we want to know God's presence, and if we want to hear His voice, we cannot constantly pursue self. At any given time, we pursue either the flesh life or the spirit life. We cannot have both.

Day 17
HOW DO I CHANGE?

> *If your right hand causes you to sin, cut it off and throw it away. For it is better that you lose one of your members than that your whole body go into hell.*
>
> **MATTHEW 5:30**

If I find myself enslaved to drugs, food, or lust, I must—at some point—realize that *I am the problem.* The fault does not lie in the world or with other people. I am my own problem. My own flesh nature is what separates the person I am from the person I want to be.

How do I change? *I realize my addiction is destructive, but I cannot stop. I have asked God to change me, but He has not. It's his fault.*

Though God allows my struggles to remain, it is not His will that I live enslaved to them. There is a vast difference between the life where my need drives me to God and the life where my need drives me back to addiction.

Jesus, in today's passage, described the difference. He did not suggest that I *let go and let God.* Jesus simply said that I must do whatever it takes to amputate whatever is causing my destruction. Am I willing to go to treatment or give up certain activities? *I do not want to do anything. I just want the miraculous fix.* However, He will allow me to remain in my addiction if I am not willing to change anything.

What does God do then? Where does His work meet my effort? This is where God meets me: "Draw near to God, and he will draw near to you" (James 4:8). If all I have is my destructive behavior, I must realize that I am not following God.

God allows me to cling to my destructive defects, but I cannot then complain that God will not fix me. If I do not have God, it is because I have not been willing to pursue Him. If all I have is my destruction, it is because I have not been willing to change.

Day 18
I'M A GOOD PERSON, RIGHT?

> *I say to you that everyone who divorces his wife, except on the*
> *ground of sexual immorality, makes her commit adultery.*

MATTHEW 5:32

Three times Jesus quoted the Old Testament law, and three times He insisted that following the rules is not enough. He said that anger is like murder, lust like infidelity—and in today's passage, that divorce is adultery.

What was Jesus' point in raising the bar? He was saying we will never earn God by following the rules; and if we make the rules our goal, we have missed God. Jesus' audience had apparently become more interested in the rules than in the God behind the rules.

I often do this. It is easy for me to look at a list of bad behaviors in the Bible and see that I am innocent of most of them. As I am not a thief, adulterer, or murderer, I must be a pretty good guy. Now, I may look down upon those who do not follow the same rules. When I focus on the list of rules, I convince myself of my own goodness . . . and thus I can convince myself that I really do not need God.

To this Jesus says, *"You just do not get it."* It is not about following external rules. It is about what is inside of me. If my life is focused on God, yes, my outward behavior will show the signs, but I do not prove my godliness by adjusting external behaviors. Even if the outside looks clean, inside I am full of imperfections. I may still have adultery and murder inside of me, even if it is never expressed outwardly.

The truth is, I was never going to be good enough to *earn* God. I can only be saved by faith, not by rule following. Jesus raised the bar so I would understand my constant need for Him. When I see my need, I remain on my knees, right where I belong. When I deny self and cling to God, my destructive behavior will change, but rule following is not the goal. God is always the goal.

Day 19

I SWEAR, I'LL CHANGE

I say to you, Do not take an oath at all. . . . Let what you say be simply "Yes" or "No"; anything more than this comes from evil.

MATTHEW 5:34, 37

When confronted with the consequences of our destructive behavior, we often swear by heaven and earth that we will never repeat our mistakes again. *Things will be different! I really promise this time. I will never do that again. I'm a changed man . . .*

I've been there. I've looked my loved ones in the eyes and sworn that I would never again engage in my addictive behaviors. It was not that I was purposely lying to them. It was just that my words were not accompanied by any actual change. Though I *meant* the words, I did not mean them *enough* to go through the pain of transformation.

I swore and I promised and then—when those around me had the audacity to doubt—I was offended. I convinced myself that I had changed (even though nothing had actually happened yet), and I expected those around me to believe it. I became resentful when they didn't accept my oath of change.

To this, Jesus tells me, *"Do not swear an oath to be different. Just be different."* It is not my hollow words that convince others of my transformation, particularly if I have been a repeat offender. It is only my transformation that will convince them. My appropriate response to my destruction is not to try to convince others that I have changed. It is to actually change.

Change is not easy or instantaneous though, which is why I would rather just *say* that I have done it. It is only through denying self and following God—for a long time—that others will come to see and believe in my transformation.

I no longer try to convince anyone with empty promises and oaths. The evidence of my transformation—and yours—does not lie in our words, it lies in the way we live our lives. Do we daily follow self . . . or do we follow God? Those around us will know the difference.

Day 20

HURT PEOPLE HURT PEOPLE

> *I say to you, Do not resist the one who is evil. But if anyone*
> *slaps you on the right cheek, turn to him the other also.*

MATTHEW 5:39

Jesus' teaching is just plain hard sometimes. I can love my neighbor. I can even act kindly to people I do not like. I know some people, however, with whom I would struggle to turn the other cheek. If they said a harsh word or raised a hand, I do not know that I would be able to remain passive.

Is it not my right to demand justice? When I am injured by some insult, I am justified in hurting back, right? It is simply my nature to strike back when offended. Except . . .

Jesus said that, as His follower, rather than responding with evil, I must allow evil to be done to me. I am not to seek revenge. Jesus insisted that it is better to maintain my right behavior than to seek justice.

I don't like this. It just seems so wrong to allow myself to become a doormat to those who would use me. Jesus' teaching is completely unnatural to me.

And that is His point. As a follower of Christ, I am not supposed to follow my own nature. I must follow Him. When I'm hurt and want to hurt back, Jesus says, *"No. Do not follow yourself. Like me, allow evil to be done to you and in doing so, your gaze remains focused on me. I know how unfair this seems to you, so take your eyes off yourself. Turn your eyes to me."*

Jesus insists that we must surrender our offense and our demand for justice. We are not to perpetuate hurt by hurting back. We are not responsible for the behavior of others. We are responsible only for our own behavior. We must continually take our eyes off ourselves and keep them on God, particularly when it is contrary to our own nature.

Day 21
THE ARROGANCE OF HATE

Love your enemies and pray for those who persecute you.
MATTHEW 5:44

Some passages do not seem to have much to say to me. I don't really have any enemies, so . . . I really don't have much to work on here. As far as I know, there are not a lot of people out to get me; and I mostly treat others with kindness and respect—except for those who obviously do not deserve it.

You know whom I'm talking about—those people who are just defective to the core. Surely God is not asking me to love them. *I do not hate them, but I am not expected to love and pray for them, am I? You have got to be kidding me. They are despicable, deplorable, and degenerate. There is something wrong with them. They are broken.*

The hateful thoughts in my head betray my condescending, arrogant attitude about those whom I think myself *better than*. The fact that I find others to be worthy of my derision because they are defective betrays my own defect.

In my defect, I believe myself to be in better standing before God than the one whom I find to be worse than I am. I am as a blade of grass, one millimeter taller than the one next to me, looking arrogantly down on it because I feel I am closer to the sun. How foolish must my arrogance look to the sun?

God, I think, looks similarly at my arrogance. He loves me despite my defect. He wants me to love Him in return. So, He insists I must love my enemy because—in my hatred and animosity—I am unable to love and focus on Him.

It is in our enmity that we focus on ourselves instead of God, not injuring our enemies, but ourselves. When we hate, we dislocate ourselves from a right position before God. In loving our enemies, we remain in communion with God. It is only in choosing love that we turn the focus from self to God.

Day 22

SMOKE AND MIRRORS

> *When you give to the needy, sound no trumpet before you, as the hypocrites do . . . that they may be praised by others.*
>
> **MATTHEW 6:2**

Have you ever done good from evil motives? Have you ever performed good works with your right hand to cover up the evil in your left hand? This is a common illusion that I am ashamed to say I have attempted.

In my worst addictive behavior, I felt awful about myself. I was terrified of being discovered—and of what others would think if they knew the truth. I loathed myself. To assuage my guilt, I did good, attempting to fool others with a facade of virtuous behavior.

Jesus warned of this kind of deception, calling out the hypocrisy of doing good to cover evil. When I do good as a show, I am not actually interested in good, I am just interested in promoting myself and camouflaging my destructive behavior.

My smoke-and-mirrors routine has had several layers over the years. First, I have hidden the destructive behavior that caused the guilt in the first place. In the case of my addiction, it was far easier to conceal it than to undergo the misery of getting sober . . . so, I constructed a false coating of good behavior, which only crumbled when the truth was revealed.

Second, I have betrayed my defective sense of self-worth when trying to control what others think. In doing good just for a show, I have revealed that I am sometimes still consumed by pride.

Third and finally, when I have used good to mask evil, I have completely missed God's grace. God is not holding a balance, measuring my good deeds against the bad. Because of Christ's sacrifice, I am forgiven once for all. I cannot earn God's love with good behavior . . . and I cannot fool him with my sleight of hand.

The answer to our hypocrisy and destructive behavior is not to distract with an illusion. The answer is to do whatever it takes to turn from self to follow God. In doing so, His love will fill us, producing authentic change, untainted by self-promotion.

Day 23

MY WILL BE DONE

> *Pray then like this: "Our Father in heaven, hallowed be your name. Your kingdom come, your will be done."*
>
> **MATTHEW 6:9–10**

When facing the trials of life, I usually ask God to deliver me from those trials. *God, fix this situation. Here is what I want, now make it happen.* This is not just how I pray. This has been my approach to life in general. I pursue and pray for whatever I want.

It's simply my self-serving nature to treat God like my *big helper in the sky.* When God doesn't answer my prayers, I am offended. *Why didn't you fix this? Why didn't you save me from this pain? I prayed, didn't I?*

I want faith, but I want it to be about me. *What good is God if He doesn't make my life better?* To this kind of thinking, Jesus said, *"Let me show you how to pray* and *how to live. It's not all about you. You're not the center of the universe."* Faith is about pointing my life at God, not at myself.

Jesus said that when I pray, I must start with, *"Our Father in heaven, hallowed be your name."* It may be that God just likes to hear me tell Him how wonderful He is . . . but I suspect this is probably more for me than for Him. I must begin prayer in proper posture before God, bowing to His will.

"Your kingdom come, your will be done." This is the hardest prayer, but it is the one we should be constantly whispering. In good times and bad, we must pursue God's will instead of our own. So many times I have this backwards, asking God to fix all my trials . . . when I should be asking instead for Him to fix me.

It isn't that God doesn't care about us. He is profoundly interested in what is best for us. It's just that what we think is best for us and what God thinks is best for us are often two very different things. We must surrender our will to the only one who knows exactly what we need.

Day 24

THE COST OF UNFORGIVENESS

> *Forgive us our debts, as we also have forgiven our debtors. . . . But if you do not forgive others their trespasses, neither will your Father forgive your trespasses.*
>
> **MATTHEW 6:12, 15**

I've always found these verses to be a little frightening. Why did Jesus say we must continue to ask forgiveness if we have already been forgiven? What if I forget to repent for something? Would God withhold His mercy if I fail to forgive another?

I thought that when I came to faith, I was forgiven (Colossians 2:13, 14) for all time. Why then, must I continue to ask for forgiveness? If I sin and forget to repent, am I going to hell?

The reality is, that when I came to Christ, I was forgiven once, for all eternity. I will never lose that. I still, however, live in this imperfect flesh, where I continue to struggle. The daily Christian walk is a daily effort to turn from self to follow Christ.

When I sin, I do not lose my status as God's child, but I do injure my relationship with Him. I do not lose my status as a husband when I do something hurtful to my wife, but I do need to ask forgiveness to heal the injury. Likewise, Jesus insisted that when we wander from God, we must repent, not to be saved again, but to return to right relation with Him.

Does God refuse forgiveness if I do not forgive another? If I remain bitter, am I eternally lost? No. God does not withhold salvation from me if I have accepted Jesus Christ as my Lord and Savior, but I do damage my communion with Him when I refuse to forgive.

When I indulge in bitterness, that is the thing I place between God and myself, focusing on my pride and resentment instead of Him. In this condition, I cannot see God. Unforgiveness always damages my relationship with God. When I fail to ask for forgiveness—or fail to forgive others—I am focused on myself and remain outside of an intimate relationship with God. When I find God distant, I may need to start here.

Day 25

DELIVERANCE: AM I FIXED OR NOT?

| *And lead us not into temptation, but deliver us from evil.* |

MATTHEW 6:13

Within Christianity, there are opposing views on sin and addiction. There are those who believe that we are delivered once for all from our defects when we come to Christ. These would believe that a Christian cannot be an addict.

The opposing view sees our defective flesh nature as something with which we will wrestle our entire lives. When we are born again, we are given a new spirit life, "but we have this treasure in jars of clay" (2 Corinthians 4:7). Jesus insisted, "The spirit indeed is willing, but the flesh is weak" (Matthew 26:41); and Paul said, "The desires of the flesh are against the Spirit" (Galatians 5:17). Thus, addiction—like other defects of our flesh—may influence us for life.

Which is it? I know those who claimed deliverance from their addiction—and I know those who have claimed deliverance, only to return to addiction. I am one of those. When I first attempted recovery, I claimed deliverance then stuck my head in the sand, only to return to my addiction.

This return brought my faith to a crisis. Like Paul, I cried out, "I do not do the good I want, but the evil I do not want is what I keep on doing" (Romans 7:19). Through Paul's writing, I realized that my flesh is diseased and will influence me until I die. When I feed the flesh life, I will sow destruction. If, however, I sow the seeds of the spirit, I will grow life. I may always live under the *influence* of my flesh, but I do not have to live *enslaved* to it. As I grow in Christ, I will abandon sin more and more because He transforms me.

Though I do not struggle with pills today, I know that if I started indulging in all-things-me, I could easily return to active addiction. As I live in a broken flesh, the only solution is to continually pursue the One who delivers me daily from myself. It is my constant need that keeps me constantly dependent on God.

Day 26

I WANT TO EAT RIGHT, BUT RIGHT NOW, I JUST WANT A DONUT

When you fast, do not look gloomy like the hypocrites . . . that [your] fasting may be seen by others. . . . And your Father who sees in secret will reward you.

MATTHEW 6:16, 18

I have been meaning to fast, but the truth is, I like eating. I knew this passage was coming up though, so I fasted the day before writing this devotion. I know that today's passage says that I should not fast and tell, but I hope God does not mind if I share my experience here.

I did not enjoy it. I was constantly hungry, and I'm not sure I would have made it if I had not been planning on writing this entry. In my hunger I realized how much my appetite still rules me. In theory, I want to fast, but in reality, I want donuts.

This, I think, is Jesus' point. Fasting is about denying self. Apparently, some hypocrites of His day made quite a show of fasting, drawing attention to self, feeding their own pride. To this, Jesus said, "They have received their reward" (Matthew 6:16).

If I do something for self-gain, then that is all I will get out of it—instant and fleeting gratification. If, however, I voluntarily sacrifice my own desires and turn to God, He rewards me by growing His life in me.

It is often only in my discomfort that I turn to God. In fasting, I induce a hunger that I may not be aware of otherwise, which reminds me of my constant need for God. God draws near to those who draw near to Him (James 4:8). When I purposefully deny self and follow God, He works in me. When I train myself to deny the constant hunger of the donut, I grow in self-control and in my focus on God.

As much as I dislike the discomfort of fasting, discomfort is the whole point. In my hunger, I turn to God. When I seek God, He draws close to me, filling me with Himself. God after all, is always the goal.

Day 27
ADDICTED TO STUFF

Do not lay up for yourselves treasures on earth, where moth and rust destroy, . . . but lay up for yourselves treasures in heaven. . . . For where your treasure is, there your heart will be also.

MATTHEW 6:19-21

I cannot blame my occupation for my mistakes in life, but I remember realizing that my previous job in the emergency room was a hard life. I could not, however, give up the paycheck. I had bills to pay and stuff to buy. My treasure lay in the temporal. Moth and rust eventually caught up with me and I paid the price. My addiction was not initially to drugs, but to stuff. It was my pursuit of things that started me down the road of the temporal over the eternal.

If I am honest, I still struggle with this. I sometimes wonder what an auditor would discover, sifting through my life. Does my heart lie in the things of heaven—or the stuff of earth?

Jesus said the meaning of my life and the purpose of my heart will be revealed by that which I pursue. *Where my treasure is, my heart will be also.* In 50 or 100 years, I will not care much about boats and cars, so why do those things seem so important now? Unfortunately, it is the nature of my flesh to pursue instant gratification. When faced with the choice of stuff now or reward later, I want stuff now.

It is not wrong to enjoy what God has given me, but when I put the pursuit of stuff ahead of my pursuit of God, I get it backwards. In my pursuit of things, I find my meaning where *moth and rust destroy . . .*

God did not say I can't own things. He just wants them to not own me. Daily, I must be honest about my pursuits. Am I chasing the temporal or the eternal? Do I put time and effort into my relationship with God—or things? If I pursue self, I will receive a fleeting reward. If, however, I pursue the eternal . . . I will store up treasure that can never be taken.

Day 28

BE CAREFUL LITTLE EYES . . .

*The eye is the lamp of the body. So, if your eye is healthy,
your whole body will be full of light, but if your eye is
bad, your whole body will be full of darkness.*

MATTHEW 6:22–23

I love road trips. The problem is that I like to enjoy the scenery as I drive. Much to my wife's terror, as I turn my head, taking it all in, I turn the wheel as well. Where my eyes go, my body—and the car—follow.

Jesus said it's the same with my life. Where my eyes look, my life follows. If I am focused on my career, that is what my life will be about. If I am focused on God, I will pursue Him above all else.

Daily I must focus on something. If I do not choose purposefully, I almost always choose self. My default setting is myself. If I do not purposefully get up at 5:30 a.m. and point my life at God, it does not automatically happen.

In my addiction and destruction, I realized that pursuing myself had just become my habit because I had done it for so long. Jesus says this must not be. I am to begin every day, doing whatever it takes to turn my eyes to the Light, following God.

As I go through each day, I must be ruthlessly aware of that which distracts. Just as with Peter walking on the water, the wind and waves are constantly seducing my eyes away from Christ. My job is to keep my gaze on Him. The secret is to realize that anything not-Christ is wind and waves. This does not mean that I do not perform my normal activities. It just means that I learn to do them with my eyes on the Light.

Turning my gaze to Christ does not change the wind and the waves around me, but it much improves my position in relation to them. Whenever I find myself sinking into the darkness of life, it is my responsibility to look once again to the Light.

Day 29

GOD MONEY

No one can serve two masters, for either he will hate the one and love the other, or he will be devoted to the one and despise the other. You cannot serve God and money.

MATTHEW 6:24

I do not see myself as a lover of money. I do not obsess over how much I have, and I really spend very little time worrying about it. My defective attitude toward money, however, may be revealed by the effort I have put into making money versus the effort I have put into serving God.

Jesus says the two pursuits are mutually exclusive. I cannot be a servant of both God and money. In my extreme thinking, I think I must be either greedy or poor. Money itself is not evil, though. It becomes evil only when it rules me. I must rule over my money as I rule over the other defects of my flesh. I can use money. I am just not to serve it.

The difference is often subtle, though. How do I know? If I spend more time at my job than I do on my knees in prayer, am I getting it wrong? Must I become a missionary in Africa? Do I need to give up a lucrative job if the paycheck is *too good*?

As with many things, it is my attitude toward money that matters. Money and possessions are not evil in themselves; they just become evil when I elevate them to become my masters. Whatever I serve becomes my god. It can be family, career, possessions, or money. Whatever it is—if I choose to find my meaning and security in it—then that is my god. If my god is not *the one true God*, I am pursuing disaster.

I must daily choose God as my master. He may keep me in the same occupation, serving Him there, or He may ask me to do something completely different. If I am truly serving God instead of money, it will not matter. Everything falls into its proper place when I put God above all.

Day 30

ANXIETY ADDICTION

Therefore I tell you, do not be anxious about your life. . . . Which of you by being anxious can add a single hour to his span of life?

MATTHEW 6:25 AND 27

Anxiety manifests itself in different ways. For some, it is an uncontrollable obsession with a specific focus like money or security. For others, it is an overwhelming sense of dread with no obvious cause or explanation. It may be something we are born with, or it may be a result of traumatic experiences. Whatever the cause, anxiety is a destructive defect, similar to other defects in that it often controls us; and despite the misery, we cannot *just stop it.*

It is not exactly like addiction, greed, or pride; but at its core, it is an uncontrolled, pervasive response to the world, which is unhelpful and destructive. Anxiety is a soul-crushing misery which God does not wish us to suffer. The Word of God says that we should be casting all our anxieties on him, because he cares for us (1 Peter 5:7).

Why then, does He not deliver us from anxiety when we ask? I would guess that if you suffer from anxiety, you have read today's verse and prayed that God would take your anxiety from you. I would also guess that you may have felt abandoned if God did not take your anxiety away.

The reality is that God often allows our struggles to remain, using them to teach us dependence on Him. Though we do not need to live enslaved to them, those struggles will always exert some influence on us. It is often only in our need that we turn to God.

This does not mean that we must live in fear. That is living in slavery to the defect. It does mean that we may daily need to turn our anxieties over to God so that we may find the peace and life that can come only from Him.

Day 31

KINGDOM OF ME

But seek first the kingdom of God and his righteousness,
and all these things will be added to you.

MATTHEW 6:33

Though my defects come in all shapes and sizes, Jesus, in today's passage, exposed the root of all my life struggles. He said that first and foremost my life must be about God and His kingdom. I, however, have always been all about the kingdom of Scott. In almost every situation, every conflict, and every decision, my first impulse has been to consider my own preference. In theory, I want to follow God; but in practice, I follow myself.

I tend to look to God for the *big decisions. Where should I go to college? What job should I take?* My interest in God's will has generally existed only when I have not known what to do. In most of my daily decisions, however, I know exactly what I want to do, and thus, I mistakenly believe that I do not require God's help.

God, though, is intensely interested in how I make my everyday decisions. I do not really want to hear how I should love my neighbor, feed the hungry, and visit those in prison. I want to do my own thing and just get a little divine help with the big decisions.

The truth is, most of us live our lives upside down. We want God, but we want Him to know His place. Jesus said, though, that our lives will always be out of order as long as we do not seek Him above all.

Our relationship with God is supposed to be the entire, all-consuming purpose of life. We are to think of Him when we wake, and we are to pray to Him as we fall asleep, seeking Him above all. Only when we do this does everything else exist in its proper order. It's not that we should abandon all else. It's just that the chaos of life falls into proper perspective when we have the faith to let God be our God.

Day 32

DO WE CHOOSE OUR STRUGGLES?

> *Therefore do not be anxious about tomorrow, for tomorrow will be anxious for itself. Sufficient for the day is its own trouble.*

MATTHEW 6:34

Occasionally I've been told that in my blog writing, I make it sound as if anxiety were a choice. *Just choose not to be anxious.*

I do not believe that I *chose* to have a predisposition for addiction, but I did put those pills in my mouth; so at some point, I engaged in voluntary behavior. When I write of anxiety and addiction both as life struggles then, those who suffer from anxiety may chafe at the comparison.

Of course, we are not responsible for which struggles we have. It does not matter much whether we were born with a flaw or it was the result of some life trauma. We are all broken in some way, and we all have different issues. We are not responsible for our specific shortcomings.

I am, however, responsible for my behavior in *response* to a weakness. I may not be responsible for my predisposition to anger; but when I yell at my family, I alone am to blame for the behavior. To call addiction or anger *diseases*, though, is offensive to those with *real diseases*, like cancer.

All of our shortcomings are symptoms of our diseased flesh nature. No one in his right mind *chooses* to be anxious, angry, or addicted. These imperfections are, by definition, pathologic. We all have our own diseases—or defects—of the flesh.

Jesus never said that it is wrong to suffer from a predisposition to be anxious. He acknowledged the reality of the struggles and told us what we must do about them. Daily we must do whatever it takes (prayer, counseling, service) to turn our focus from ourselves to God. He may or may not relieve us of our flaws. That is up to Him. We are not responsible for our defects. *We are responsible for how we respond to them.* When we use our anxiety to daily turn ourselves to God, He grows life and peace in us.

Day 33

THE GIFT OF BEING JUDGMENTAL

> *Judge not, that you be not judged. . . . Why do you*
> *see the speck that is in your brother's eye, but do not*
> *notice the log that is in your own eye?*
>
> **MATTHEW 7:1, 3**

Here, in perfect metaphor, Jesus sums up the defect of being judgmental, a defect that is so pervasive in our faith. When I first read this, I thought of 15 people who need to read what I have to say on this topic. *Perhaps I should ask them to read my blog. Some people are so blind to their own defects.* These thoughts, of course, reveal the log in my own eye to which Jesus is referring.

No one likes being judged, yet we all have this tendency of criticizing others. We are gifted at detecting defects in others while remaining blind to our own.

Christianity lends itself to this. We identify the big sins, and we feel innocent of them, giving us a false sense of holiness. *I am not a murderer or an adulterer, so I am better than . . .* however, Jesus reveals our hypocrisy by insisting that anger and lust are sins, just like murder and adultery (Matthew 5:21–22 and 27–28).

We all have some struggle that disqualifies us from the right to judge. If I find myself thinking that I am good enough to be critical, I have certainly succumbed to blinding pride. If I find myself being constantly offended by the stupidity of others, then I have a colossal log in my own eye.

I will someday have to address the destruction of those around me, but there is a vast difference between lovingly engaging in the discussion and simply being judgmental.

I know the difference between the two approaches. It's just that it makes me feel better about myself to be judgmental. Jesus said, however, that I can only engage in the work of helping others when I am honest about my own defects.

Day 34
SELLING GOD

> *Do not give dogs what is holy, and do not throw your pearls before pigs, lest they trample them underfoot and turn to attack you.*

MATTHEW 7:6

Early on in our marriage, my wife and I *won* a free carpet cleaning. In our ignorance, we invited a vacuum salesman into our home. This sad salesman had no idea that we were just poor newlyweds who had no hope of affording his fancy vacuum cleaner. It was a fine vacuum, but from the beginning, it was a colossal waste of the salesman's time.

As a Christian, I often feel that I must be God's salesman. Jesus, however, was no salesman—and in this passage, He said that I do not have to be either.

I am often asked, by a certain family member, to speak with someone or other who is struggling with addiction. My first question is always the same. *Does he want to talk to me?* I will do what I can to help someone find recovery, but I am no salesman. At some point, the seeker has to do some seeking. I cannot recover for someone else.

I have come to understand today's passage in this light. Christ wants me to share what He has done for me. It is not my job, however, to sell God to those who reject Him. Though I often feel the burden to argue, I have yet to argue someone into faith or recovery.

Jesus' approach was more about *attraction* than *promotion*. He loved, healed, and spoke the truth. He did not chase after those who rejected Him. He preferred to take His message to those who knew their need, which meant that he was associating with prostitutes, lepers, and the like.

Everyone needs God as much as the addict. Not everybody sees it. There are plenty around me, though, who see their need. If anyone believes he does not need God, he will never seek God, and I am unlikely to change his mind.

I go, then, to those who see their own need. This may mean that I have to live among those who are needy. It is precisely for the needy (including me), that Christ came.

Day 35
SEEK AND FIND

Ask, and it will be given to you; seek, and you will find; knock, and it will be opened to you.

MATTHEW 7:7

I have often attempted to use this verse to twist God's arm, praying for cars, success, and athletic skill. In doing so, I missed out on one of the most important principles in the Bible: *God desires that I seek Him and rewards me in measure with my seeking.* It is only in seeking God that I know Him, and I will know Him only as much as I seek Him.

I can have a little God in me or I can have a lot. He is constantly seeking me; but in His wisdom, He allows me to pursue my flesh life or my spirit life. Whichever one I pursue is the one I will find. When I pursue self, I find destruction. When I seek God, I find life.

I am always pursuing something. If I do not fill myself with God, self naturally fills the void, causing me injury. For some, this is not so obvious. For me, however, if I do not pursue God daily, I pursue my flesh life, which leads inevitably to painful consequences.

The problem is that I often want only enough God to be saved from my big defects—but not enough to upset my life too much. *I do not want Him changing everything.* I hold back and do not truly pursue God.

To this half-hearted seeking, God responds in kind, allowing me to feel distant from Him. When God seems withdrawn, I must realize it is not God holding back. I'm at fault. He has moved heaven and earth to reach me. Now, I must pursue Him.

I must be radically honest about my seeking. Am I holding out on God, clinging to part of self? I cannot simultaneously pursue God *and* pornography, anger, pride, bitterness, money, or self. When I pursue self, I find myself and all my disaster. If, however, I pursue God, He promises that I will find life in Him.

Day 36

THE NARROW PATH

The gate is wide and the way is easy that leads to destruction, and those who enter by it are many. For the gate is narrow and the way is hard that leads to life, and those who find it are few.

MATTHEW 7:13–14

I sat in the restaurant one evening with good intentions. I meant to eat healthy. Then the familiar voices started. *You're on vacation, live a little.* I caved. *Fried macaroni and cheese? Yes, please . . .*

I remember those same voices talking me into much worse behavior not all that long ago. I don't mean to equate food with drugs, but my path to each was strikingly similar. *You only live once, enjoy it! Indulge now, pay later . . .*

Everyone who recovers from active addiction looks back at some point and asks, "What was I thinking?" Once on the narrow road, it is easy to look over at those on the path to destruction with incredulity. *What is wrong with you?*

It's this way with anything worthwhile: exercise, recovery, or faith. The harder the path, the higher the price required to travel it—and the fewer who will take it. I should not be surprised when many do not follow. Though I feel compelled to share my story with those on the path to destruction, their choice is not my burden to bear. My job is to continue on the narrow path.

On that path, complacency is my constant enemy. *Thank God, I'm not like those losers over there. I've got life figured out—and don't have much to work on anymore.* Reality, of course, is the exact opposite. As I grow closer to God, the path narrows even more . . . and I become much more aware of how far I have to go.

Am I living in sobriety, only to be enslaved by food, sex, money, or approval? Am I trying to keep one foot—or even one toe—on the broad, easy path? Knowing the path and following it are two different things. It's a daily choice to continue walking on the right path. The narrow one.

Day 37

DOES THE BAD GUY KNOW HE'S BAD?

Beware of false prophets, who come to you in sheep's clothing but inwardly are ravenous wolves. You will recognize them by their fruits.

MATTHEW 7:15–16

As my family left the movie theater one night, I asked, "Does the bad guy *know* he's the bad guy?" My kids rolled their eyes, but I genuinely wanted to know. Does the wolf know he is the wolf—or does he believe himself to be a sheep?

I know many who claim faith but who also act in a manner contrary to that faith. Their destructive fruit varies, but they all have one thing in common. *They are convinced they are good.* They all have a righteous conviction that—though they produce destructive fruit—they are still in the right.

I look at the wolf and think, *He must know. How could he not?* I am sure there are some who know they are evil and embrace it; but the truth is, most who bear destructive fruit still think themselves to be good.

These wolves sit in our church, believing themselves to be sheep, all the while deceiving themselves—and some of us. How am I to know? Jesus said that it is not just what we confess to believe that matters. Our belief must translate into a changed life *or it is not real.*

Suddenly, I am a little uncomfortable.

What if I am an imposter? I have used God's grace to live as I pleased. I do not think I am a wolf, but that is exactly what a wolf would think.

Jesus' words require painful introspection. What if Jesus stood in front of me and examined my life? Have I loved God above all else? Have I loved my neighbor as myself? Have I been a sheep or a wolf? This is terrifying.

I must honestly ask if I truly follow Christ . . . or do I just confess a belief in him? There is always grace and forgiveness when I fail, but I do not want to use God's grace as an excuse to be the wolf.

Day 38

THE TWISTED SPAWN OF GRACE

> *Not everyone who says to me, "Lord, Lord," will enter the kingdom*
> *of heaven, but the one who does the will of my Father who is in*
> *heaven. On that day many will say to me, "Lord, Lord, did we not*
> *prophesy in your name, and cast out demons in your name, and do*
> *many mighty works in your name?" And then will I declare to them,*
> *"I never knew you; depart from me, you workers of lawlessness."*
>
> **MATTHEW 7:21–23**

When my life fell apart due to my addiction, those around me questioned whether or not I knew God. They wanted to know if my claim to faith was all a sham. I couldn't blame them. My beliefs and my behavior were incompatible. Looking back, I believe I was a Christian, but as I was abusing grace, it was fair to ask the question.

Many of us embrace only the grace of Jesus, insisting that He's all about forgiveness. Today's passage, however, is a sobering reminder that we can distort grace. This false grace is born out of the twisted desires of our flesh.

We may be saved by faith, but Jesus insisted that just *saying the words* is not faith. Faith is a belief followed by action. I can sit in church on Sunday morning and sing of how I love God, but those words ring hollow if I don't live it out.

I may embrace grace, but if I abuse that grace to continue in my destructive pursuits, then I haven't really changed—I don't have faith and I don't know God. I just have a thought in my head. However, I am not saved by a thought. I'm saved by faith. For a thought to become faith, it must manifest itself in my behavior.

This doesn't mean I must be sinless to have faith. I'll always fall far short of perfection. Jesus' point was that there are some who think they know Him; but as they never follow, they're deceived. When they finally encounter Christ, it will be a bitter shock. I don't daily wring my hands over whether or not my faith is real, but I'm right to ask the question when I insist on repeatedly following self over God.

Day 39
THE APPROACHING STORM

*Everyone who hears these words of mine and does not do them
will be like a foolish man who built his house on the sand. . . .
And the winds blew and beat against that house, and it fell.*

MATTHEW 7:26–27

When I first started working in the emergency room, I was struck
by how often I encountered tragedy. I remember thinking, *"My day will
come. It's inevitable."* As time passed and tragedy did not brush too near
me personally, I grew less concerned.

Jesus insisted, however, that it is not a question of *if* the storm will come,
but *when* it will come. The world is broken, and following God does not
mean I escape that brokenness. Jesus, in today's passage, explained where
my strength must lie when disaster hits.

Before I came to God, my meaning and purpose rested in that which is
fallible and unstable. This approach is inevitably destructive, as when the
storm strikes, my foundation will dissolve. Calamity visits all eventually.
So . . . what is my foundation? If my security is in self and the world, I
will be wrecked.

The unbeliever will be quick to point out that I only need God because
I'm so weak. To this, I say, *"Absolutely. I need God precisely because I am
weak."* I cannot imagine what I would have done in my addiction without
God. When my career and family were taken away—and I had no guarantee of their return—I had only my foundation of God (weak as it was)
on which to rely.

The challenge is to build my foundation *before* the storm. It is during
times of calm, however, that self-sufficiency tempts me the most. Every
day, I must choose to build my life on God, reading, praying, and following.

With the right foundation, I may well avoid causing my own destruction. I cannot avoid all of life's ruin, though; so today, I will build my life
on God—in preparation for the approaching storm.

Day 40

WHY WON'T GOD FIX THIS?

A leper came to him . . . saying, "Lord, if you will, you can make me clean." And Jesus . . . touched him, saying, "I will; be clean."

MATTHEW 8:2–4

I am, at times, a child. One night, on the drive home, as the slow pickup ahead of me sped up whenever I tried to pass, I clenched the steering wheel and muttered a few naughty words. I almost prayed for a flat tire on that pickup before I realized I was being ridiculous.

In my self-focus, I expect God to cater to my preferences. *He's in control and He loves me, so He should take care of that pickup, right?* It's easy, reading today's passage, to get the idea that Jesus' purpose is to iron out all my life's wrinkles. Jesus' multiple healing stories give the impression that He has the power and the desire to remove all of my discomfort.

Then, I look at the lives of those around me and see the horrible things they're going through, and I question God. *Why? If you care, then why have you not healed those illnesses, addictions, and defects?*

Some will read these verses and *claim* them, insisting that if they just . . . believe . . . enough—God will heal them. *He must.* Using God's own words, they believe they can twist God's arm, forcing His hand. I cannot twist God's arm, though, and I misuse this story when I try. The leper had the correct approach: "Lord, if you will . . ." I often confuse my will for God's will. I desire a thing so badly that I assume God wants it too. Then when I don't get what I want, I act like a child.

God's purpose in my life, however, isn't health, wealth, or comfort. He wants me to pursue Him above all. Because it's my need that keeps me dependent on God, He often allows my need to remain. So often I've prayed for God to fix my situation when really I need Him to fix me.

Day 41

HOMELESS JESUS

> *A scribe . . . said to him, "Teacher, I will follow you wherever you go." And Jesus said to him, "Foxes have holes . . . but the Son of Man has nowhere to lay his head."*
>
> **MATTHEW 8:19–20**

As I sat in a coffee shop one day, a disheveled man approached me and mumbled something. I removed my headphones apprehensively, not really wanting to engage. He repeated his question, (sigh) asking for money for coffee.

I considered refusing, but since I was writing a Christian blog at that moment, I felt a certain obligation; so, I gave him enough for a cup of coffee. I considered asking him to sit down and talk, but he smelled a little; so I was relieved when he moved along. After all, I had a blog to write…

Consider now, that this was Jesus' sales pitch in the passage above. In the story, this scribe impulsively attempted to follow Christ. At first it seemed to me that Jesus should have taken advantage of the moment.

Jesus, however, reading the scribe's lack of commitment, instead told him that He was homeless, suggesting that the scribe too, would be homeless if he followed. Jesus turned the man away, insisting that he count the cost of following.

Turning followers away seems bizarre to me. The rich young ruler (Matthew 19) could have funded Jesus' ministry for life if Jesus had just allowed him to keep some of his money. Jesus insisted, though, that his followers crucify themselves daily and turn the other cheek when offended. Frankly, it's surprising that anyone followed Him.

How different is this from the pitch I've used at times to sell Christ? I have, with good intentions, told others, "Just say the magic words of the sinner's prayer and you're in. It's that easy."

Jesus insisted, however, that following Him is anything but easy. I wanted a little of God in my life, enough to help with my addiction. I would have preferred to manage the rest of my life by myself. Jesus insisted, though, that half-hearted measures fall short.

Day 42
THE STORMS OF LIFE

*There arose a great storm on the sea, so that the boat was being
swamped by the waves; but he was asleep. And they went and
woke him, saying, "Save us, Lord; we are perishing." And he said
to them, "Why are you afraid, O you of little faith?" Then he rose
and rebuked the winds and the sea, and there was a great calm.*

MATTHEW 8:24–26

I'm a fixer—or at least I like to think I am. When confronted
with a problem, I focus on it and try to figure out how to manipulate a
solution. I'll often expend much time and energy trying to figure out a
problem, only to discover that I can't fix it. What's worse, is that I'll turn
to God only when all my efforts fail.

There are many storms in life that are beyond me. The disciples found
themselves in one such predicament while Jesus slept in their boat. This
was no metaphorical storm, but rather a very real one that threatened
to destroy them. They had the Creator of the world with them, but they
fought the storm until they were nearly swamped by it. Finally, they woke
Jesus as a last resort.

I think I hear a sigh—and maybe see an eye-roll—in Jesus' response. I
imagine him saying, *"Why are you afraid of the storm when you have the
Creator here with you? Where is your faith?"*

Jesus says the same thing to me when I manipulate instead of first going
to Him. Faith is to turn to God first, instead of myself.

Most of my angst in life has been caused by my focus on myself or the
world. To this, I hear Jesus say, *"Oh you of little faith. Look to me and give
me your fear."* Faith doesn't mean that God will calm every storm. Faith
is looking to God to give me what I need, even in the midst of the storm.

Day 43

WANTS AND NEEDS

Some people brought to him a paralytic, lying on a bed. And when Jesus saw their faith, he said to the paralytic, "Take heart, my son; your sins are forgiven."

MATTHEW 9:2

I often approach God as I would Santa Claus. I don't pray for a new car. I just have a very specific idea of how the world should be. It isn't wrong to ask God for what I want, but today's passage reveals the gap between what I want and what I need.

In the story, a paralyzed man was brought to Jesus for healing. Instead of physically healing him, though, Jesus used the opportunity as a lesson. He didn't give the man what he wanted. He forgave his sins—giving him what he needed.

I can imagine the look of disappointment on the man's face. It would be like getting a Bible instead of a toy for Christmas. *Thanks Jesus, that's really nice . . .*

The religious leaders in attendance recognized that Jesus was claiming to be God. They accused Him of blasphemy. Seeing that they had taken his bait, Jesus asked them which was harder, to heal spiritually or to heal physically?

The scribes, like the paralytic—and me—got it wrong, of course. They saw the more impressive feat to be physical healing. To prove His authority, Jesus then healed the man's body, making him whole—physically and spiritually.

That I too would have been more impressed by the physical healing betrays the gap between what I see as important and what God sees as important. I go to God with my wants—He gives me what I need.

God, I need you to fix my predicament.

"No, I need to fix you."

Can't you do both?

"It is through your predicament that you are being fixed."

Nuts.

Faith is looking to God for what I need. Faith is not trusting that God will work everything out according to my specifications. I must keep my eyes on Him always, particularly when life isn't working out as I want.

Day 44

DIRT ON MY HANDS

> *Many tax collectors and sinners came. . . . And when the*
> *Pharisees saw this, they said to his disciples, "Why does*
> *your teacher eat with tax collectors and sinners?"*
>
> **MATTHEW 9:10–11**

In college, I once volunteered at a homeless shelter. I saw it as a chance to serve God by *getting my hands dirty*. My attitude about ministering to those *beneath me* betrayed my pride. The truth was, I had plenty of dirt on my own hands.

Jesus, who was without sin, did truly lower Himself to those beneath him. He rubbed elbows with tax collectors, prostitutes, and all manner of sinners. The Pharisees saw this and took offense. *Why would Jesus associate with such people?* Their pride—like my pride—revealed the reality they were missing. We're all sinners. We're all below Jesus . . . and we all need him desperately.

The Pharisees needed Jesus as much as the prostitutes and tax collectors did, but their pride blinded them. Likewise, I need Jesus as much as those staying at the homeless shelter or those sitting in jail. I do not *descend to their level* when I visit them. We're on equal ground.

Though I can't identify with the inmate's incarceration, I can identify with being enslaved to my flesh nature. I can be honest about my own addiction and destruction. This humility opens the door to engaging like a brother on the same level. I'm not above them, and I don't dirty myself to be near them. Like them, I'm a sinner in need of Jesus.

I must be honest about the dirt on my hands, and I must be honest about what Jesus has done for me. I'm not better than those who sin differently from the way I sin. We all need God the same. As Jesus is quite comfortable among those in jail, I share Him there with those who know their need.

Visiting inmates is not some noble task of reaching the lowly. It's simply meeting with those who know their need. Everyone needs God, but not everyone sees it. I prefer to spend my time with those who can see the dirt on their own hands.

Day 45

TERMINALLY ILL

Those who are well have no need of a physician, but those who are sick. . . . For I came not to call the righteous, but sinners.

MATTHEW 9:12–13

Modern medicine sees addiction as a disease, a view which chafes some. The rub is that addiction appears to involve choice. Cancer doesn't usually cause people to lie, cheat, and steal . . . whereas addiction does. When I compare addiction to cancer, it seems to excuse the addict's behavior.

When I was in medical school, I had a minor cancer, which stayed minor as long as I treated it. Had I refused to recognize my illness, it would have eventually killed me. In this way, addiction is similar to cancer. If I don't admit the problem and actively seek treatment, it will be progressive and fatal. Addiction in this sense is a terminal illness.

Jesus pointed out the painful reality that we're all terminally ill. We all live in this flesh, and we're all in a state of decay. Our flesh nature is rotten, and without God we are spiritually dead. In this sense, we all have something in common with the addict.

We're all diseased in our addiction to self. We may not all go to jail or treatment, but we all follow self—separated from God—and are thus, quite sick. It's only in recognizing our illness and seeking God that we find hope. If we refuse to acknowledge our disease, we'll never come to know God. It's only in coming to God that we can know freedom from our destruction.

Jesus came for the sick. The problem is that we're all sick—we just don't all see it. It's difficult to convince a man to undergo a painful treatment if he doesn't see his need. No one of right mind chooses daily crucifixion . . . until it's the only option left.

I follow myself to disaster—or I follow God. There is no alternative treatment for my condition. I can wallow in self-destruction, or I can find true life in God.

Day 46

WHEN GOD FEELS DISTANT

> *"Why do we and the Pharisees fast, but your disciples do not fast?" And Jesus said to them, "Can the wedding guests mourn as long as the bridegroom is with them?"*
>
> **MATTHEW 9:14–15**

During our engagement, my wife and I lived 600 miles apart. As it was the olden days, we wrote letters. Now that we live together, we don't write letters because we communicate face-to-face. Once married, it would have been ridiculous to continue our communication via snail mail.

This is exactly why the Pharisees were irritated with Jesus' disciples in today's passage. They believed fasting was necessary to draw near to God. Thus, when Jesus' disciples didn't fast, the Pharisees considered them uncommitted, even though Christ was right there with them.

Jesus pointed out that fasting—while He was with them—was akin to begging God to come near while He sat right there with them. They didn't need to find God, as God was literally with them. Jesus explained that He would eventually leave, at which time they'd need to make some effort to draw near to Him.

Therein is the lesson for me. Though God is not with me as a physical person, when I came to faith in Him, His Spirit began to dwell in me. Though I'm supposed to have an intimate relationship with God, I often simply ignore Him. He's in me, but He allows me to connect with Him—a little, or a lot—it's up to me.

God longs for intimate communion with me. James 4:8 tells us, "Draw near to God, and he will draw near to you." It's my responsibility to do the drawing near. When I find God distant, a little honesty will usually reveal that I've been ignoring God and pursuing self.

If I want to be close to my wife, I must spend time with her. Likewise, If I want to be close to God, I must keep up my end of the relationship, daily turning from self to pursue Him. When I fast, pray, and read His Word, I grow my relationship with the Father. He draws near when I pursue Him.

Day 47

TOUCHING GOD

> *A woman who had suffered from a discharge of blood*
> *for twelve years came up behind him and touched the*
> *fringe of his garment, for she said . . . "If I only touch his*
> *garment, I will be made well." Jesus turned . . . and said,*
> *"Take heart, daughter; your faith has made you well."*
>
> **MATTHEW 9:20-22**

I've always found this story to be peculiar, but I'm not sure I ever understood it; so I needed to work on it one night. I usually go out for a run to do this, but the January temperatures were well below freezing, so I stayed inside. Instead I shut off the lights and sat in my chair. I did what I had to do to clear my mind and connect with God.

In the story, this *untouchable* had suffered for 12 years with bleeding and thus, came to Christ out of desperation. Her dire need drove her to touch Jesus's robe, believing this would heal her. The healing came from God, but Jesus said it was her faith that triggered the event. *"Your faith has made you well."*

I cannot miss this point. It was in the woman's misery that she reached out for Christ. *This is faith*: To see my need, to believe that God is the answer, and to do whatever it takes to connect with Him. It's only through my faith that I touch God.

Though I'm not thankful for the destruction I caused in my addiction, I am thankful for the need I couldn't ignore. It was only in my own desperation that I desperately pursued God. Without my need, I would never have come to know God as I do.

Fortunately, I'm not going to run out of need anytime soon.

I can recall a time when I couldn't feel or hear God. The truth was, I was making virtually no effort to touch Him. I did nothing to find Him, and then I had the audacity to complain about His distance. Whether I go running or sit in my chair, I must do whatever it takes to touch God daily.

Day 48

KNOWLEDGE OR FAITH?

> Two blind men followed him, crying aloud, "Have mercy on us,
> Son of David." . . . And Jesus said to them, "Do you believe that I
> am able to do this?" They said to him, "Yes, Lord." Then he touched
> their eyes, saying, "According to your faith be it done to you."
>
> **MATTHEW 9:27–29**

It's the responsibility of every father to pass on wisdom to his children. One such lesson that I may have repeated too many times is the difference between knowledge and faith. I may know that a chair exists, but I do not exercise faith in it until I sit on it. Faith is not just knowledge, it is knowledge followed by action. My kids aren't as impressed by this analogy as I am, but it has helped me understand my faith better.

The two men in today's passage, though blind, could see who Jesus was. They didn't only *believe* He was the Messiah. They *followed* their belief, acting *accordingly*. Jesus asked if they believed, but they had already proven this in their following.

God asks me the same question, *"Do you believe?"* If I believe, do I follow with my behavior . . . or do I simply know of Him but continue to follow self?

Jesus said that, like the blind men, I'll receive in keeping with my faith. "According to your faith be it done to you." If I keep my eyes on God, following Him, I will find Him. If I pursue myself, I will find . . . myself.

I have a friend who speaks of his cancer as an opportunity to *lean into God*. He doesn't just know of God. He rests in God, receiving grace *according to his faith.*

This is a life lesson that I must relearn frequently, and it's perhaps why I repeat the chair analogy so often. It's only when I choose to act on my knowledge that I exercise faith. It's only when I lean on God that He holds me up.

Day 49

VIOLENT JESUS

> *Do not think that I have come to bring peace to the earth.*
> *I have not come to bring peace, but a sword. . . . Whoever*
> *loves son or daughter more than me is not worthy of me.*

MATTHEW 10:34, 37

Sometimes Jesus didn't sound very Jesus-like. I have a very clear idea of what Jesus is all about. He's loving, He's kind, and He's a peace-maker. Jesus would never carry a sword, right?

I often embrace the side of God that I prefer, and I dismiss those attri-butes that I dislike. When I fail, I remind myself that God is love. I don't want to hear about wrath. I just want God to make me feel good.

So then . . . I prefer to ignore this passage. I desire a Jesus who tells me how family should be the most important thing in life. I don't want to hear about my upside-down priorities. I'm supposed to be a good dad, right?

In my distorted view of Christ, I imagine Him to be an extension of my own will. *Jesus just wants me to be happy . . . following Him is easy . . .*

Jesus must have known that his message of grace would lead many to view him as a pushover. In this passage, He set the record straight, insist-ing that following Him would be anything but easy. Choosing to follow Christ must absolutely and violently change the way we live our lives.

Jesus said that to follow Him is to put Him above everything—even my family. I object to this. Vehemently. *How could I put anything above my wife and children?* To my objection, Jesus points to my past, showing me how I followed self to destruction in my addiction, never considering my wife and children.

The truth is, I've always pursued myself above all. The violence that Jesus perpetrates isn't to my wife and children. The violence done to my life has been removing me from its throne. This may seem painful and vicious; but it is necessary . . . and in the end, beautiful.

Day 50

DIE IF YOU WANT TO LIVE

Whoever finds his life will lose it, and whoever loses his life for my sake will find it.

MATTHEW 10:39

In today's passage, Jesus articulated the great paradox of our faith. If I pursue self to find life, I will fail. It's only when I forfeit myself in the pursuit of God, that I truly live. This isn't just some far-off promise of life after death. This is the promise of God in me now, trading death for life.

I used to think that following God was like an eternal diet, abandoning all fun in this life. *I'll accept misery now so I can go to heaven later.*

Christ dispelled this myth, reminding us of the anxiety and misery we cause in the pursuit of self. This may be where addicts are actually more fortunate than others. We know the destruction of self so we don't find it foolish to give up the old.

The reality is, this isn't my life to live. When I came to Christ, I became His. 1 Corinthians 6:19–20 tells us, "You are not your own, for you were bought with a price." If I want to know God and life, this is not optional.

This is how I get there. Self-sacrifice is a daily practice. It's not just my addiction that needed to go. I had to continually abandon self to follow God. If I'm not doing this, I'm not living as a disciple.

Does this mean I need to give up my dream of sky-diving to feed the poor? No, I need not be so dramatic. It does mean that I must start every day by pursuing God: reading, praying, and listening.

I still fail often, but there is always forgiveness when I do. I must be honest about it, though. If I struggle with pride, anger, anxiety, or pornography, I must do *whatever it takes* to leave it and turn to God. I can't pursue both my life and God. It's only in my surrendering the old life that God can grow the new one.

Day 51

CHRIST'S OFFER

*Come to me, all who labor and are heavy laden, and
I will give you rest . . . and you will find rest for your
souls. For my yoke is easy, and my burden is light.*

MATTHEW 11:28–30

I've often been skeptical of Christ's description of following Him. It seems to me that the Christian life is anything but restful. When I think about the daily sacrifice of self and the cost of obedience, I waiver. This faith thing isn't easy. It costs all of me.

The alternative to giving my mess to God, of course, is that I carry it. By myself. As one who has been crushed under the weight of my own disaster, I find that it's worth giving up. The words of Christ are a beautiful comfort to those who've come to know the misery of following self. If following Christ meant nothing other than being daily delivered from the mess of myself, it would be worth it. If following Christ meant nothing more than being free from the guilt of my own sin, it would far outweigh any cost.

At times, I balk at surrendering self, but this is nothing more than what I wanted in the first place. I must remind myself of where following my desires got me. In the end, I was begging God to deliver me from myself.

To my begging, Jesus says, *"Come to me. Give me your misery, anxiety, and pursuit of self. You don't have to bear this weight. Know the rest, peace, and forgiveness of following me. It will require all of you, but you'll find it no sacrifice . . . because you'll gain everything."*

It's easy to see how necessary it was to give up my addiction. It's more difficult today to see how I should continue to sacrifice self. *Thanks for helping me with that addiction thing, God. I've got it from here . . .* I must continually choose to give up self, or I'll return to the disaster of myself. The reality is, I always need God.

Day 52

DO I FOLLOW GOD OR DO I FOLLOW THE RULES?

| *I desire mercy, and not sacrifice.* |
MATTHEW 12:7

What does a good Christian look like? I have, at times, thought that what set me apart as a Christian was a list of behaviors from which I refrained. Never mind that I did nothing to honor God—or that I was engaging in hidden, destructive behavior. I still pointed to my *sacrifice* as evidence of my faith.

This is what Jesus chastised the Pharisees for doing in today's passage. When the Pharisees *caught* Jesus' disciples picking grain on the Sabbath, they were technically right, objecting to working on the Sabbath.

Their mistake was in holding the rules above God. In their rule-worship, the Pharisees insisted that the disciples go hungry instead. The rule followers didn't care that this would inhibit the disciples' ability to worship God on the Sabbath. *Only the rules matter!*

We often think the most pious and holy among us to be those who live by the strictest rules. *He doesn't drink or smoke so he must be holy.* To this, Jesus says, "*I desire mercy, and not sacrifice.*" It's not the things we *don't* do that make us followers of Christ.

Christ does ask me to abandon the destructive behaviors of my flesh. This passage isn't a green light to do whatever I please. It's just that He said if I stop at *following the rules*, I'll make a *god* of the rules.

Jesus insisted that following Him meant doing as He did, showing His love, mercy, and forgiveness to others. I can follow the Ten Commandments my entire life and still be a complete stranger to God if I don't do as He did.

This point was a slap in the face to the Pharisees—and it will be a bitter shock to those who depend on rule-following to define their faith. Faith isn't just about what I don't do. I must live out Jesus' love for others, or I don't follow God; I just follow the rules.

Day 53

UNFORGIVABLE?

> *Every sin and blasphemy will be forgiven people, but the blasphemy against the Spirit will not be forgiven.*
>
> **MATTHEW 12:31**

Have you, like me, ever feared that you are, in the end, unforgivable? Whether it's a painfully public failure or a deep, dark secret locked away in the mind, each of us has our own painful history. Have you ever looked in the mirror with despair and wondered if your collection of sins disqualifies you from God's grace?

Buried in this strange passage about the unforgivable sin, is this comforting promise: *Every sin and blasphemy will be forgiven.* I find much peace and comfort in knowing that my destruction is cancelled and was nailed to the cross with Christ (Colossians 2:13–14).

This means that the dark deeds of anyone—no matter how evil—can be forgiven. I may find the evil of some too repulsive to be forgiven, but I had better be thankful that God forgives all. I too, have a dark collection of misdeeds.

Still, this passage speaks of that one *unforgivable* sin. I've lost sleep over this one. I recall, as a child, worrying that just saying *holy cow* was blaspheming the Holy Spirit.

I shouldn't have worried, as Jesus explicitly described this unforgivable offense. In the story, the Pharisees accused Jesus of using Satanic power, attributing His work to Hell. Jesus insisted that in doing so, they betrayed their own opposition to God, committing the unforgivable sin.

Have I ever done this accidentally? No, anyone worried about such a thing isn't capable of it. The condition described here is one of malignant and complete opposition to Christ. This person—if he or she believes in Jesus—hates Him. God cannot or will not forgive such a one. The one guilty of this sin doesn't care, however, as he or she doesn't see the need—or want God's forgiveness.

If you and I read this and have any concern for our own souls, we need not worry. We may take comfort in knowing that if we have faith in Christ, we are, in fact, completely forgiven.

Day 54

THE SUM OF MY LIFE

The tree is known by its fruit. . . . The good person out of his good treasure brings forth good, and the evil person out of his evil treasure brings forth evil.

MATTHEW 12:33, 35

When asked how I find time to write every day, I always think of how much time I've wasted on corrupt behavior. I have put so much effort into pursuing my flesh, that now, I must put that same effort into pursuing God.

The fruit I bear stands as evidence of what I pursue. When I wonder about the fruit I've produced, I have no farther to look than that which I have been pursuing. If I pursue my flesh, I find myself. If I pursue God, I find Him.

I must daily read, pray, and meditate. I don't do it perfectly, but by the time I get up to write, I have worked on a passage for the previous 24 hours. This habit has been revolutionary for my thinking. I don't write this to tell you how great I am, but rather just to provide some insight into how God has renewed my mind.

If I want to produce different fruit, I must be a different tree. This isn't a once-for-all decision . . . and it's not a hobby. This will consume the rest of my life.

The fruit I produce flows out of what I am inside. If I'm filled with God's Spirit, that life will grow out of me. If I'm filled with the pursuits of my flesh, death blooms. I don't set out to grow fruit. I set out to grow God in me. Fruit is the result.

Jesus insisted that faith must lead to something. If, at the end of a life, that life has never produced the fruit of faith, then there was never any real faith in the first place. Real faith will produce fruit. Jesus said that by this, I will be judged.

Day 55

DANCE JESUS, DANCE

Then some of the scribes and Pharisees answered him,
saying, "Teacher, we wish to see a sign from you."

MATTHEW 12:38

Many times, I have asked God to prove Himself. *If you're real, flicker the lights.* Nothing. I just wanted some assurance of his existence, and I couldn't understand why He didn't reveal Himself. If He can prove Himself, why does He not? I just want some assurance before I put too much faith in Him. I will follow, but only if God will prove Himself first.

I walked a path for years, arrived at a place I didn't want to be, and then asked God to magically transport me out of my disaster. *I will follow you, God, if only you do this thing for me. Just this one thing.* I studied for a C but prayed for an A.

The Pharisees did the same. They didn't follow Jesus, and they wanted a demonstration. *Dance, Jesus, dance. We'll believe . . . if you can prove yourself.*

Jesus rebuked them, insisting that this isn't how faith works. Faith doesn't demand of God. Matthew records Jesus performing many works of healing, but they all occurred *after* the individual went to Jesus in faith.

The Pharisees were certainly not acting out of faith, and they wouldn't follow Jesus until he performed for them. However, Jesus rejected their demand . . . and simply walked away.

Faith doesn't mean I get to demand magical signs from God. I don't get to study for a C and pray for an A. If I want God in my life, I must put in the daily effort of pursuing a relationship with Him.

I can't walk a thousand miles toward disaster and then expect to circumvent God's laws. I reap what I sow. This is how God made the universe to work. Faith is pursuing God daily and then watching Him work in my life. I used to say that I would have faith when I saw God move, but God often doesn't move until I show my faith. God doesn't dance for me.

Day 56

THORNS IN THE GARDEN

This is the one who hears the word, but the cares of the world and the deceitfulness of riches choke the word, and it proves unfruitful.

MATTHEW 13:22

There are some passages that I just know are about me. I'm pretty sure Jesus, in today's parable, was somehow looking directly at me two thousand years later.

In the parable, Jesus described Himself as a sower, planting His Word. The story goes on to explain the possible responses to the Word of God. In some people's hearts, the seed never takes root. In others, it takes root, but at the first sign of pressure from the world, it is abandoned.

Then Jesus gets to me. I'm the one in whom the seed has started to grow . . . but then it just doesn't get to its full potential as the cares and riches of the world choke it out. My growth was stunted as I repeatedly allowed my gaze to be seduced by my self-interests.

This is a passage that I read on my first day home from treatment in 2014. It was as applicable then as it is now. It may have had more painfully obvious thorns back then, but the thorns aren't gone. They're just different.

I still—daily, if I want to grow—must put in the effort to avoid the diversions of the world. Pride, resentment, anger, and greed all continue to pull at me. As long as I'm in this flesh, I'll wrestle with its appetites.

If we're choked by the cares of the world, and if we find we're drowning in self, we have no further to look than our own responses to God. I have so often complained of being distant from God, only to realize that I was the one who had neglected the relationship. Faith and growth are not passive. If we don't purposefully choose to focus on God, we'll by default be distracted and choked by the thorns of the world.

Day 57

I DON'T HAVE A PROBLEM

For this people's heart has grown dull, and with their ears they can barely hear, and their eyes they have closed.

MATTHEW 13:15

I don't have a problem! Almost everyone who has ever been addicted to anything—whether it was drugs, pride, anger, self-image, or pornography—has uttered these words. Denial is a universal expression when confronted with our own defects.

If loved ones and family come to me suggesting that I'm a workaholic, I have a problem. (Oddly, no one has ever accused me of that one.) Insisting that I don't have a problem doesn't make it true. It just makes me blind.

Working with addicts can be maddening, but working with addicts in denial is just futile. This, I think, is the frustration Jesus felt in the passage above. He spoke of those who chose to close their eyes and ears. Their condition was *self-imposed*, preventing them from knowing Christ.

If I'm honest, I must acknowledge that I do this too. That which keeps me from honesty about my defects is the same that blinds me to God. *I* am the obstruction in my own ears and the cataracts in my own eyes. It is my self-focus that distracts me from knowing Christ and being healed.

Honestly, I do not want change and I do not want to be healed. I like indulging in my appetite, as it brings me pleasure. And change can be excruciating, so I'd rather just remain blind and deaf. Jesus, though, longs for me to know healing and life . . . if I will but open my eyes to Him. If I continue to refuse Him, by default I will continue to focus on myself, pursuing misery.

When God is distant, God is not the problem. I've chosen to be deaf and blind to him. I cannot keep one eye on self and the other on God. I must pursue painful honesty about my own struggles if I want to see God and know His life in me.

Day 58

TREASURE HUNTER

> *The kingdom of heaven is like treasure hidden in a field,*
> *which a man found and covered up. Then in his joy he*
> *goes and sells all that he has and buys that field.*

MATTHEW 13:44

What would I give to be free of my defects? What would I give to be able to look back at my life and see that I pursued God above all? I may claim that God is the most important thing in life . . . but I must ask myself if I actually live that way.

This choice is mine to make—nobody else's. There's no one on earth who can choose this for me.

At one time I told God that I'd give anything to be free from my defects. Even so, my words were empty, as I knew I wouldn't do any of the things I knew I needed to do. What I was really saying was, *I just want you to fix my problems without any disruption to my life. I still want to follow myself, just without the consequences.* At that point, my will was simply worth more to me than His was.

In this passage, Jesus explains what the kingdom of heaven is actually worth. *It is worth everything. Everything.* I don't sacrifice anything to relinquish the things that cause me destruction. In surrendering my own disaster, I gain the kingdom of heaven in me.

When we give up our defects to pursue God, we're relieved of our misery and filled with His life. So then, why wouldn't we take this deal? Because we're often satisfied with so little of God, we just can't surrender the right to do what we want. We may *want* to be free from our defects, but when it comes down to it, we wrestle with surrendering our right to live the way we want.

If I truly want to be free . . . and if I truly want to love God above all, then I must be willing to live that way. Like buying the field with a hidden treasure, I must give all I have to find God.

Day 59
ETERNAL CONSEQUENCES

Again, the kingdom of heaven is like a net that was thrown into the sea. . . . When it was full, men . . . sorted the good into containers but threw away the bad. So it will be at the end of the age. The angels will . . . separate the evil from the righteous and throw them into the fiery furnace.

MATTHEW 13:47–49

I have difficulty with delayed gratification. I'm not good at sacrificing now for a reward later. I prefer buffets. I'm not inclined to wait for a meal or think about tomorrow's consequences.

With that, Jesus' perspective in today's passage, is a little alien to me. Jesus insisted that what we do in this life matters in the next. As Christians, we believe that though our flesh will end in the grave, our spirits live on for eternity. In this view, our spirit life is our greater reality.

This isn't a natural perspective for me. My nature says this is all there is, so I might as well do what feels good now. If I want a dozen donuts, why not? I naturally seek my own pleasure, and I seek it in the quickest manner possible. Tomorrow's consequences are not my concern.

Most of us have this problem, just with different manifestations. Some will indulge in alcohol while others turn to anger, pride, anxiety, or affirmation from others. Whatever it is, most of us are *now-focused*. It's not natural for us to neglect our impulses today for gain tomorrow.

This is not to say we can't do it. It just takes effort. We do have the capacity to understand the necessity of delayed gratification. We understand working today for a paycheck tomorrow.

It's to this capacity that Jesus spoke. He said that "at the end of the age" there will be a day of reckoning. What we do in this life will actually matter *forever*. It may not be natural for us to think this way, but Jesus insisted that the consequences of our actions today will reverberate for eternity.

Day 60

WHEN I MOVE GOD

> *Coming to his hometown he taught them in their*
> *synagogue. . . . And they took offense at him. . . . He did not*
> *do many mighty works there, because of their unbelief.*
>
> **MATTHEW 13:54, 57–58**

I've always thought this passage made Jesus sound like a Santa from the movies who remained powerless without the belief of children. God, of course, is not empowered by my faith; but still, this is a curious passage. In it, Jesus went to his hometown where familiarity bred contempt and disbelief. "Is not this the carpenter's son? . . . And they took offense at him" (Matthew 13:55, 57).

Prior to this, Jesus had performed many miracles—always in response to faith. "Your faith has made you well" (Matthew 9:22). In his hometown, Jesus didn't perform miracles, as those who knew Him would not believe in Him.

God often moves only in response to my faith. It's not that He is dependent on me (like Santa), but that He longs for me to depend on Him. He first reached out to me so I could know Him, but now, He desires that I respond in faith.

This means that if I want God to move in my life, I must practice faith. Like Peter, I must walk on the water *while keeping my eyes fixed on Christ.* It's often only after I get out of the boat that He moves in my life.

Faith isn't doing nothing—and then expecting God to move. Faith isn't sitting on the couch, playing video games, praying for a job. I don't get to study for a C and pray for an A. Faith means I follow God in obedience. God often waits to move until I act in faith.

In my flesh, I have prayed for God to change me, while I was unwilling to *change anything.* I never wanted to have to move toward God. I just wanted to stay in the comfort of the boat, rocking though it was. Jesus said this isn't how faith works. If I want to see God move, I need to get out of the boat.

Day 61

FIVE THOUSAND MOUTHS TO FEED

> *The disciples came to him and said, . . . "Send the crowds away to go into the villages and buy food for themselves." But Jesus said, "They need not go away; you give them something to eat."*
>
> **MATTHEW 14:15–17**

A few years ago, my son and I were in Washington D.C. walking quickly down the street on a brisk fall day, when a disheveled woman asked us for money to buy food. My son paused. I did not. I grasped his hand and directed him across the street.

He asked me why we didn't help her. *She will probably use the money for alcohol or drugs.* He suggested that we go back to the food vendor on the corner and buy her some food. *Sigh . . . I can't help the whole world. Plus, we are in a hurry.*

When we got to our destination a few minutes later, I could see the hurt in his eyes, and asked about it . . . knowing his answer, "I just wish we could have helped that lady." I had blown it. I had missed the opportunity to help someone and missed the opportunity to allow my son to be a part of it. We looked for her on the way back but never saw her again. I felt terrible.

Jesus' disciples had their excuses too. *What can we do? We have barely enough for ourselves.* Jesus, though, insisted that the disciples do what they could. They knew the futility of the effort, but they obeyed Jesus and took Him what little they had.

Jesus didn't lecture the crowds on the necessity of being responsible. He just had compassion and insisted that the disciples give what they had in order to do what they could. He had a miracle up his sleeve, but the disciples didn't know that when they obeyed. They just obeyed.

I think this is often what Jesus asks of us—not to perform miracles, but just to do what we can with what we have for those He has put in our lives. He has yet to ask me to feed 5,000, but He does ask me to obey. Daily.

Day 62

WIND AND WAVES

*Peter got out of the boat and walked on the water . . . But when he
saw the wind, he was afraid, and beginning to sink he cried out,
"Lord, save me." Jesus immediately reached out his hand and took
hold of him, saying to him, "O you of little faith, why did you doubt?"*

MATTHEW 14:29–31

In today's passage—a faith-defining passage for me—the disciples
were in their boat, battling a storm, when Jesus came—walking on the
water. Unsure and terrified, Peter asked, "Lord, if it is you, command me
to come to you" (Matthew 14:28). Jesus called, and to Peter's credit, he
obeyed while eleven other disciples watched from the safety of the boat.

Peter literally stepped out in faith, not really knowing if the water would
hold him up; but he kept his eyes on Jesus and obeyed. Then, as the wind
and waves distracted his gaze from Christ, he sank. Terrified, he cried
out, "Lord, save me!" Jesus must have sighed, *"Why did you look to the
wind and waves?"*

I am Peter. I long to follow Jesus, but like Peter I am easily distracted. I
start out every day with eyes on God, but quickly become consumed by
the wind and waves of the world. Here's the secret: *Everything that isn't
Christ is wind and waves.*

I hear Jesus saying, *"Just keep your eyes on me."* He doesn't promise that
there won't be storms. He allows me to be distracted—and He allows me
to sink, choking on the sea—but He's always there to lift me up when
I return my gaze to Him.

Only when I keep my eyes on God can I have the faith to walk on the
water of life. When I abandon Him, focusing on the wind and waves, I
struggle. Faith isn't pretending that the wind and waves don't exist. Faith
is learning to navigate the storms of life—with eyes fixed firmly on Christ.

Day 63
MY CHURCH FACADE

*This people honors me with their lips, but their heart
is far from me; in vain do they worship me.*

MATTHEW 15:8–9

Have you ever, out of obligation, said that you'd do something
that you had no desire to do? Lacking the courage to say *no*, have you
found yourself half-heartedly participating?

I must admit, I've felt this way in church worship many times. I love
music, but I dislike facade and hypocrisy. Few places have exposed my
hypocrisy like standing in church, singing about how I follow God above
all . . . when I know that I don't.

It's church, though, so I feel obligated to recite the lyrics, even when
I know I haven't been living them. It's not that I disbelieve the words. I
want for them to be true. I just know they are not always true.

This is exactly the kind of thing that frustrated Jesus in today's passage. The Pharisees (of whom Jesus was speaking) were notorious for
pretending to be obedient to God while following their own paths. With
their mouths, they proclaimed God, but with their deeds they followed self.

No one tries to be a hypocrite. I don't set out to falsely proclaim God on
Sunday mornings. I just want two opposing things. I want God, and I also
want to follow my own will. So, six days a week, I pursue myself, and on
Sunday morning—for one hour—I sing my little heart out. As miserable
as I find my facade, I imagine God is even less impressed.

I often wonder what it would be like if my thoughts and deeds were
displayed on a screen above my head on Sunday morning. A better question, however, is this: *What would it be like if I actually lived out what I
was singing?* Instead of closing my mouth to avoid hypocrisy, what if I
changed my life to match my actions with my words?

For that, I must prepare today—and every day—for church next Sunday.

Day 64

SHINY ON THE OUTSIDE

> *Out of the heart come evil thoughts . . . These are what defile a person. But to eat with unwashed hands does not defile anyone.*
>
> **MATTHEW 15:19-20**

In today's passage, Jesus' disciples failed to wash their hands prior to dinner, which offended the Pharisees. In response, Jesus observed the hypocrisy of one who cleans on the outside, only to remain filthy on the inside.

If I had known of this verse as a child, I would have told my mother that I was just acting like one of Jesus' disciples when I failed to wash. Now, though, this passage makes me think of the vain efforts I go through as an adult, to appear clean.

Every Sunday, I shower and dress for church. How awkward would I feel if I showed up in my sweaty workout clothes? My heart may be filled with treachery and destruction, but if I wear nice clothes, at least I *look* nice. Clean. Pure.

Jesus pointed out the hypocrisy of this facade, saying it isn't what the outside looks like but what's in the heart that condemns a person. "Out of the heart come evil thoughts . . ."

It may be obvious to others only when expressed in action; but make no mistake, the evil I do starts in my heart. If I'm filled with anger, resentment, jealousy, hate, and bitterness, it doesn't matter how well I dress. Even if it's never expressed in deeds, my dark heart betrays that I'm still a mess on the inside. Nice hair may fool those in church, but it doesn't fool God.

What if we dressed for church according to the evil thoughts we've had in the last week? What if we were honest on Sunday about our struggles on Saturday? We all struggle with something. We just don't readily admit it in church. We may not wear sweaty clothes to church next Sunday, but it would do us good to be more concerned with the condition of our hearts than the style of our clothes.

Day 65

REPUTATION

He said to them, "But who do you say that I am?" Simon Peter
replied, "You are the Christ, the Son of the living God."

MATTHEW 16:15–16

I often wonder . . . would I have answered Jesus' question correctly? Peter had seen Jesus perform many miracles, so when Jesus asked Peter about his identity, he got it right.

Under different circumstances, though, Peter failed the same test. When confronted by a young servant girl after Jesus' arrest, Peter denied even knowing Him. When in Jesus' presence, Peter got it right. When confronted with fear, he lied through his teeth to save himself.

I can identify with fearful Peter. When I feel the need for God, I claim to follow. When life came apart, I promised God that I'd go to Africa to be a missionary if He would just get me out of my mess. I have done this many times to God. When it has worked for me, I've declared my faithfulness. When I'm in distress, I boldly declare my intended obedience.

Like Peter, though, I've historically gone soft on commitment when confronted with the world. I have this desire to not be a *religious nut*. I want to follow God, but I don't want to be a *Bible thumper*. In church, I am all bravado. Put me in a situation where my faith may be mocked by man, though, and I go all weak in the knees.

The underlying defect is my continued focus on self. I still prefer to be popular and well-regarded. I want to follow God, but I never wanted to *get too crazy with my faith*. Ironically, as my destruction has been quite public, I think God chuckles a little when I tell Him how worried I am about my reputation.

If our faith is worth anything, then it's worth everything. In our pride, reputation seems monumentally important. When we keep our focus on God, though, we see how ridiculous that concern is.

Day 66

WHAT I EXPECT FROM GOD

> *Peter . . . began to rebuke him, saying, . . . "This shall never happen to you." But he turned and said to Peter, "Get behind me, Satan! You are a hindrance to me. For you are not setting your mind on the things of God, but on the things of man."*
>
> **MATTHEW 16:22–23**

I sat, not long ago, talking with a man in jail who believed in the existence of God but who would not follow Him, as he believed that God had never done anything for him. He had prayed many times for God to deliver him from jail, and God had let him down every time. *What good is believing in God if He does not answer my prayers?*

Many of us harbor this dissatisfaction with God. We feel frustrated. He has failed to deliver on our expectations. Our disappointment betrays our distorted view of God. We erroneously think that *He exists to serve us.* We pray, and when God does not deliver . . . we feel rejected. In our supposed rejection, we reject God.

In today's passage, Jesus reveals that He had come to die. This offended Peter. His reaction? "This shall never happen to you!" Peter tried to bend Jesus to his own will. Jesus reacted passionately to the temptation, "Get behind me, Satan!" If Peter wasn't following God's plan, he was following the Devil's.

The lesson for me here is that no matter how good my intentions are, if my will stands in opposition to God's, I have become an agent of evil. If my focus is on what I want instead of what God wants, then I am in the wrong.

It was necessary for God's will to be done for Peter to find redemption. If Peter had had his way, Jesus would not have gone to the cross—and neither Peter nor I would have found God. Only in following God's will do we find that which is ultimately in our best interest.

God's will is the path to life. My path, when it opposes God's, is the path to destruction.

Day 67

HOW DO I CHANGE?

If anyone would come after me, let him deny himself and take up his cross and follow me.

MATTHEW 16:24

I've tried to change a thousand times . . . and failed a thousand times. I've prayed repeatedly for God to change me, yet He remains silent. What am I to do? Most of us can relate to Paul's frustration, "I do not do what I want, but I do the very thing I hate" (Romans 7:15). We likely all have some destructive behavior that we wish we could stop.

Is it God's responsibility to change me? Do I just wallow in my misery until He decides to fix me? Or . . . am I left alone to do it myself?

Jesus, in today's passage, described the two necessary steps to transformation. It's no coincidence that the process by which I am transformed is the same process as becoming a disciple. God works through these two steps, which—though profoundly simple in concept—are radically difficult in practice.

First, Jesus insisted that transformation is not passive. If I want authentic change, I must take up my cross daily. Taking up my cross—a symbol of death—means that if I truly want change, I must do whatever it takes to kill my old destructive behavior.

If I'm an alcoholic working as a bartender, I need to quit my job and go to treatment. If I can't stop looking at pornography on my phone, my phone needs to go. If nothing changes . . . then nothing changes. Half-measures are of no use here.

Step two is following Christ above all. Just as the first step requires radical effort to deny self, this too, is anything but passive. I must daily pour myself into reading, praying, listening, meditating, and obeying God.

When we leave self and pursue God, He transforms us and grows His spirit life in us. He delivers us daily when we deny self to follow Him. If we want to change, we must do whatever it takes. He always does His part.

Day 68

WHAT WOULD I GIVE TO CHANGE?

Whoever would save his life will lose it, but whoever
loses his life for my sake will find it.

MATTHEW 16:25

Half-measures are of little use in the battle against the flesh nature. I still struggle with some things (donuts) because I've not been desperate enough to change. In other areas (addiction), I've been desperate enough to make radical change.

It's often only in our desperation that we become willing to do what it takes to change. This is why most of us don't ever find transformation. No desperation. We simply remain unwilling to do what it takes to get there.

Some believe that God transforms us without any effort on our part. I've even been told that I didn't need to go to recovery meetings, counseling, or treatment—that those were all faithless, vain efforts at change. *All you need is prayer.*

We do this with other defects quite often. We want God to magically change us, so we just pray. We ask God to take away our anxiety, appetite, lust, anger, and pride; but we do nothing ourselves. We just sit and pray.

Should I not pray about everything? Absolutely. We must take everything, including our flaws, to God. Just as with addiction, though, we must *pray and do* whatever it takes to abandon the destruction. If I pray for change but remain unwilling to change . . . I will remain in my defect.

We can choose to do nothing. We can remain in the same job, habits, TV watching, and internet surfing. If nothing changes, though, nothing changes. Being a Christian does not mean we can indulge in anxiety, anger, or lust today . . . and then pray that God make us magically different tomorrow.

If we want to follow God, we must continually abandon self. We don't get to pray that God will make donuts taste bad. I must change my life if I want to stop eating donuts. The defects we still struggle with remain because we remain unwilling to change. God always does His part. We have to do ours.

Day 69
FAITH OR FANTASY

If you have faith like a grain of mustard seed, you will say to this mountain, "Move from here to there," and it will move.

MATTHEW 17:20

As a kid, I thought today's passage meant that I could move things with my mind. I took Jesus' words literally and tried to move stuff by faith. I planned to work my way up from ink pens to mountains . . . but I never got past the pens.

At the time, I thought it was my lack of confidence that thwarted my efforts. I understood faith to be positive thinking. Had I only believed harder, I would have been successful. This idea seems silly now, but what did Jesus mean? What is faith if it's not believing *really hard*?

My childhood folly now helps me see the error in my understanding of God. Faith isn't believing that God will do what I want. Faith is—like Peter walking on water—keeping my eyes on Christ. Peter *waited* on Jesus' command, and then he *obeyed*.

Faith doesn't mean that I'll always get the outcome I want. Faith is following God—even when the outcome appears terrifying. When I was a child, it was fantasy, not faith, that led me to think that I could use God to enforce my will. Fantasy is the opposite of faith, as fantasy is focused on myself.

This is easy to see when it concerns moving pens. However, when a loved one is sick, it's harder to separate my will from God's. My will isn't necessarily wrong. God desires that I bring my needs to Him, believing He will answer my prayer. Faith is praying, expecting God to work but also accepting His will when He says no.

I often ask of God . . . and then feel as if my faith must be broken when He doesn't answer the way I want. I must remember the lesson of the pen and keep my eyes on God, even when the outcome is uncertain. Faith isn't using God to enforce my will. Faith is following God even when it's contrary to my will.

Day 70
MASSAGING MY EGO

> *The disciples came to Jesus, saying, "Who is the greatest in the kingdom of heaven?"*
>
> **MATTHEW 18:1**

In jest, I once told some coworkers that the key to feeling good about yourself is to stand next to someone who makes you feel better. If you feel short, stand by someone shorter. If you feel heavy, stand next to someone heavier. If you feel unattractive . . . you get the idea.

Shortly thereafter, while sitting at my desk, I felt the obnoxiously close presence of two people behind me. With big smirks plastered on their faces, they informed me that I was making them feel better in almost every way. I had that coming.

In today's passage, this is the situation Jesus found Himself in with His disciples. Of all the discouraging moments for Jesus, this one had to be near the top. It wasn't enough that they were arguing about who was who in the kingdom, they tried to drag Jesus into it. Ignoring His words on humility, love, and dying to self, they asked Jesus to participate in their contest.

Jesus responded by informing them that they were engaging in behavior that wasn't even worthy of the kingdom of heaven. As they were arguing about who was the greatest, Jesus told them that in their pride, they were not even in the running.

I must admit, I do sometimes compare myself to those around me. *Am I smart enough? Am I successful enough?* This need to compare—turning my gaze from God to myself—always breeds some kind of destruction.

In our need to feel good about ourselves, we compare. Then, when we don't measure up, we criticize and mock. Jesus pointed out how ridiculous and destructive this is. If we want the kingdom, we must daily abandon self. When we keep our eyes on God, we're relieved of the burden of worrying about our status.

Day 71
THE HAMMER OF TRUTH

*Whoever causes one of these little ones who believe in me to sin,
it would be better for him to have a great millstone fastened
around his neck and to be drowned in the depth of the sea.*

MATTHEW 18:6

Years ago, I walked into the office of my campus pastor and quoted this verse to him. He had, in my estimation, been leading his children astray—and I told him as much. I informed him that it would be better for him to have a millstone fastened around his neck.

I'm not proud of that story. I was even more arrogant back then than I am now, convinced that I knew everything. *Everything.* While I still think I was right regarding that particular issue, I handled it terribly. I was a colossal jerk, using Jesus' words as a weapon, not considering that my own behavior mattered as well. I carried the truth like a hammer.

I tend to read the Bible like this: I read a passage . . . and I think about how it applies to everyone else. *I know a few people who need to read this.* It's easy for me to see the fault in another while remaining blind to my own. This is particularly true with destructive behavior that I don't understand.

When I see someone wrestling with a gambling addiction, I just don't get it. *How stupid. Why would you do that?* It's so easy to see defects in others. The challenge of Jesus' words, however, is to be introspective, to see how they apply to *me*. When I read the Bible, it does me little good if all I do is attempt to apply its truth to those around me.

When I read this passage now, I try not to dwell on *others*. I ask what God is trying to say to *me*. God's truth must always be applied to my life first.

Day 72

RUTHLESS AND VIOLENT

And if your hand or your foot causes you to sin, cut it off and throw it away. It is better for you to enter life crippled or lame than . . . to be thrown into the eternal fire.

MATTHEW 18:8

Whenever someone tells me a story of personal failure, I ask if he can identify how it started. No one sets out to drive drunk. Few engage in severely destructive behavior without making a thousand small choices leading up to *the big one.* If being honest, one can usually identify a multitude of progressively destructive choices leading up to it.

The problem is, I think that I can get away with secret, "insignificant" sins. *No one will know. God will forgive me tomorrow. No consequences.*

After indulging in my flesh once, though, I'm much more likely to do it again. I don't eat just one potato chip. I don't stop until only crumbs remain. I promise not to do it again, but I do. After a few repetitions—or maybe many repetitions—this pattern of behavior can become an addiction.

Now, potato chips may not lead to the collapse of my career or marriage, but indulgence in the flesh in little areas leads to more destructive ones. If, instead of potato chips, I indulge in lust, anger, pride, or a chemical, it can—and will—lead down a progressive road of destruction.

Jesus knew our propensity to tolerate our own destructive behavior. Thus, He taught us how we must deal with our flesh. We must be ruthlessly violent with those desires that distract us from God and keep us from a right relationship with Him.

Of course, Jesus wasn't teaching self-mutilation. My foot in itself is not inherently evil. His point was that this is how seriously I must take *any indulgence* of my flesh nature. If it distracts from God, it has to go. I cannot pursue life and death at the same time. If I want life, I must amputate that which brings death.

Day 73
FORGIVEN AND FORGIVING

> *"Lord, how often will my brother sin against me, and I forgive him? As many as seven times?" Jesus said to him, "I do not say to you seven times, but seventy-seven times."*
>
> **MATTHEW 18:21–22**

Jesus' teaching in today's passage was difficult. No one likes forgiving someone over and over for recurrent hurtful behavior. I know that I've been forgiven much; but still, I chafe at the idea of letting go of my right to be offended when someone injures me repeatedly. It's a bitter irony that the same defects in me that require so much forgiveness are the same defects that *prevent* me from forgiving others.

I, having required so much forgiveness, should be the most forgiving person in the world. Still, I cling to my own sense of justice. If I forgive, I surrender my resentment; and often, I'm just not ready to do that.

Make no mistake. Forgiveness means giving up my bitterness and resentment. Truly giving it up. It's a disposition of my mind in which I let go of my right to hold another in my debt. Forgiving doesn't require repentance . . . or even a request on the part of the offender. The one who wrongs me may never say he is sorry, but for my own spiritual health, Jesus said that I must forgive.

Forgiving doesn't mean that I return to the relationship as if nothing had ever happened. If someone borrows and wrecks my car five times, I can forgive without handing over my keys the sixth time. In my addiction, I repeatedly hurt my wife. Though she has forgiven much, it would be ridiculous of me to ask her to forget past lessons. Forgiveness doesn't mean she has to embrace future destructive behavior.

Jesus simply insisted that, as I have been forgiven, I must forgive. Clinging to my anger grows a cancer that consumes my faith; and thus, forgiving is critical for my own spiritual health. If I want to grow spiritually, I must accept God's continued forgiveness and continually forgive others. For the one forgiven by God, forgiving others isn't optional.

Day 74

THE PROBLEM WITH MY MARRIAGE

> Because of your hardness of heart Moses allowed you to divorce your wives, but from the beginning it was not so.
>
> **MATTHEW 19:8**

When reading today's passage on divorce, it's easy to come away with rules and miss this principle: *The reason marriages fail—and the reason I have conflict in my marriage—is the hardness of my own heart.* Jesus' point is that if I have marital conflict, I must look to my own part in it.

Unfortunately, in conflict, it's natural for me to blame my wife. I can admit now that I'm a handful to live with, but I didn't naturally see it that way. I tend to see myself as completely reasonable and loving. I've been slow to see my own fault in any conflict, and I'm quick to take credit for any success. In my self-focus, I'm always biased in my own favor. *I'm not the problem here.* The reality is, I am my own problem.

Jesus said the reason I have conflict is the hardness of my own heart. It's not that my spouse has no flaws, it's just that my responsibility is not to fix her. It's to fix me. If my plan for making my marriage work is to fix my spouse, I'm in trouble.

This doesn't mean that your spouse may not have serious issues that must be addressed. If your spouse is engaged in highly destructive behavior, you may have to go so far as to remove yourself from the situation.

I cannot, however, fix my spouse. I can fix only me. In my bias toward myself, though, I often fail to see the corruption of my own behavior. As in the rest of life, it's my focus on self that brings destruction. If I want to continue to grow life and love in my marriage, I must turn from self and follow Jesus' instruction. I love my wife—it's my job to act like it.

Day 75

PICK YOUR GOD

> *"Teacher, what good deed must I do to have eternal life?" . . . Jesus said to him, "If you would be perfect, go, sell what you possess and give to the poor."*
>
> **MATTHEW 19:16, 21**

I used to think this passage taught that I must take a vow of poverty to be a Christian. Jesus' story of this rich young man revealed an even tougher truth, however. In the story, Jesus met a successful man who *sort-of* wanted God . . . but was still addicted to his stuff. He followed the rules, obeying God's commandments . . . but recognized that something was missing.

I think that Jesus should have given him the *saved-by-faith* talk, letting him off the hook of his self-sufficiency. Jesus instead upped the game, telling him that to be perfect he must give away everything. Jesus, reading the heart and cutting to the bone, saw that this man's god was his own success. The very question asked by the man betrayed that he was enslaved to his own self-sufficiency. Success and wealth prevented the man from knowing God.

This terrifying truth should concern me more than any vow of poverty. Christ insists that I surrender *anything and everything* that I hold above him. Whatever it is that I put above God becomes my god— and it's the very thing that Jesus will always insist must go. It may be my family, career, sexuality, or drug use. If I follow it above God, it must be removed from His rightful place.

I may think myself better because I've put away my drug addiction, but I must remember—that which kept the rich young man from God was not a pill or the bottle. It was the good life. Wealth was his god, and it prevented him from finding *the* God.

Jesus always insists that I must choose my god. Do I want self or Him? Anything above Him is not to be tolerated. It's not in my success that I find God. It's only in surrender of self.

Day 76

PICK ME!

> *Whoever would be great among you must be your servant
> . . . even as the Son of Man came not to be served but to
> serve, and to give his life as a ransom for many.*
> **MATTHEW 20:26–28**

Most of us have an innate desire to be praised. Our flesh nature craves recognition for good and avoids blame for bad. It's our natural inclination to honor self at the expense of others. There are those few who are truly humble, but most of us would just like a little recognition for our humility.

Jesus taught the opposite of self-promotion, but His disciples struggled with this one. In today's passage, two disciples—or rather their mother—asked Jesus for recognition, "Say that these two sons of mine are to sit, one at your right hand and one at your left, in your kingdom" (Matthew 20:21). This request offended the other ten. The fault of the two and of the ten was the same, though, both being motivated by pride.

I'm guilty of this. My flesh nature is still very interested in self-promotion. I've had my name in the paper for good deeds and bad. I love being the center of attention when it's praiseworthy, and I want to hide under a rock when the attention focuses on my misdeeds.

When I have *humbled myself* to serve the poor and needy, I've felt perverse pride at helping *those poor souls*. When—in treatment—where *I* was the one being served, I felt the sting of humility. It wasn't the morality of the situation that hurt. It was my pride that hated being on the receiving end of a handout.

Jesus says that we must get over ourselves if we want to follow Him. He says that in His kingdom, the last are first and the first, last. If we truly want to follow, we must deny our desire for self-promotion, serving others instead—without getting credit for it. If we want to truly know God and His spirit life in us, we must be servants.

Day 77
ANGRY LIKE JESUS

Jesus entered the temple and drove out all who sold and bought in the temple, and he overturned the tables of the money-changers.

MATTHEW 21:12–13

I'm generally not an angry person, but when I get angry, it's always justified—surely, I am always right and the one frustrating me is always wrong. In my anger, my *rightness* validates my wrath. If the conflict involves a matter of faith, then I'm even more convinced that my response is appropriate. I may even convince myself that I have *God-given anger.*

Even Jesus got angry, after all. In today's passage, Christ saw salesmen turning a profit in the temple and threw them out. In my own anger, I've used Jesus' anger to endorse mine. In my rage, I have followed angry Jesus.

Here's the problem. My anger is usually more about my will than it is about right and wrong. Even when I'm discussing spiritual matters, my anger is less about God than it is about me. I don't get angry because I feel that God is offended. I get angry because *I* am offended.

My anger is one more defect of my flesh nature, like pride, lust, greed, and addiction. To pretend that my anger is from God is to lay my defects at his feet and to blame Him for my corrupt behavior. *That is obscene.*

While there may well be a place for righteous anger, I doubt very much that I'm actually capable of wielding anger in a righteous manner. In my fury, I almost always say or think things that are anything but righteous. In my anger, I indulge my flesh nature and I lose self-control. Then I blame it on God: *When I see bad behavior, I just get mad, like Jesus.*

In my anger, I'm nothing like Jesus. In my anger, I indulge in a defect as surely as if I were using drugs or pornography. God never asks me to indulge in my defects for Him. He does ask that I continually turn away from my will and my anger . . . to follow Him.

Day 78

KINGDOM OF THE BROKEN

> *Truly, I say to you, the tax collectors and the prostitutes*
> *go into the kingdom of God before you.*
>
> **MATTHEW 21:31**

Jesus, at times, offended those around Him. When religious leaders challenged His authority, He responded in a manner that must have cut them to the bone. He told of two sons whose father asked them both to work in his vineyard. One son said he would obey but then did not go. The other son refused the father's request but later repented and obeyed.

Jesus pointed out that the one who followed the father was not the one who said the right words, but the one who *obeyed*. He told these priests that *they* were the imposters . . . and that the repenting tax collectors and prostitutes were the real followers of God. This blistering attack must have infuriated the priests.

The chief priests thought their pedigree and their words would get them to God. They followed in ceremony, but that wasn't enough. However, the prostitutes and tax collectors realized how broken they were and thus, knew exactly how much they needed God. In their desperate need, they turned to God, truly following Him.

I've found this to be true in my own life. I'm not proud of the destruction I caused because of my addiction. I'm sure the prostitute wasn't proud either. I am, however, very thankful for my desperate need, as it was only in my desperate need that I became desperate for God.

It wasn't until I saw my utter depravity that I was willing to give it up. *Enough. I am a broken mess. I need you, God.* It was only in that condition that I became willing to even begin abandoning myself to follow Him.

Jesus was not, of course, endorsing prostitution or drug addiction. When He encountered destructive behavior, He called it out. Even so, He didn't shy away from the broken. He said that those were the exact people for whom He had come. His is not a kingdom of the perfect. It is a kingdom for the broken, for it is only those who can see their own brokenness who seek Him.

Day 79

LIFE LESSONS FROM COUNTY

I tell you, the kingdom of God will be taken away from you and given to a people producing its fruits.

MATTHEW 21:43

In our county jail Bible study, I meet many who confess to follow God, only to return to a life of corruption when released. I find it all too easy to express frustration at those who follow God when in need, only to abandon Him when life returns to "normal."

I was frustrated by this thought on the way into the jail one Sunday when God pointed me to my own life. I've often pursued God in my need, only to lose interest in Him when focusing on my successes. Like those inmates though, I *always* need God. Faith isn't just a *Get-Out-of-Jail-Free* card.

As I pondered that lesson, God hit me with another. That Sunday I met a young inmate who'd been sharing his faith with a cellmate, whom he also brought along to our Bible study. The second man was someone I knew—someone with whom I would honestly never have shared my faith. I would've thought it a wasted effort.

In jail, though, this man came—with his cellmate—to Bible study. To be completely clear, the very *kind* of person whom I had criticized in my heart just minutes earlier turned out to be the very same kind of person to share his faith with someone whom I'd been unwilling to approach. The first inmate was more obedient than I was.

This, I think, is exactly what Jesus was teaching when He told the chief priests that the kingdom would be taken from them and given to those who follow Him. Those who truly follow God, obey Him, and produce His fruit—those are the ones in whom the kingdom of God dwells.

If we're frustrated by not knowing the kingdom of God inside us, then we must do what it takes to grow His kingdom in our hearts. This doesn't mean we should sit on the couch and pray. This means radical obedience, even when we don't feel like it.

Day 80

SEX, DONUTS, AND GOD

"Teacher, which is the great commandment in the Law?" And he said to him, "You shall love the Lord your God with all your heart and with all your soul and with all your mind."

MATTHEW 22:36-37

Every day, I look at the numbers for my blog's performance. I can see which entries do well and which ones tank. I assume that it's usually the title that hooks the readers—or loses them. Titles like *Sex and Lust* perform well, while titles like *God Above All* are snoozers. I'm tempted to title every blog something like *Sex, Drugs, and Rock 'n' Roll*. Sadly, the more salacious the title, the more likely we are to read it. Sex sells—and we, apparently, are buying.

Therein lies the question for me. *What catches my eye and what distracts me?* When asked what the most important commandment was, Jesus answered, "You shall love the Lord your God with all your heart and with all your soul and with all your mind." My preoccupation with God is to be above all, consuming every part of me.

If I'm unaware of what may be distracting me from that goal, I need to wonder, *What is keeping me from loving God with all of my heart? What is distracting me?*

For me, it's the basic appetites of my flesh. Once it was drugs, but now it's the routine things: sex, food, pride, selfishness, and materialism. Some of these things may not be particularly bad in and of themselves. I need to eat, and sex in marriage isn't wrong. It's just that when my appetites control me, I lose sight of God.

Even if the only injury those appetites cause is to distract me from God, this is still profoundly destructive. Success can be just as disastrous as drug addiction if it keeps me from loving and following God.

Daily, we must ask if we are following our own appetites for sex, donuts, and stuff—or are we following God? We find God—and life—only when we pursue Him above all.

Day 81

ADDICTED TO ME

| *You shall love your neighbor as yourself.* |
MATTHEW 22:39

If I'm painfully honest, I must admit that I don't act as though I love anyone as much as I love myself. Though I love and would die for my family, my day-to-day behavior betrays that I often pursue my own interests first. My neighbors aren't often even on the radar. *Surely Jesus didn't mean that I must love them* above *myself?*

My difficulty in loving others is, at its core, a *me* problem. I am a *me-addict*, and it's my self-interest that prevents me from loving others as I should. As long as I'm hooked on myself, I'll never love God and neighbor as Christ commanded.

The only solution for this problem is to recover from my me-addiction. How do I do this though? I was born to put my own interests above all. It just comes naturally to me. It's natural for all of us. This is the very definition of my flesh nature—to want what I want.

This, in essence, is our primary life problem. It's the principal defect that keeps us from the faith and love that God intended, and it's the root of all the destruction we cause ourselves. Our selfishness is what keeps us from being who God intends us to be.

This isn't a problem that we resolve once and for all. It's something we'll struggle with until we're freed from this flesh at death. It is, however, something that we can improve. Daily, we can choose to deny self, follow God, and love others.

In every decision, I must practice asking if I'm following myself or following God. Then daily I must purposefully live, not according to my flesh nature, but according to God's Spirit in me. This won't be easy, but recovery from addiction never is. It's what God commands me to do, though. If I want to love God above all *and* love others as myself, I must continually work at recovery from my addiction to myself.

Day 82

I'D RATHER NOT GET INVOLVED

*Well done, good and faithful servant. You have been faithful over a
little; I will set you over much. Enter into the joy of your master.*

MATTHEW 25:23

Early in my residency, I was on a flight with my wife when a woman
seated behind us began having chest pain. I was technically a physician
. . . but my paper-thin license and shaky voice were less than inspir-
ing. Nevertheless, I examined her as best as I could, decided she needed
a hospital, and asked the pilots to divert.

During this time, my wife moved to another seat where she was engaged
in conversation by a man who turned out to be a cardiologist. She
informed him of the situation, but he declined involvement. When I
learned this later, I was more than a little irritated. He may have had ten
times my knowledge and skill, but in his apathy he was utterly useless.

As frustrated as I was with his indifference, the parallel to my life was
obvious. I too have spent much of my life watching opportunities pass
by. Jesus, in today's passage, told a parable of such apathy. He spoke of
a man and the three servants he trusted—each with a portion of his
money. Two of them used the money to produce more, but the other
buried his.

When the master returned, he praised the two who had been productive. His words were less kind, though, to the one who did nothing with
his money, "You wicked and slothful servant!" (Matthew 25:26).

According to Christ, my obedience isn't optional. As part of the body
here on earth, I have a duty to follow Him. My refusal to obey won't
thwart His ultimate will, but it can cause—and certainly has caused—significant misery.

If I claim to follow God, I must obey Him. I cannot be His servant
without serving Him. At the end of my life, I don't want to look back on
wasted opportunities. I want very much to hear God say, "Well done,
good and faithful servant."

Day 83

BUT JESUS, THAT'S NOT MY GIFT!

*I was hungry and you gave me food, . . . I was in prison
and you came to me. . . . As you did it to one of the
least of these my brothers, you did it to me.*

MATTHEW 25:35–36, 40

Though it's sometimes tempting for me to define my faith by denomination, political affiliation, or the big sins that I avoid, Jesus defined those who followed him in radically different terms. He said that if I truly follow Him, I'll love and care for those around me.

Today's passage is part of the story in which Christ explains the final judgment, when He will divide all humanity into two groups, the sheep and the goats. To the sheep, He'll say, "Come . . . inherit the kingdom" (Matthew 25:34). The sheep are those who fed the hungry, clothed the naked, and visited those in prison. What the sheep did for the poorest among them, they were doing for Christ.

To the goats, however, Jesus will say, "Depart from me, you cursed, into the eternal fire" (Matthew 25:41). The goats are those who refused to feed the hungry, clothe the poor, or visit those in prison. As they turned their backs on the poorest among them, they turned their backs on God, sealing their own fate.

In the end, Jesus won't divide the world into political parties or denominations. All distinctions will be stripped away, and the *only* thing that will matter is whether I followed Christ or not. If I claim to be His follower, I must follow Him. If I *say* I am a Christian, but I never lift a finger to help the unfortunate around me, then—like the goats—I'll be in for a shock.

Now, I'm not talking about politics or denominations—and I'm not talking about the sins I have or have not committed. I'm talking about examining my life to see if I'm participating in the work of Christ. If I claim to follow Him but I live for me, then I'm not His disciple. I'm just fooling myself. I certainly won't fool Christ.

Day 84

AT LEAST I'M BETTER THAN JUDAS

> *Judas . . . said, "What will you give me if I deliver him over to you?" And they paid him thirty pieces of silver.*
> **MATTHEW 26:14–15**

The name Judas ranks up there with the great villains of history. He may not have the volume of blood on his hands that some tyrants do; but he turned on the Son of God, and thus, his name has become synonymous with betrayal.

One of the twelve disciples, Judas participated in Christ's ministry and could easily have had a gospel named after him . . . had he not turned traitor. He presumably made great sacrifice to follow Christ, and there is no doubt that he was one of His dedicated followers. Yet he chose to betray Christ for *thirty pieces of silver.*

I may think Judas to be a monster . . . but I have to ask myself, *Which disciple do I resemble most?* I'd like to be like Peter—the rock—but I'm afraid that if I had to honestly examine my life, I'd be more akin to Judas.

It's not that I've literally betrayed Christ. Daily, though, I have this choice: to pursue Christ or to follow my own desires. Whom do I usually pursue? Am I one of the eleven, denying self daily, sacrificing all to follow Him? Or, like Judas, do I pursue silver, pride, lust, anger, or bitterness at the expense of the Messiah?

Judas claimed to follow Christ but then betrayed Him for money. I claim to follow Christ but then turn my back on Him in pursuit of self. The moral difference between betrayal and hypocrisy is not as significant as I'd like it to be.

As far as we know, Judas never repented and returned to Christ, which is the difference between Judas and me. Daily, I must throw myself on the mercy of God and follow Him desperately, realizing that I'm not better than anyone, including Judas.

Day 85

EATING JESUS

Jesus took bread . . . and said, "Take, eat; this is my body." And he took a cup . . . saying, "Drink of it, all of you, for this is my blood of the covenant, which is poured out for many for the forgiveness of sins."

MATTHEW 26:26–28

I frequently insert myself into a story to understand what the characters experienced. I imagine that, like the disciples, I would have been utterly confused with Jesus at Passover.

Jesus had told the disciples of his approaching death, but here He was telling them that, to receive forgiveness and life, they must eat His flesh and drink His blood. It wasn't enough that He die. They must rely on Him for sustenance. Even figuratively, this had to seem grotesque and confusing.

Eating Jesus sounds offensive, but these are His words, not mine. Though we regularly celebrate communion, we don't often speak of it in graphic terms. We've sanitized communion to the point where it has lost some of its meaning. Jesus meant for this to be a radical idea that shook us with its truth.

The reality is this: *Just as we all must regularly consume food to maintain our physical lives, we must continually fill ourselves with reading, praying, and meditating to maintain our spiritual lives.*

I don't eat only once in life . . . and I don't claim faith once and walk away. The supply of Christ is endless—and I must continually fill myself with it for my spiritual survival. If I want His eternal life in me, this is not optional.

When I starve myself from Christ, my spiritual life withers, becoming emaciated and weak. In His place, I fill the void with the desires of my flesh, sowing the seeds of my own destruction.

I've many times wondered where God was during those times when it seemed that He was absent. I starved my spiritual life and then had the audacity to wonder why it was anemic and powerless. If I want a vibrant spirit life, I must consume Christ daily.

Day 86

ANXIOUS JESUS?

> *Then Jesus . . . said to his disciples, "Sit here, while I go over there and pray.". . . He began to be sorrowful and troubled. Then he said to them, "My soul is very sorrowful, even to death."*
>
> **MATTHEW 26:36–38**

It's tempting for me to be dismissive of struggles when I don't identify with them. Admittedly, anxiety isn't my primary struggle, so when I see someone struggling with it, my first thoughts are predictable. *Just stop worrying.* If you know anxiety, you know how helpful this is.

Some will go so far as to suggest that just to *be* in a state of anxiety is sinful. *Jesus said we're not to be anxious, so anxiety is a sin, right?*

Anxiety can be an unhelpful response; but by itself, it's no more sinful than sorrow, or even hunger. It's a predisposition to feel a certain way, which may or may not be in response to some stressor.

Just as my appetite for food isn't in itself sinful (but can lead to destructive behaviors), anxiety can lead to appropriate or inappropriate responses. I can, in my hunger, make healthy or unhealthy choices. Responding incorrectly to any predisposition of my flesh nature—including anxiety—can result in destructive behavior.

Jesus, on the night of his betrayal and arrest, showed us how to respond appropriately to our natural impulses. Without sinning, Jesus was anxious. He knew that He was about to be tortured, and His flesh nature rebelled against it. He was "sorrowful and troubled . . . even to death." So, what did Jesus do about His sorrow and anxiety? Did He just suck it up?

No, Jesus gathered his friends and told them of His sorrow. He asked them to help bear His burden. Then, He prayed. Jesus—the Son of God— spent time on his knees, communing with the Father. In His anxiety, Jesus could have sinned, but instead He chose to respond constructively. Therein lies the lesson for me.

Day 87

WAR OF THE WILLS

My Father, if it be possible, let this cup pass from me;
nevertheless, not as I will, but as you will.

MATTHEW 26:39

I often find myself in conflict between two wills in opposition to each other. I want to lose weight, but I really like donuts. I want to be in good shape, but I would rather sit on the couch. I intend to spend time with God, but I am very busy—perhaps on the couch eating donuts.

I want what is right, but I would rather have immediate gratification. I lack self-control, so I settle for satisfying my appetite with immediate pleasure, which almost always leads me away from who I want to be. Then I get frustrated with myself and promise to do better next time. When next time comes around, nothing has changed—and I repeat the cycle for the thousandth time.

Life is an ongoing battle of wills. As long as we live in these bodies of ours, we will be subject to their flawed desires. We all struggle with something, be it food, pride, image, greed, lust, anger, or affirmation.

Jesus knew this war of the wills. In the garden of Gethsemane, on the night of His betrayal and arrest, He was deeply troubled about His imminent torture and death. He knew the higher purpose of what was coming, but that didn't mean that it wasn't going to hurt. Jesus was anxious about the coming pain, and He wanted out.

What was Jesus' response? Did He give in to self? No. In His conflict of will, He honestly took His struggle to God. He told His Father that frankly, He would rather avoid the coming pain. Then, in magnificent example to us all, He surrendered His will for the Father's. "Not as I will, but as you will." Jesus was honest about his conflict; but in the end, He surrendered to God.

This is how we must learn to live. We must continually be honest about our struggles and examine ourselves to see if we are following our wills . . . or surrendering to God's.

Day 88
JUST STOP IT

| *The spirit indeed is willing, but the flesh is weak.* |
MATTHEW 26:41

Some preach that the solution to my sin is to *just stop it.* I've always found this to be nonsense, as I have known the slavery of my flesh. My defects may be somewhat amusing when they involve donuts, but my flesh has far more destructive, addictive manifestations.

Why are we addicted to destructive behaviors? Why do we surrender control to anger, drugs, greed, pride, sex, status, approval, and appearance?

In regard to my addiction, many wanted to know why. *Why would you do this?* I don't know that there's any way to help someone understand, other than to point to his or her own defect and ask that they never indulge in it again. *If you are angry, never get angry again. If you lust, never lust again. Just stop it . . .*

Why do any of us repeatedly engage in harmful behavior? It's because we have sown the seeds of our flesh nature to the point where it controls us. We have the perfect spirit life of God, but we carry it in this defective flesh. We can grow our spirit life—or feed the flesh life to the point where it owns us. We sow the seeds of our own life—or our destruction.

Jesus, in today's passage, insists that, though our spirit desires right, the flesh opposes it. On the night of His arrest, Jesus struggled with His own will, which did not go peacefully. In distress, He wrestled His will to the ground and surrendered to His Father. He did *whatever it took* to follow God and to kill His own will.

When we struggle, we don't need to look far for the *why.* If we spend hours in front of the TV but give only five minutes to God, we need not wonder at our lack of faith. When we feed our flesh, we shouldn't ask why it controls us. If we want to have a vibrant spirit life, we must—like Christ—do *whatever it takes* to abandon self and pursue God.

Day 89

SKELETONS IN MY CLOSET

> Now the betrayer had given them a sign, saying, "The one I will kiss
> is the man. . . . " And he came up to Jesus. . . . And he kissed him.

MATTHEW 26:48–49

It would appear that even as Judas betrayed Christ, he hoped to get away with it. He tried to get his silver and retain his status as one of the twelve. Working in the dark, masquerading as a friend, he greeted Jesus with a smile and betrayed him with a kiss.

It's easy to judge Judas for his treachery and greed. He was a thief (John 12:6) and a traitor. In the end, he hanged himself (Matthew 27:5). He was a tragic, despicable figure who met his deserved end.

Still, it's difficult for me to write about Judas, not because I feel bad for him, but because his corrupt behavior mirrors mine. How often do I think that I can get away with it? What if all of my evil motives and deeds were on display for the world to judge?

It's convenient to point back to my addiction and dismiss it. *That's all in the past.* However, in reading Judas' story, I have just enough honesty to ask which skeletons I'm still hiding in my closet. Stopping off at the grocery store for a donut and discarding the evidence before I get home may sound funny to you, but it only promotes my *I-can-get-away-with-it* attitude.

I may insist that my business is private, but it's a good exercise to ask myself if I'd be okay with my wife and children observing all my behavior. If I engage in conduct that I want to hide in the dark, then I'm sowing seeds of corruption.

In the darkness of my addiction, I wanted to hide from the world—and from God. I hated even looking in the mirror. Though I don't live perfectly now, I like not hiding from God—or the mirror. If I want to live in the Light, I can't dwell in the dark.

Day 90
MY FAILURE

> *Then he began to invoke a curse on himself and to swear, "I do not know the man." And immediately the rooster crowed. And Peter remembered the saying of Jesus, "Before the rooster crows, you will deny me three times." And he went out and wept bitterly.*
>
> **MATTHEW 26:74–75**

I sympathize with Peter. I too have turned my back on God and have felt the bitter sting of regret. Peter was bold when he was with Christ, but with the arrest of Jesus, his faith wavered. Peter was again consumed by the wind and the waves; only this time, Jesus wasn't there to save him.

Just a few paragraphs earlier, Jesus predicted that Peter would deny him not once, but three times. Peter, in a moment of false bravado, insisted, "Even if I must die with you, I will not deny you!" (Matthew 26:35).

Peter's faith held strong when they came to arrest Jesus, drawing a sword in Christ's defense. With Christ present, Peter was bold. Once he could not see Jesus, though, he crumbled.

The first lesson here is that I exercise faith when I keep my gaze on Christ. When I take my eyes off Him, I become distracted by the wind and waves of the world. With God above all, everything is in its proper place. It's in taking my gaze off Christ that, like Peter, I become consumed by the world.

The second lesson is that God sees past my failures. Jesus was Peter's biggest cheerleader, even though He knew of Peter's imminent unfaithfulness. Jesus saw past Peter's weakness to see that he would become the foundation of the church.

My vision is often so shortsighted. In the mess of life, it's so easy to lose faith. Like Peter, I fail and weep bitterly over my failure. I think all is lost simply because I can't see the big picture. Thankfully, God works, even through my failure. Even when I stumble and lose faith, God is always faithful.

Day 91

ANATOMY OF AN ADDICTION

> *Judas . . . brought back the thirty pieces of silver . . . saying,*
> *"I have sinned." . . . He went and hanged himself.*
>
> **MATTHEW 27:3–5**

Maybe it went like this.

I doubt that Judas *set out* to betray Christ. Judas genuinely wanted to *follow* Jesus, but like all of us, he had his defects. Judas loved money, and in John we're told that he routinely stole from the disciples' money bag.

He likely had some guilt the first time. *Just this once. I'm no thief. I just need it right now.* Then afterward, he probably felt awful as the guilt consumed him. *I swear, I'll never do that again! However,* as he realized that he had gotten away with it, the remorse didn't last. *No consequences!* The guilt faded.

The next time, it was easier. *I'm not hurting anyone.* Soon, Judas was living off stolen money. Sin became routine, and his conscience numbed to the repeated insults. It was never enough, though. One day, he struck up a foolproof scheme to fleece the priests out of a fortune by betraying Christ. Jesus could show His power, save Himself, and Judas would get paid.

Then everything went sideways as Jesus was condemned to death. Judas' world came apart as he finally saw the monster he had become. In his guilt and shame, he ended himself.

I do not tell Judas' story this way to invoke sympathy. He was a miserable figure who met a miserable end, but Judas didn't set out to kill Jesus or himself. It started with an appetite, which he indulged—until it owned him. By the end, Judas didn't control his flesh nature. It controlled him, driving him to destruction.

This brings up an important question. *How much Judas is in me?* I'm not speaking of betrayal. I'm referring to the pursuit my own appetites. Pride, lust, self, anger, and affirmation are all addictions that can own me as surely as Judas' greed owned him. Have I become so comfortable with my defects that they no longer even bother me?

Judas abandoned Jesus for self. If we want to avoid his fate, we must abandon self for Jesus.

Day 92

I CANNOT BELIEVE IN A GOD WHO . . .

> *The chief priests, with the scribes and elders, mocked him,*
> *saying, "He saved others; he cannot save himself. . . . Let him*
> *come down now from the cross, and we will believe in him."*
>
> **MATTHEW 27:40–42**

As Christ hung naked and dying on the cross, those watching assuaged their guilt by concluding that if He really was God, He would save Himself. Those responsible for His torture and death mocked Him, saying they would follow Him if He would just come down. *We cannot believe in a god who would allow Himself to be crucified.*

I hear this echoed often today. *I cannot believe in a god who allows . . . I cannot believe in a god who says . . .* I do this myself when I insist that God must be what I demand Him to be. *God must satisfy my sense of reason, or I will reject Him.*

The chief priests and elders found their own logic to be inescapable. They knew that God could not die on a cross; therefore, Jesus was not the Son of God. As He was not God, they felt comfortable killing Him. They were, of course, horribly mistaken.

Likewise, my best thinking has led me to destruction. Yet I still sometimes have had the arrogance to insist that God satisfy my sense of logic and justice. *If you are God, you must . . .*

Like a petulant child, I have demanded that God meet my expectations—or I would withhold my faith. What must God think of my mandate? *Oh, this doesn't make sense to you? Well, I apologize. Please allow me to meet your expectations . . .*

It's in my self-centered addiction to myself that I demand that God bend to my will.

Faith isn't forcing God to meet our understanding or expectations. Faith is us bending to His will—even when we don't understand. Faith is focusing on God, particularly when we don't get it.

Day 93

OUT OF THE WRECKAGE

> *But the angel said . . . , "Do not be afraid, for I know that you seek Jesus who was crucified. He is not here, for he has risen."*
>
> **MATTHEW 28:5–6**

Jesus predicted His own death and His resurrection, but His followers didn't understand. When He was crucified and buried, they must have felt profound despair with the thought that they may have wasted their lives. *We followed a failed messiah.* Still, they loved Him and they went to pay their respects.

In their mourning, they harbored a spark of hope. That flicker fanned to a flame when they found an angel and an empty tomb. The hope they dared to indulge in was realized as they met the risen Christ. In that moment, they went from complete despair to profound joy.

This is what Jesus does for those who follow Him. He doesn't make us perfect or guarantee wealth. He does promise, though, that He will meet our deepest needs and free us from slavery to ourselves.

When asked why I follow God, I tell of how I followed self to despair and how, in that despair, I turned to God. I wasn't promised that my career or family would return to normal. I was only promised that if I followed Christ, my life would be better than it was when I was following only myself. Jesus saves me from the wreckage of myself.

I look back at the misery and despair of following myself and remember how, in that situation, I couldn't see that my life could ever be repaired. I did believe in God, though, so I turned to Him, the only one capable of handling it. In following God instead of myself, I found that life, joy, and hope returned.

This doesn't necessarily happen all at once. Growth for us is sometimes painfully slow, and life isn't made easy just because we follow God. Once we turn from self to God, though, we stop sowing the seeds of our own destruction. Only then does life grow out of the wreckage.

Day 94
BLESSED ARE THE LOSERS

> *Those who are well have no need of a physician, but those who are sick. I came not to call the righteous, but sinners.*
>
> **MARK 2:17**

I got lost once on vacation. Miles from our hotel, in a strange city, my phone died; and I had absolutely no idea how to get back. I must have driven in circles for an hour, thinking I was on the right road—only to find that Orange Blossom Avenue is very different from Orange Avenue. I was lost.

Jesus, in today's passage, said He came for the sick and the lost, associating with tax collectors and prostitutes. The Pharisees were offended by this, unable to see that they themselves were lost. Meanwhile, Jesus surrounded Himself with the losers who knew they were losers.

The world would tell us one thing: *Blessed are the wealthy and successful,* but Jesus contradicted. *Blessed are the losers, as only they know their own need.* Those who feel they have no need for God are, in the end, truly lost.

If I don't think that I need God, then I'll never seek Him. Even if I want God or think He's a good idea, if I don't realize my need, I'll never find Him. It's only in my need that I go to God in my proper posture—as one who is lost, in need of salvation.

There are those who see no need for God and thus, have no interest in Him. There are also those who imagine their need to be gone because they once confessed faith long ago. Both groups have a hard time knowing God, as they remain blind to their true need.

It's only in recognition of my continual need for God that I continually seek and find Him. The Pharisees were just as lost as those who refused to follow God, as they were blind to their own sickness. They thought themselves *righteous* and thus, had no further need for healing.

Lost in the city, it did me no good to insist that I wasn't lost. It was only in admitting my need (and asking for directions) that I could begin to find my way.

Day 95
ANXIETY CURE?

Do not fear, only believe.

MARK 5:36

Though donuts are my favorite metaphor for my flesh nature, not everyone shares my defect (weirdos). For many, anxiety is far more relatable. As it turns out, Jesus said quite a bit more about anxiety than donuts.

In today's passage, a religious leader came to Jesus requesting healing for his daughter, only to learn that he was too late. His daughter was already dead. In that moment of despair, Jesus said, "Do not fear, only believe." He said that the answer to our angst is to believe, taking eyes off self, looking to God continuously.

What happens when I do this? Does God cure me of my anxiety? Some will insist that coming to Christ means our anxiety is gone forever. *Real Christians are not anxious.* While it is true that I must focus on God in my defects, this absolutely doesn't mean that I'm delivered from them once and for all. I'm never promised that my anxiety or my appetite for donuts will be removed. Jesus just commanded that I turn to Him in my need.

It's not my donut appetite that makes me gain weight. It's my donut eating. Likewise, it's not my predisposition to anxiety that is destructive, it's my response to it.

As often as we're tempted to indulge in our defects, we must use them to turn ourselves toward God. He can bear the burdens that we can't. He has transformed us so that we don't feel the gravity of our defects as much as we used to, but our flesh nature is never gone while we live in these bodies.

When we pursue God, He grows life and diminishes the flesh. The answer to our defects isn't to pretend they don't exist. The answer is to use them to turn us toward God. "Do not fear, only believe."

Day 96

POTTY-MOUTH

For from within, out of the heart of man, come evil thoughts,
sexual immorality . . . envy, slander, pride, foolishness.

MARK 7:21–22

I said bad word one day. This wouldn't be worth including in this book, except that I didn't just say it, I yelled it—in a gym full of people. It wasn't that the word itself was inherently so bad, it just surprised me that it shot out so easily. In thinking about it, I realized that I say that word under my breath and not infrequently.

This got me thinking about what else is inside of me. I wish that word was the worst thing lurking in my mind. I've many times wondered what it would be like if my thoughts were displayed on a sign above my head. That would be terrifying.

If we think we have no evil in us, we need look no farther than our own thoughts. Jesus, in today's passage, said that our hearts and minds are corrupt. Though we may never act on them, we all harbor angry, covetous, lustful, prideful, or deceitful thoughts.

Some will say that I'm too hard on myself and too obsessed with our defects in general. *We're just human, after all.* This was Jesus' point. It's our human nature that is, by definition, broken. To be human is to have a desperately defective flesh nature.

"But I'm not that bad!" This is the battle cry of the man blinded by pride, who might as well say, "I don't need God!"

This is the height of self-deception, to convince myself that I'm not that bad and just don't really need God. *I swear only occasionally. I'm a pretty good guy. I don't need to get crazy with this faith thing.* Jesus said that if I want to be His disciple, I must deny self and follow Him. If I don't see the need to deny self, I will never truly follow Him.

Day 97

IGNORING GOD'S VOICE

> And Zechariah said to the angel, "How shall I know this?
> For I am an old man, and my wife is advanced in years."

LUKE 1:18

I was driving down the interstate one day when my phone spoke, warning me of an accident ahead, suggesting an alternative route to save time. I couldn't see any accident, so I ignored the voice . . . and spent the next hour crawling three miserable miles. I should have listened to the voice. My phone knew what I did not.

In today's passage, Zechariah, a priest in the temple, heard the voice of God speaking through his angel, Gabriel. The angel told Zechariah that his wife, who had been unable to conceive for many long years, was going to have a son.

Zechariah was no fool. He and his wife had been unable to have children in their prime, which was long past. He doubted the angel and asked God to prove Himself. "How shall I know this?" God was apparently unimpressed—and struck Zechariah mute for his disbelief.

There are always consequences for my disbelief. When God speaks, I can follow His voice, or I can follow my own. He allows me the choice, but each path I choose has its own consequences. Just as on the highway, I may end up at the right destination eventually, but following *my* route takes longer . . . and is much more painful.

Each day, I have this choice to follow God or to follow me. Each decision I make can be in faith, pursuing God's will, or in pride, pursuing my will.

But I don't know God's will. If an angel told me what to do, I would do it. His will is no secret, though. I must turn from self to love God and love my neighbor. He has told me what I must do, and He has told me of the consequences of refusing. When I follow myself, I find the disaster of me. When I follow God, I find life, joy, and peace in Him.

Day 98

IF YOU LOVED ME, GOD . . .

And she gave birth to her firstborn son and wrapped him in swaddling cloths and laid him in a manger, because there was no place for them in the inn.

LUKE 2:7

I know it's immature to do so, but sometimes, when I'm frustrated, I lash out at God. When I can't find my keys, I ask God for help. Then, when my keys do not miraculously appear, I have the audacity to get angry at God. *Why God? If you loved me . . .*

We often treat God this way. We believe He is all-powerful, so we know He could fix everything if He wanted. Following God means that we should be wealthy and healthy, right?

This fantasy about God comes neither from the Bible nor from observing reality. It's simply an invention of our flesh nature. It's what we want God to be, because deep down we are still obsessed with self. We want God to be a genie in a lamp, existing only for our comfort.

I wonder if Joseph and Mary thought this way. They went along with His plan, so, why did God not arrange a place for them to stay while in Bethlehem? *OK, God. Would it be too much to ask for a room in the inn? The barn? Seriously?*

God's own Son came into the world in a barn, greeted not by dignitaries, but by shepherds. It seems that God is pleased to use humble people and humble circumstances for His will. Those who find themselves successful often feel no need of God and therefore are not useful to Him.

It's not that God isn't interested in what's best for us, it's just that our version of what's best is very different from God's. Following God doesn't mean that we'll have all the desires of our flesh met. Following God probably means the opposite. It does, however, mean that God will work out what is ultimately best for us, precisely because He loves us.

Day 99
TURNING MY BACK ON GOD

> *Soldiers also asked him, "And we, what shall we do?" And he said to them, "Do not extort money from anyone by threats or by false accusation, and be content with your wages."*
>
> **LUKE 3:14**

Though I clearly recall the events of my relapse into addiction, I am hesitant to include it in this book, as it's painful to remember. It's important, though, to understand how destructive my purposeful disobedience to God has been.

Long before I took the first pills, I turned my back on God in an act of defiance that sparked my relapse. One day in the spring of 2014, my appetite for chewing tobacco, a vice I had previously surrendered, returned. I felt that I could indulge *just once.*

I felt God tugging at me. *This is destructive. Do not do this.* I knew it was wrong, but I wanted it anyway. I felt his response deep in my gut. *So basically, you are just turning your back on me?* And my retort? *Yes, but you are God, so you must forgive me when I repent.* God did forgive when I finally repented . . . six long, destructive months later.

When I choose defiance, I turn my back on God. I thought I could do this with no consequences. *God will forgive.* The bomb I dropped in my mind, though, was devastating. The next day, I could not bring myself to look to Him or repent. I just wanted more of my sin.

In today's passage, John the Baptist had a simple message. *Stop defying God! You know what is right. Now do it!* His audience knew right, but they chose wrong *because they wanted it more.*

How often do I do this? The reality is, when I choose *my* way, I decimate my own faith. I can't follow God while also defying Him. If I'm tired of my own destruction, I must repent, doing whatever it takes to deny self and follow Him.

Day 100
ADDICTED TO BUSYNESS

| *He would withdraw to desolate places and pray.* |
LUKE 5:16

I'm not patient and I do not sit still well. I relax by engaging in what my kids call work. Don't get me wrong. I enjoy sitting at the beach as much as anyone, but after five minutes . . . I have stuff to do.

For me to just sit and pray is not natural. Jesus found prayer to be an important part of his life, though, so I must ask why. What did He even pray about? He could turn water into wine. What need could have driven him to God?

As I was thinking about that, I realized my question itself could be wrong. I think of prayer as asking God for stuff; so naturally, Jesus must have been praying because He needed stuff too, right?

Today's passage refers to the crowds who pursued Christ, which I'm sure was draining and distracting. Jesus' greatest need wasn't stuff, but to find time alone with God. Living in an earthly body, Jesus came to know the confines, defects, and distractions of the flesh. In the flesh, even Jesus needed to take time to pursue His Father.

How much more must I need time in prayer? The most important relationship in my life is with God. Do I act like it? If I audited my time, what small percentage would be devoted to Him?

I am just so busy. Family, exercise, work, leisure, sleep. I just don't have time, God. Sorry, I have TV to watch. The truth is, I have time for God. I just don't give it to Him. I'm addicted to busyness.

If we find our faith to be weak and our connection with God to be lacking, we have no further to look than the effort we've put into our relationship with Him. We can live either near to or far from God, but we too often choose distance by default. If we long to know God, we must pursue Him. We have the time. We must daily take the time.

Day 101
APPETITE FOR DISTRACTION

Blessed are you who are hungry now, for you shall be satisfied.
LUKE 6:21

Occasionally, I meet those who are unsure of their defects. This always astounds me, as I have so many, and they're so obvious to me. There are those, though, who have no obvious struggle with pride, food, greed, drugs, anger, or selfishness. They seem to avoid any evident destructive behavior. Do they have no defects?

It's safe to promise this: *We all have defects that distract us from being who God wants us to be.* None of us live a perfect life, pursuing and obeying God as we should. So how do we know what our defects are?

I must identify what distracts me from pursuing God as I should. Jesus said those who hunger for God are the blessed. Those who need God will pursue Him. The opposite is true as well. Those who pursue satisfaction in anything other than God are blinded to their need for God, as they still think it can be found elsewhere.

The more obviously destructive my appetites are, then the more likely I am to recognize and confront them. Though I am not thankful for the destruction I caused, I am profoundly thankful for my addiction, as it revealed my need for God. It was only in my desperation that I pursued Him. If my worst defect had been a small, unrecognized one, it may never have been severe enough to turn me to God.

Anything that takes the place of God is sinful and destructive. It may be a secret lust that no one ever sees, or it may be something that hides in plain sight. A successful career and family can be as devastating as drug addiction . . . if it keeps someone from God.

I must be painfully honest with myself, asking what appetite I pursue above God. The appetite I feed is the one that grows. If I expend my life pursuing God, my hunger for Him will grow as I come to know the joy and satisfaction that only He can provide.

Day 102
HATING FOR GOD

> *Love your enemies, do good to those who hate you, bless those who curse you, pray for those who abuse you.*

LUKE 6:27–28

When I read this passage, I thought, *I don't have any enemies. Everyone loves me, right?* On second thought, I realized I could be missing something, so, I checked in with a friend. *Who are my enemies?*

Our conversation turned to those who believe differently: those who don't believe in God, those who believe in a different god, and those who believe in God *differently.* Faith is a divisive topic, exposing divisions—and sometimes producing enemies.

As a Christian, I've created enemies needlessly. There certainly will be those who hate me because I follow Christ. However, most of my enemies exist because I have *treated* them as enemies. I have disobeyed Christ's command to love.

I have seen myself as a bearer of a divine truth, thinking that those who believe differently don't just oppose me, they oppose God. In the name of my faith, I have treated others as adversaries.

Absolute truth can lead to destructive arrogance. We tell ourselves that the most loving thing we can do is to tell someone the truth. *I don't need to be kind. I just need to tell you that you are going to hell.*

Jesus, in today's passage, explains how we must love. He said that we must bless those who consider us enemies. We should be kind, praying for and giving to them. We must love them despite their disdain for us. For our part, we are not to consider them as enemies. If there be enmity between us, it's to be their choice, not ours.

This absolutely doesn't mean we abandon the truth. It just means that we don't use the truth as an excuse to hate. Once we begin to hate in the name of the truth, we have become as wrong as if we had abandoned the truth altogether. The truth is that we are called to love our enemies.

Day 103
A PAINFUL LESSON

*Judge not, and you will not be judged; condemn
not, and you will not be condemned.*

LUKE 6:37

It's dangerous to pray for some things. As I read this passage,
I asked God to show me how I am judgmental. Not long afterward, God
answered as I met with a sex offender. I won't provide the details of the
meeting except to say that I judged him. I found myself looking down
most of the time—literally and figuratively.

I'm far from perfect, but there are those who've failed in ways that even
I look down on, finding myself to be *better than*. It's the essence of being
judgmental—elevating myself and condemning those I find to be inferior.

Jesus, in today's passage, warned me of this. Being a Christian doesn't
mean I have the power or responsibility to condemn another. It isn't my
place to hate a sex offender for his sin, though I certainly should hate
the sin.

To avoid being judgmental doesn't mean I can't identify destructive
behavior. Sin is still sin, and I'm not asked to pretend otherwise. I may
well need to confront destructive behavior in others. Not being judgmental does not mean I ignore sin. As a Christian, though, I tend to divide the
world into good and bad people. I believe that I'm good and those who
commit horrific crimes are bad. The fact that I too have done awful things
doesn't matter . . . I draw the line just beyond my bad behavior.

This shouldn't be about a hierarchy of sins to alleviate my guilt. This
is about recognizing God as the only judge. I make myself out to be a
god when I look down on others, hating them for sin that's different from
mine. Jesus said I must love my neighbor regardless of how he sins. He
didn't say it would be easy.

Day 104
STUPID PEOPLE

> *Why do you see the speck that is in your brother's eye,*
> *but do not notice the log that is in your own eye?*

LUKE 6:41

One summer, I was hauling a load of four-by-four posts in my pickup when I pulled away from a stoplight—and left the load in the intersection. Horrified, I parked on the shoulder and hurried to remove the debris from the road, obstructing traffic for blocks in every direction. Embarrassed and racing to pick up my mess, I was thankful to see a man come out of a local business to help. Instead of assisting, though, he stood by his shiny pickup, about 20 feet away from mine and informed me that if I scratched his vehicle, he was not going to be very happy.

I was already frustrated, but this just made me mad. *What an idiot!* I began fantasizing about taking out one of his stupid headlights with a post. My frustrations now had a focal point. This man was the cause of my misery. Never mind that I had been the one who failed to secure the posts. Not about to be distracted by facts, I blamed this jerk for my life problems.

I often do this. Being guilty of my own defects does not prevent me from being offended by the defects of others. *It's different when I do it!* In my me-addiction, I lend myself grace that I offer to no one else. Never mind the destruction I have caused. I recovered from drug addiction, so I'm now the authority on everyone else's defects.

Jesus warns us of this, "First take the log out of your own eye" (Luke 6:42). It's not my responsibility to fix that guy with the shiny pickup.

We're responsible only for our behavior and our relationship with God. All we can do is work on ourselves and our defects. Focusing on the defects of those around us is destructive, as it distracts us from God. Jesus said we must keep our eyes on Him, not on the defects of our neighbors.

Day 105

GUTS

For no good tree bears bad fruit, nor again does a bad tree
bear good fruit, for each tree is known by its own fruit.

LUKE 6:43–44

We all know those who live paradoxical lives. On the one hand, they do great things for God, but on the other, they remain tremendously defective. They may be wonderful leaders—or even pastors—but they're still prideful, difficult, or lacking self-control.

How do I understand such people? How can someone who does so much good remain so defective? Is this person an imposter? Did Jesus not say that a tree is either good or bad, bearing only good fruit or bad?

It's my tendency for extremes that interprets today's passage to say that a person is either all good or all bad. It's easier if I can divide the world into good and bad people. The problem is that I don't know anyone who's all good—or all bad. None of us produces only one type of fruit. Each of us is a mixed basket.

If you knew me only from my writing, you may have imagined that I have life all figured out. Then, after you met me, you'd be disappointed to find that I am still prideful, I eat too much, and I can be short tempered.

The truth is, the world is not divided into good and bad people. That line runs through each of us. Jesus insisted that what we do comes from inside us. If we pursue the works of the flesh, we grow a predictable fruit. If we instead pursue God, we produce a completely different result. When we participate in destructive behavior, it's not some random occurrence. It comes from inside us.

When I find someone else to be a paradox, I need to look no farther than my own life for understanding. Though I produce good fruit, I still retain defects that, when indulged in, produce destructive consequences. This perspective gives me grace and understanding for the failures of others and reminds me that I am still capable of stumbling.

Day 106

JAIL OR TREATMENT, ANYONE?

> *As for what fell among the thorns, they are those who*
> *hear, but as they go on their way they are choked*
> *by the cares and riches and pleasures of life.*

LUKE 8:14

One doesn't need to go to jail or treatment to meet God, but it can help. In treatment, I had little contact with my family, I wasn't working, and I had no internet access. It was a giant time-out that forced me to focus on God and myself. It was there that I finally learned to start every day by turning my gaze to Him.

Today's passage was one that I read on my first day home from treatment. Looking back at that journal entry reminded me of the lessons learned. I could see that meeting God in treatment was the easy part. Reentering the real world was the danger zone. I wasn't wrong to worry. When I'm in pain, I seek God. When life turns around, my recognition of my need fades.

Many inmates find themselves desperate for God. They attend Bible study and swear that life will be different when they get out. When they're released, they initially promise that they'll remain hungry for God. It rarely lasts. Why?

Jesus, in today's parable, explains. God, the sower, plants the seed, but we bear no small responsibility. However, we often abandon the sprouting plant when life goes well. In our own success, we strangulate our spirit life, pursuing self. Our interests don't need to be obviously evil to distract from God. An honest career can be just as destructive as a dishonest one if it consumes our life focus.

The tragedy of the inmate who leaves God at the jail gate could be our tragedy. It's our responsibility to continually ask which thorns are choking the spiritual life out of us. If we prefer to avoid future self-destruction, we must remember the lessons we learned from our past destruction.

Day 107
AFRAID OF THE LIGHT

*For nothing is hidden that will not be made manifest, nor is
anything secret that will not be known and come to light.*

LUKE 8:17

When I was five or six, I was camping with my family when my sister and I were sent to the camp store on an errand. We also bought a snack, which was not included in the errand. In guilt, we hid the evidence under a log. I spent the rest of that vacation convinced that my parents would roll that log over and know.

Had I just told my parents, I'm sure all would have been forgiven. I covered up my crime, though, and so, every time we walked by that log for the rest of that week of camping, I panicked. By the end of the week, I was a wreck.

You may laugh at my over-developed conscience, but you likely also know what it's like to live in fear that the real you will be discovered. *What if my deepest, darkest secrets were revealed for all to see?*

Most of us know what it's like to live in fear of the Light. We think, say, and do things in the dark that would mortify us if dragged into daylight. The guilt and fear are miserable, but we don't want to change—change is worse than discovery. Change is profoundly painful, so we keep the facade up, continuing in our secret hatred, anger, resentment, arrogance, lust, or addiction.

I'd like to say that I got help voluntarily; but the truth is, I had to be dragged—kicking and screaming—into the Light. I'm thankful now though, as I like being able to look in the mirror.

I'm not saying that we should print all our misdeeds in the paper. I am saying that the only real solution is to do whatever it takes to stop. This may require confession, and it will certainly involve painful change. For some it will mean treatment. For all of us, it will require radical, daily work to abandon the dark in pursuit of the Light.

Day 108

PRACTICING FOR FAILURE

| *Where is your faith?* |

LUKE 8:25

When I first read today's passage, I didn't understand why Jesus had chastised the disciples. In the story, Jesus and company were all traveling across the lake when a storm hit, threatening to swamp their boat. As Jesus slept, the disciples lost it. In a panic, they woke up Jesus, who calmed the storm and reprimanded them, "Where is your faith?"

What? The disciples were terrified of dying in a storm and had turned to Jesus for help. What had they done wrong?

Here's where the disciples failed: When the storm hit, the disciples panicked. They claimed faith, but when disaster struck, they were spooked and became obsessed with saving themselves. This is natural, of course, which is why Jesus rebuked them. Faith is unnatural.

If faith is keeping my gaze on God, then faith is anything but intuitive—and it must be learned *before* the storm hits. Waiting for the storm is a terrible way to find out if I have faith. I must learn faith by practicing it daily, in the small things, so that when the storm does hit, I already have it.

I often hear men claim that they will be following God when they get out of treatment or jail. *What are you doing today to practice faith?* They plan to follow God someday . . . but today, they practice for failure. They plan to follow God in the big decisions . . . but in the little everyday decisions, they still follow self.

If I prepare for failure by pursuing self today, then I will not suddenly find faith when the storm hits. Instead I'll panic—and I'll continue to follow self.

If the disciples had been prepared for the storm, they wouldn't have panicked. They would have known that whether they lived or died, Christ held them in His hand. If I want to have that kind of faith in the storm, I must prepare for it in the little, everyday decisions—continually keeping my eyes on Christ.

Day 109

WHAT HAVE YOU DONE FOR ME LATELY?

| *Return to your home, and declare how much God has done for you.* |

LUKE 8:39

God delivers me from myself. This is what I tell people that God does for me. When I visit inmates in jail or when I meet struggling addicts, I tell them that they don't need to live like this. I tell them of my struggle and what God has done for me. In today's passage, this is what Jesus commanded me to do.

In the story, Jesus met a violent, psychotic man who lived naked, in the cemetery. He had his demons. Then he met Jesus and was made whole, returning to his "right mind" (Luke 8:35). In love with Jesus, he wanted to follow. However, Jesus instructed the man to go and tell others what He had done for him.

We too, are to bear witness to what Christ has done for us. The problem, of course, is that we often have little to tell. When asked what difference God has made, we hesitate. *Well, I'm thankful for my stuff and for not going to hell . . .*

I've been there. It wasn't that I didn't have my demons. It was that I had never allowed God to heal me. "He who is forgiven little, loves little" (Luke 7:47). If I have been forgiven for only a little, it's not because I don't need forgiveness. It's that I haven't repented. I remain enslaved to secret pride, anger, lust, or addiction . . . and so I have no happy tale to tell.

If we want to be whole, we must allow God to deliver us from ourselves. Our part is to do whatever it takes to abandon our defects and follow Him. In response, He'll always do His part and grow His life in us. As we follow, God delivers us from ourselves daily. When we're obedient, God uses our stories of transformation in the lives of those who need it themselves. "Return to your home, and declare how much God has done for you."

Day 110

OFFENDED FOR GOD

*Lord, do you want us to tell fire to come down
from heaven and consume them?*

LUKE 9:54

The angriest I have been in my adult life—and the closest I have come to physical violence—has probably been over matters of faith. Though I'm embarrassed by it, my worst tantrums have stemmed from disagreements about church or God.

When someone disagrees with me about my football team, I may argue a little . . . but when someone disagrees with my faith, the gloves come off. *You're not just offending me, you're offending God.*

In today's passage, Jesus and His disciples found themselves in such a situation as they traveled through a Samaritan village where Christ was rejected. The disciples took offense, reacting hatefully. *Should we kill them for you? Would that please you?*

The disciples thought they were doing right. Christ had been rejected, which could not go unanswered. *The pagans must burn.* In their pride, the disciples were offended for Jesus and wanted vengeance.

We often do this. When someone rejects our faith, we take the offense upon ourselves and we lash out. We claim we're offended for God . . . but God can take care of Himself. He doesn't require our retaliation.

Being offended is often a defect itself, as it's usually my own pride on the line. I declare the offense to be God's, but when I act badly over a religious disagreement, it has nothing to do with God. He never asks me to sin for Him.

Jesus must have shaken his head at James and John. *What is wrong with you? Have you ever seen me call down fire from heaven to kill those who reject me?* How did Christ respond to rejection? When rejected, He simply moved along, shook the dust off his sandals, and left the results up to the Father.

God never asks us to behave badly for Him. When someone disagrees with us about our faith—or when someone rejects God—we must, like Christ, keep our eyes on God and leave the consequences up to Him.

Day 111

GOOD INTENTIONS AND THE ROAD TO HELL

> *I will follow you, Lord, but let me first say farewell to those at my home.*

LUKE 9:61

As I had to figure this out in treatment, I often pose an important question to those new in recovery. *What's going to be different this time?* I generally get the same answer. *I'm going to live for God and stop using drugs.* I answered much the same way when I was in treatment, but my counselor was wise enough to ask exactly what I was going to do differently.

I told her that I was willing to change everything. In fact, if God wanted me to sell all my possessions and become a missionary, I would do it. She suggested that I had other things to work on first. I first needed to stop using drugs.

In today's passage, this would-be disciple tried to get away with making a similar grand commitment. He intended to follow Christ, but . . . he had some other stuff to do first. This sums up my entire life. I plan to follow God. I just have some other stuff to do. I call myself a disciple, but when it comes to the doing, I must first (insert generic excuse).

We all have reasons not to follow. We want a little bit of God . . . but we don't want to disrupt our normal lives. We want God to be in our top-ten list of life—but rarely are we willing to put Him above all else.

This leads us to some level of destruction, even if it isn't immediately obvious. Putting anything above God in my life is distracting and destructive. It's only in following God above all that everything is in its proper place.

If we say we follow God, it must impact our behavior *right now*. When we get up in the morning, we must point ourselves at God. Through the day, we must keep our eyes on Christ and make our feet follow. If we say we follow God, we must stop making excuses, or our faith is nothing more than good intentions.

Day 112

CAN'T I JUST TAKE A PILL FOR THAT?

Ask, and it will be given to you; seek, and you will find; knock, and it will be opened to you.

LUKE 11:9

In junior high, I watched one of those heroic sports movies where the underdog overcomes ridiculous odds. I'll spare the details, except to say that I was inspired. I decided that night to do whatever it took to become a high school state wrestling champion. Before training, though, I needed a bowl of ice cream. I did not win state.

As an adult, I've probably not matured much. I still want to be in good shape, but eating right is hard work. If there were a pill to make me athletic, I would be interested.

I have always tried to take the easy way out. When forced to go to treatment, I tried to pick the shortest program. I wanted sobriety, but I didn't want the hard work of getting there. If someone had offered me a sober pill, I would have taken it.

This kind of thinking crept into my theology. I have never wanted to work hard, I have just wanted God to miraculously transform me. No one finds God by doing nothing, though. Spiritual growth is not a spectator sport.

Ask, seek, knock. These are all action words. Spiritual growth is not a passive process in which we sit back and allow nature to take its course. Our nature always pursues the destructive. We're on an escalator, constantly moving down toward our fleshly desires. God longs for us to live life at the top with Him, but we don't get there by doing nothing. We abide in Christ only when we continually put forth the effort to pursue Him.

Day 113

THE CHOICE WE ALL MAKE

| *Whoever is not with me is against me.* |

LUKE 11:23

I'm tempted to think today's passage does not refer to me. I became a Christian long ago, so I've already made my choice, right?

In treatment I begged God to save me from my destruction. He said I needed only to point my life at Him every day, and I would never follow myself to this destruction again. Though I was already a Christian, God insisted I still must make my choice daily. Do I live for God or for self? He made it clear that I must daily choose Him or—by definition—I will have chosen opposition to Him.

But I am not opposed to God! This is the cry of those of us who want God but continue to pursue self. In doing so, we find ourselves, by default, opposing God. Apathetic opposition is still opposition, though.

But I am a Christian! I cannot be opposed to God! Yes, I have a new life that nothing can take away, but I still have this old life—and daily, I must choose between the two. The temptation is to think that, because I have chosen once, I no longer need to do so.

The problem is, I turn my gaze back to self constantly. In writing my blog and this book, I can either write honestly about my walk with God— or I can get caught up in the numbers, writing for my own success. This is how I tend to turn a good thing into elevation of self.

It's not that I can continually lose and regain my salvation. God loves me regardless of my behavior. I don't earn his grace by good behavior or lose it with bad. Daily, though, I must choose to focus on Him, or I naturally focus on myself. I'll never find intimacy with God by pursuing self.

We all make this choice. We can choose opposition to God, or we can live as we were meant to, with the Creator of the universe on our side.

Day 114

PORN

> *Your eye is the lamp of your body. When your eye*
> *is healthy, your whole body is full of light, but when*
> *it is bad, your body is full of darkness.*

LUKE 11:34

When I was in junior high, a classmate brought a certain magazine into the locker room. The fact that those images are still burned into my brain decades later stands as testament to the impact of the event. Men are highly visual, and pornography is a drug in our testosterone-soaked brains.

I don't know that Jesus was specifically referring to lust in today's passage, but His words are certainly applicable to our current epidemic of pornography. We currently have churches full of men who are paralyzed spiritually by pornography.

The problem, as Jesus described it, is that I follow my eyes. I cannot look at the dark and the Light at the same time. If I'm pursuing the dark, my spiritual life will follow. I may want God, but if I'm regularly viewing porn, my spiritual development will inevitably be arrested.

You're being a little ridiculous. . . . At least I'm not out having an affair. . . . Jesus must have encountered such thinking. "Everyone who looks at a woman with lustful intent has already committed adultery with her in his heart" (Matthew 5:28). I can't consume garbage and expect to grow spiritually.

I'm not addicted to pornography! I said the same about my pills once, creating a facade of excuses that allowed me to continue in my behavior. Refusal to accept the truth has often been my choice.

What do we do if we find ourselves addicted to porn? It is our responsibility to do whatever it takes to stop pursuing the darkness and turn toward the Light. For some, this will mean going to treatment. For others, it will mean getting rid of a phone or computer. (Gasp!) Anyone who truly wants to change must make a radical commitment to turn from the darkness, toward the Light.

Day 115
ADDICTED TO RULES

> *Woe to you Pharisees! For you tithe mint and rue and
> every herb, and neglect justice and the love of God.*
>
> **LUKE 11:42**

Admittedly, I see addiction everywhere. Because of my own experience, I have come to see defect in everyone. In my defense, it's just a fact that we all struggle with some destructive behavior. This is simply how I define addiction. *We all struggle with something that controls us.*

Some defects are more obviously destructive than others. If we don't know our own struggles, then our condition is perhaps worse off than we think.

The one who has no *obvious* defect is often just blind to it. If a man never knows a struggle with drugs, gluttony, or lust, then he will likely succumb to pride. Following the rules often breeds arrogance in the one who follows them so well. Rules themselves becomes an addiction when they are elevated above even God.

This is the condition that Jesus describes in today's passage. The Pharisees were notorious for enforcing their preferred rules, but this made them prideful, condescending, and judgmental. Worshipping the rules above God, they completely missed God.

We call this legalism and we despise it. We cheer Jesus chastising the Pharisees. *Yes, no rules!* Those of us who have been rule-breakers are tempted to think that Jesus was giving us the green light to do whatever we want. But Jesus was not encouraging us to indulge in our destructive defects. He was just pointing out that rules can be their own addiction.

Though we despise legalism in others, we all tend toward legalism when it comes to defects with which we don't struggle, looking down on those who sin differently. This is rule-addiction: *I keep these rules, so I'm better than you.*

The underlying defect of rule-worship is the same as every other defect. It's a focus on self instead of God. It's as destructive as any other addiction. It just masquerades as holiness. The only way to recover from it is to daily do whatever it takes to deny promotion of self—and to turn to God.

Day 116
MANIPULATOR

> *Do not seek what you are to eat and what you are to drink, nor be worried. . . . Instead, seek his kingdom, and these things will be added to you.*
>
> **LUKE 12:29, 31**

In Alcoholics Anonymous, I learned the Serenity Prayer: *God grant me the serenity to accept the things I cannot change; courage to change the things I can; and wisdom to know the difference.* I've always thought there should be another line: *Keep me from manipulating the things I could change but should not.*

In treatment, my life was a mess. My marriage and career were on the brink, and I became obsessed with fixing them both. My primary need, though, was to figure out my own life. What I couldn't see was that the only way to fix anything was to turn myself to God first. My wife and my career needed me to radically change before I did anything else.

This conflict came to a head over my discharge date. It was perhaps my final lesson in treatment. Because I was to be discharged two days *after* my daughter's twelfth birthday, I became obsessed with manipulating events so I could get out early.

In the end, I had to let it go. I finally had to accept a hard fact. There are some things that I can *possibly* change . . . that I should simply let go.

This is how I've come to understand the words of Christ in today's passage. "Do not be anxious about your life" (Luke 12:22). Jesus says I must focus first on the things that truly matter. I must put God before everything, including family and career. It's only in seeking Him above all that everything else is in its proper place. When I put even good things (family) above God, they become destructive to me, and I become destructive to them.

There are some things we can manipulate, and there are some things we cannot. We can, however, always choose to look to God and His will, believing that He loves us and holds us in His hands.

Day 117

WHOSE SIN IS WORSE?

*Do you think that these Galileans were worse sinners than
all the other Galileans, because they suffered in this way?*

LUKE 13:2

Are some sins worse than others? Is the drug dealer more despicable than the thief? Is stealing worse than outbursts of anger? Is anger more destructive than overeating?

In today's passage, Jesus was asked a similar question. Some Galileans had apparently been killed by Pilate, which stood as evidence to some, that the victims must have been guilty of some egregious sin. Those who posed the question sought to make sense of evil by blaming those killed. *They must have really offended God.*

We see this with natural disasters. After the 2004 Indian Ocean tsunami, which killed thousands, internet articles circulated, attributing it to God's wrath on *those godless pagans. They must have deserved what they got. It's the only thing that makes sense.*

Jesus objected, insisting that we're all in the same boat. We all engage in destructive behavior and we all need God. We may try to assuage our consciences by comparing ourselves to those we think to be worse than we are. But in the end, we all need God the same.

This doesn't mean that all sins have the same practical consequences. If I think mean thoughts, that's not as destructive as if I use drugs. Not all destructive behavior has the identical results.

This doesn't mean that I should use a hierarchy of sin to condescend to those who sin differently. I need God as much as the man sitting in prison. It's only in my pride that I find myself to be *better than*. It is, of course, ridiculous to stand before God, thinking myself to be better than anyone in His eyes.

Jesus pointed out the absurdity of comparison, as we're all on the same level in relation to God. "Unless you repent, you will all likewise perish" (Luke 13:5). We all fail and we all need God. Thankfully, He has grace enough for us all.

Day 118

LOVE'S COST

When you give a feast, invite the poor, the crippled, the lame, the blind, and you will be blessed, because they cannot repay you. For you will be repaid at the resurrection of the just.

LUKE 14:13-14

I recently turned into a coffee shop, only to see a man on the corner holding a sign. *Help, homeless, hungry. God bless.* I didn't want to help, and I didn't want his blessing. I just wanted a cup of coffee. In the end, I soothed my conscience by giving him a couple dollars. I thought about buying him something to eat, but I had stuff to do. *I can't help everyone. He will take advantage of my generosity.*

I don't mind giving to my friends. I'm happy to loan my pickup to those who can afford to fix it if they break it. Those who can give back to me are much more likely to experience my "generosity."

Jesus said this isn't how real love works, though. In today's passage, He insisted that when we do only for those who can return the favor to us, we're simply investing . . . or performing a service for a fee.

When we do for those who cannot repay, however, we show authentic love. Real love costs me time, effort, kindness, or perhaps money. When I love those less fortunate—the poor, the imprisoned, or the addicted, I will likely never be repaid. I give because Jesus told me to give, and because He gave to me when I had nothing to offer.

In my me-addiction, I object. I want to love only those who look nice, smell nice, and can repay my kindness. I don't want to get my hands dirty and I don't want love to cost me anything. Jesus almost guarantees, however, that real love will not be paid back.

Jesus Himself promises the repayment, though. He said that when I love those in need, I will be filled with His life, peace, and joy—which are worth infinitely more than the few dollars I may sacrifice.

Day 119
I'D LIKE TO, BUT . . .

A man once gave a great banquet and invited many. . . .
But they all alike began to make excuses.

LUKE 14:16, 18

I used to have many excuses to refuse time with God. *I need to get some sleep. I work today. I have to spend time with the kids.* Reasonable excuses piled up, one day at a time, into months and years. Then, when my life fell apart, I had the audacity to wonder why I didn't feel close to God. *Where were you, God?* Instead of pursuing my relationship with God, I followed self and found inevitable disaster.

In today's passage, Jesus told the parable of a man who planned a great banquet—but when the date of the event arrived, the guests all had similar excuses. One needed to inspect his land, one had to examine his oxen, and one used his new bride as an excuse.

This greatly angered the host, who declared that those who refused his invitation would receive exactly what they chose—nothing. "None of those men who were invited shall taste my banquet" (Luke 14:24).

We are those men. The Creator of the universe calls us to commune with Him in a very real, intimate relationship. He longs for us to answer His invitation, focusing our lives on Him instead of self.

The men in the parable didn't chase obviously evil things. They pursued career, possessions, and family. These were not wrong pursuits . . . until they used them as excuses to refuse the invitation.

Anything, no matter how good it may be, becomes destructive to me when I put it before God. I may daily make excuses to follow self, or I may choose to pursue God. I don't do it perfectly, but every day, I now get up early and spend time with God. This doesn't mean I abandon career and family—or that I live perfectly. It just means that I make a genuine, daily attempt to point my life at God instead of self.

God is calling. Will we answer—or will we continue to make excuses? If we insist on following ourselves, Jesus says we will get exactly what we pursue.

Day 120

I DESERVE A DRINK

*Any one of you who does not renounce all
that he has cannot be my disciple.*

LUKE 14:33

I clearly recall the justifications I made in college for drinking. I was conflicted about it because I had grown up in a home where no one consumed alcohol, so I had to perform a few contortions of conscience to excuse my behavior. *It's harmless. I deserve it. I'm just having fun.*

I felt that drinking was destructive for me, but my preference won out . . . so I lived in a perpetual state of conflict. I wanted God—but I also wanted other stuff.

Most of us can identify with this. We like the idea of God, and we know we need a little help—but we don't want to get too crazy with this *faith* thing. We want just a little bit of God.

Jesus warned us of this kind of thinking. He insisted that we must count the cost. Faith is an all-or-nothing kind of deal, in which we must be willing to sacrifice all to follow. Christ said this God thing was just not going to be for everyone.

God doesn't demand perfection of me prior to going to Him, but He does ask that I be willing to abandon myself in pursuit of Him. If I insist on holding out on some part of my life which He asks me to surrender, that pursuit will cause some distraction and destruction.

Alcohol isn't evil for everyone. Jesus turned water into wine (one of my favorite justifications). I'm just telling my story, which includes significant destruction due to my use of chemicals. God wants all of me. When I hold out in one area, that thing inevitably leads me to some injury as it turns me away from God.

For most, the area of holdout is not a chemical, but some other defect of the flesh. It may be pride, security in money, lust, sexuality, anger, appearance, or even a career. Whatever we keep from God will distract us from Him, causing us destruction. God wants every part of us.

Day 121

THE PRODIGAL SON PART 1: WHY?

> *The younger son gathered all he had and took a journey into a far*
> *country, and there he squandered his property in reckless living.*

LUKE 15:13

I sympathize with the Prodigal Son in Jesus' parable. In it, a man had two sons. The younger, afflicted by wanderlust, wanted the good life without delay and asked his father for his inheritance. Once he had the money, he took off for an exotic land, living lavishly.

I imagine his family wanted to know why. *Why would he take his money and run?* In the worst of my own destruction, this is what my family wanted to know. *Why would you do such a thing?*

There is, of course, no answer that satisfies—because the only answer is as miserable as it is true. We engage in destructive behavior, at least initially, because *we want to*. Make no mistake, we do these things because they bring us pleasure.

We seek joy in money, sex, alcohol, food, possessions, or beauty because these things deliver some pleasure . . . for a time. The problem with the instant gratification of our flesh nature is that it always requires payment later. Like the hangover after a night of drinking, cheap thrills deliver pleasure but, in the end, demand payment.

That payment often involves a kind of slavery. When we engage in a behavior repeatedly, it becomes habitual. Psychological dependence develops . . . and soon, we can't stop.

Neither the Prodigal Son nor I was unaware of the consequences of our behavior. He knew that the party would end when the money ran out. He just couldn't stop. This is the essence of addiction—engaging in destructive behavior despite knowing the consequences.

Does this mean that we're allowed no pleasure in this life? No—but there is, of course, a right and wrong way to pursue pleasure. We can pursue it through instant gratification with destructive payment later . . . or we can choose discipline now, reaping joy later. Only in following God do we find ultimate joy and peace.

Day 122

THE PRODIGAL SON
PART 2: DESTRUCTION

> *When he had spent everything . . . he began to be*
> *in need. . . . And no one gave him anything.*
>
> **LUKE 15:14, 16**

As I mentioned in the previous devotion, I identify with the Prodigal Son, who wanted to enjoy all life had to offer. He didn't set out to find destruction. He just couldn't see past his own desires and so fell victim to his flesh nature.

I've been there and can imagine his thoughts. He knew his money would run out, but he thought he had time to change. As he indulged in wine and women, he told himself that every night would be the last. *I will change . . . tomorrow!* He tried to stop but instead found himself addicted to the life. He saw the storm coming but thought there was still time. Then one day, the storm was on him. His money evaporated and he went from playboy to pauper. In his desperation, he took a job feeding the pigs—pigs that ate better than he did.

Only in his misery and humility, could he see that he alone was to blame for his ruin. As great as his misery was, though, the worst consequence was that he had severed his relationship with his father—the only one who truly loved him.

It was only in his destruction that he was able to realize his condition and change it. Only when he hit rock bottom could he see his need for his father.

As miserable as rock bottom is, there are worse places, like living apart from the Father and not realizing it. When we're just successful enough to avoid complete disaster, we don't see the need for change. We may *think* we want God, but if our pain isn't great enough, we lack the motivation to truly commit to transformation.

Looking back, I can see that, like the Prodigal Son, I wouldn't have changed without consequences. Though I'm not thankful for the pain I caused, I can be thankful for pain and the opportunity to change. As long as I could draw breath, I could still repent. *Destruction was the beginning.*

Day 123

THE PRODIGAL SON
PART 3: REBIRTH

> *He arose and came to his father. But while he was still*
> *a long way off, his father saw him and felt compassion,*
> *and ran and embraced him and kissed him.*

LUKE 15:20

I clearly remember the despair of my addiction. Like the Prodigal Son, I pursued self and suffered the consequences. In our consequences, we both found rebirth.

The Prodigal, in his poverty, decided to return home and throw himself on his father's mercy. He planned his words carefully. "Father, I have sinned. . . . I am no longer worthy to be called your son" (Luke 15:18–19).

It was only in his need that the Prodigal was able to choose several things. First, he chose *honesty*. He had to accept that he desperately needed help. Second, he chose *humility*. He could not return home and demand his old life back. Third, he chose to *change everything*. He had to abandon the old to embrace the new.

The Prodigal thus returned to his father. "But while he was still a long way off, his father saw him and felt compassion, and ran and embraced him and kissed him." There was no anger. There was only inexpressible joy that the lost had been found.

The son began to deliver the prepared speech, but the father had other plans. "Let us eat and celebrate. For this my son was dead, and is alive again; he was lost, and is found" (Luke 15:23–24).

To be reborn, the son's old life had to die. It was only out of the ashes of the old that the new could arise. The new life, by definition, was accompanied by a radical change in behavior.

This is where I found myself. It was only in my destruction that I could see my need for the Father, and it was only in my destruction that I became willing to change. Thankfully, the Father embraced me upon my return. Now, like the Prodigal Son, I must daily choose to continue to live a new life as one reborn.

Day 124

THE PRODIGAL SON
PART 4: THE BITTER END

> *Now his older son was in the field, and as he came*
> *and drew near to the house, he heard music and*
> *dancing. . . . But he was angry and refused to go in.*

LUKE 15:25, 28

I love the story of the Prodigal Son. I'm the wandering son who found new life in the Father. I've often thought that Jesus should have ended the story there, but He didn't. Not everyone has wandered like the Prodigal, so not everyone identifies with him as I do. Because some don't see their own destructive behavior in his story, Jesus went on to tell the story of the older brother.

Unlike the father, the older brother wasn't happy about his brother's return. When he came home from working in the field to find the household in full celebration, he was furious and refused to participate. His father tried to explain; but, filled with resentment, the older brother fumed. "These many years I have served you. . . . But when this son of yours came, who has devoured your property with prostitutes, you killed the fattened calf for him!" (Luke 15:29–30).

I don't mind identifying with the younger brother, but I loathe that I am, at times, the older brother as well. As I have recovered from my drug addiction, I've earned the right to condescend to those still struggling . . . right?

We so often do this. We repent of our *big sins* (or never had any *big sins* in the first place), and we think quite highly of ourselves. *These many years I have served you.* Then, when the Prodigal returns home, we're bitter. We wallow in our pride and refuse to celebrate. In doing so, we injure our own relationship with the Father.

In a bitter twist of irony, it was the older brother who left the father, while the younger son embraced him. We're never told if the older son eventually joined in or not. In the telling of the story, Jesus left him standing there as a reminder to us all. None of us has *earned* a place as His child. It is a gift freely given to those will accept it. End of story.

Day 125

FORGIVING THE REPEAT OFFENDER

If your brother sins . . . seven times in the day, and turns to you seven times, saying, "I repent," you must forgive him.

LUKE 17:3–4

Though I have been forgiven much, I still find it hard to repeatedly forgive others. When someone wrongs me repetitively, I find forgiveness a bitter pill to swallow. Jesus, though, insisted that as I have been forgiven much, I must forgive even repeat offenders.

It's worth noting what forgiveness is and what it isn't. Forgiving means that I no longer hold a wrong over someone's head. It means I let go of my anger and resentment, canceling the debt. I do not continue to bring it up with every new conflict.

Forgiveness does not mean forgetting. I'm not capable of erasing my memory, and Jesus didn't ask me to try. My wife may forgive me for my past drug use while remaining vigilant about future temptation. This does not mean she doesn't forgive me.

Forgiveness doesn't mean having no boundaries. In sobriety, the addict is often frustrated when others don't trust him. Though he has repeatedly wrecked the car, he expects to get the keys back.

Forgiveness doesn't mean that I must allow another to continue to hurt me. I can forgive *and* develop healthy boundaries. Forgiving doesn't mean allowing injury to continue.

Still, it's difficult to let go of the anger. When someone says he's sorry but repeats the behavior, it doesn't feel as if he's really sorry. Jesus said, though, that if others repent, we are to forgive. He doesn't say that we should wait to see that they never fail again. We must forgive and let go of the resentment.

As God has forgiven us, He commands that we forgive others. In our pride, we don't want to let go of the debt. We want justice. The reality, though, is that we've been forgiven more than we will ever forgive . . . so we must choose to let go of our resentment.

Day 126

WHEN GOD MOVES

*When he saw them he said to them, "Go and show yourselves
to the priests." And as they went they were cleansed.*

LUKE 17:14

In my addiction, I hated who I was. I begged God to take my addiction from me, and I was angry with Him when He didn't. Why did He not move? Why did He allow me to continue in my destruction? I became bitter at God for His failure.

Today's passage tells of ten men afflicted with leprosy who asked Jesus for healing. He responded—not by healing them, but by giving them a command that they could either obey or disobey. "Go and show yourselves to the priests." The narrative is clear. They weren't healed until they moved. "As they went they were cleansed."

God didn't heal until they obeyed. Had they refused Jesus' command, they would have remained in their miserable condition. This is where I found myself in my addiction. I wanted instant healing with no disruption to the rest of my life. However, I was unwilling to tell my wife, go to treatment, or change anything. I demanded that God fix me as I continued to wallow in self.

To this, God said *no*. Had He magically changed me, I wouldn't have understood *my* part. I always desperately need God. I need Him now as much as I did then. Had He instantly removed my defect with no disruption to my self-centered life, I would never have come to understand this truth.

God loves us and longs for us to daily abandon self to follow Him. If He just removed every need we have, we would only become further addicted to self. We would just use God as a *genie in the lamp*.

If we have needs, we must go to God for His help, but we also must ask what He wants us to do. This will mean radical change on our part. If nothing changes, nothing changes. Radical transformation requires radical obedience. God moves in us when we obey.

Day 127

THE OTHER NINE

> *Then one of them, when he saw that he was healed, turned back, . . . giving him thanks. . . . Then Jesus answered, "Were not ten cleansed? Where are the nine?"*
>
> **LUKE 17:15–17**

One day when I was in line at the gas station, the patron ahead of me bought a pack of cigarettes. I began to look down on this *tobacco addict*. I should be forever humble, but in my recovery, I found myself to be *better than*. Though God has shown infinite grace to me, I found myself looking down on this one still struggling.

Jesus, in today's passage, healed ten lepers, but only one of them returned to thank Him. The other nine were obedient when it suited their needs, but after they got what they wanted, they continued on their self-centered paths. They forgot where they came from, and they forgot who had healed them.

This is the attitude I adopted at the gas station. In my recovery, like the nine, I abandoned gratitude and humility. I took my eyes off God and turned them toward myself, ignoring my other defects. *Thank God, I am not like this loser.*

The arrogance I find in recovery is just another form of addiction. When I turn my gaze from the God who brought me out of my destruction, I'm just trading drug addiction for me-addiction. My pride that day in the gas station was every bit as destructive as those cigarettes.

So, how do we avoid the pitfall of pride that so often comes with recovery? The answer lies in choosing gratitude like the one leper. He remembered who healed him, and thus he kept his gaze focused on Christ. It is in daily choosing to remember who we are and what God has done for us that we can avoid the arrogance of the nine. It's in daily thanking God for what He has done for us that we keep our focus on Him.

Day 128
THANK GOD, I'M BETTER THAN . . .

> *The Pharisee . . . prayed thus: "God, I thank you that I am*
> *not like other men. . . ." But the tax collector . . . beat his*
> *breast, saying, "God, be merciful to me, a sinner!"*
>
> **LUKE 18:11–13**

I love the tax collector's prayer. It was the honest prayer of a man who knew what a wretch he was. Despised by all, the tax collector cried out to God. "Be merciful to me, a sinner!" It was the desperate prayer of a broken man.

I've been there, on desperate knees. When I got there, I realized that—had I been there all along, I wouldn't have pursued self to such destruction. Even in my desperation, though, I imagined that if my situation ever improved, I would likely be tempted to stand proud, assuming the posture of the Pharisee.

The Pharisee's prayer is the antithesis of the tax collector's. The Pharisee did not kneel. He stood tall before God and man. "Thank you that I am not like other men." He was *better than*, and he wanted everyone to know it.

When I was at the bottom, it wasn't difficult to remain on my knees. A few years of sobriety, however, and arrogant thoughts crept in. My pride rose from the grave and I assumed the posture of the Pharisee.

Jesus warned of this dangerous attitude. He said the tax collector, in the end, was the one who went home restored to God. The Pharisee, who chose arrogance, went home alone, in opposition to God. Those addicted to pride cannot be restored, as they can't see the need. *I am fantastic! I don't need God like these poor losers.*

It's not that pride is unforgivable. It's that pride does not see its own need for forgiveness. The surest sign of being horribly afflicted by pride is thinking myself to be free from it. *Thank God I'm not proud . . .*

God, be merciful to me, a sinner! Daily, I must choose to remain on my knees with this prayer on my lips.

Day 129
RICH AND WRONG

"Sell all that you have . . . and come, follow me." But when he heard these things, he became very sad, for he was extremely rich.

LUKE 18:22–23

In Luke, we're told of Christ's encounters with two rich men—encounters leading to two very different outcomes. The first was a rich young ruler who went to Jesus asking what he must do to be saved. Seeing that the man was self-sufficient, Jesus instructed him to sell everything he had. Only then could he stop relying on self and discover his need for God. Only in radical obedience could he break his addiction to his own success. The man walked away sad because he just couldn't do it. He didn't need God that much.

The second man, Zacchaeus (yes, the *wee little man*), also went looking for Christ. His approach was radically different, though. In his humility, he dared not talk to Christ. He knew what a mess he was . . . so he climbed a tree, just to look upon Christ as He passed. Then Jesus called him out. Zacchaeus saw his own need, recognized the disaster of self, and turned to God. In the end, he gave half his possessions to the poor. He repented from his destructive pursuits and received a new life.

My life has mirrored that of each of these men. I have, like the rich young ruler, depended on self, ignoring my need for God. I found what I had pursued, the disaster of me.

I've also been like Zacchaeus, recognizing my disaster and being a little afraid—in my mess—to turn to God. God received me willingly, of course, waiting with open arms.

The difference between the two men wasn't that one kept his possessions and one gave them away. They didn't earn God by their actions. Their actions were an expression of their hearts toward Christ. One simply did not feel the *need* for Him and thus, couldn't follow Him. The other, in his desperate need, fell in love with Christ and no longer needed all his stuff.

It's only in recognizing our desperate need that we find and follow Christ.

Day 130

HOW IT ALL FELL APART

But watch yourselves lest your hearts be weighed down
with dissipation and drunkenness and cares of this life.

LUKE 21:34

I didn't set out to become an addict. If you had asked me ten years ago if I was capable of such destructive behavior, I would have felt confident that such a thing was impossible.

So what happened? How did I get there? When everything fell apart, I desperately needed to answer those questions. The simple answer lies in today's passage. I got where I was by doing nothing. The terrifying reality is that destruction is my natural state, and if I do nothing to avoid it, gravity will work its inexorable effect.

Jesus' words here reveal a universal principle that I desperately need to understand. *I must live purposefully.* The life God intends for me does not happen automatically. Though God took the first step toward me, it's my responsibility to daily pursue that relationship if I want to live the life He desires.

Dissipation is the natural loss of heat or energy, which is irreversible unless acted on by some outside force. Life is like an escalator moving me continually down toward my flesh life at the bottom. Standing still, I will always move toward myself. The Spirit-filled life, at the top, must be purposefully and continually pursued—or I will never live there.

Not everyone's natural state will be as obviously destructive as mine has been. Subtle destruction may, in the end, be a worse condition because one does not ever see the need to address it. When I hit bottom, I could not avoid radical changes. Secret addictions, however, may continue for years. It's a pitiful state to wallow in behavior that's just bad enough to keep me from God—but not severe enough that I absolutely must deal with it.

If we want God, we must purposefully pursue Him, or we will naturally pursue self. It's only in pursuing Him that we can abandon the natural disaster of the flesh.

Day 131
EATING RIGHT

> He took bread . . . and gave it to them, saying, "This is my body,
> which is given for you. Do this in remembrance of me."

LUKE 22:19

I am what I eat, and frankly, I eat a lot of junk food. It's not that I don't know what's good for me, I just have an appetite for things that are bad for me.

My spiritual life is not dissimilar. I want God and I want to live the Spirit-filled life, but I also desire the spiritual equivalent of junk food. Some pursuits are obviously evil, but not all are. Even so, I can be distracted from God by family, work, or even exercise. If my effort at the gym distracts me from God, I may be doing it wrong.

Today's passage describes the first Communion, when Jesus told His disciples that the bread was symbolic of His body, which would be broken for them. He explained that, just as they consumed bread for their physical lives, they must "consume" Christ for their spiritual lives.

I sometimes wonder if we do Communion wrong. Is it possible that our ritual of prayer before every meal is closer to Jesus' intent? As often as we eat or drink, we must remember that as we feed ourselves physically with bread, we are to feed ourselves spiritually with Christ (1 Corinthians 11:26).

I struggle to stay connected to God through the day. Incidentally, I never forget to eat. Though I'm often too busy for God, I'm never too busy for food. This, I think, is what Jesus was saying: *As often as you fill yourself with food, choose to fill yourself with me.*

As my physical health can improve or decay, my spiritual health can do the same. I am what I consume, and I can consume a little bit of God or a lot of God. In the act of Communion, I find a practical way to stay connected with God all day. As often as I eat or drink, I can choose to keep my gaze on Christ, continually eating right, filling myself with Him.

Day 132

ALL I NEED IS PRAYER?

Pray that you may not enter into temptation.

LUKE 22:40

When I once told someone that I went to a Christian drug treatment program, she sarcastically asked, "Is that where they teach you all you need to do is pray?" The implication was that Christians deny the reality of addiction, ignorantly relying on *silly prayer* to fix everything. I understand what she meant. I too, have been frustrated watching others struggle alone, rejecting help, and refusing to *do anything*. They're just going to *pray it out*.

Jesus, though, in the garden of Gethsemane, on the night of his arrest, twice told His disciples to pray, lest they *enter into temptation*. As He was purposefully taking time to connect with the Father, He insisted that they follow His example.

Jesus taught that it is our responsibility to turn our minds to God. However, Jesus didn't teach that *prayer is all I need*. He taught that I must also take radical action, doing whatever it takes to avoid sin. "If your right hand causes you to sin, cut it off" (Matthew 5:30). I don't get to use Jesus' command to pray as an excuse to do nothing.

It's in the secret thoughts of my mind that I first begin to travel down the road of destruction. Adultery and murder begin in my imagination in the forms of lust and hate (Matthew 5). Whatever my struggle is, it starts with a desire that I either feed or starve. I must do what it takes to starve my dark thoughts.

For many of us, this is a foreign concept. We have, out of ignorance or apathy, surrendered the battle for our minds. We haven't realized that we are responsible for choosing our thoughts.

It's our responsibility to continually connect with the Father in prayer, pointing our minds at Him instead of self. Jesus didn't teach prayer as a substitute for action. He did, however, teach that we need to pray continually, focusing our minds on Him, making our feet follow. This kind of prayer may well lead to *radical* action.

Day 133
LET GO AND LET GOD?

> *In agony he prayed more earnestly; and his sweat became*
> *like great drops of blood falling down to the ground.*
>
> **LUKE 22:44**

As I finished my workout one day, I noticed that both of my shins were bleeding. Though they looked dramatic, they were just painless abrasions, so I wiped them off and moved on. Later, I reflected on this. *What if I put as much energy into my spiritual health as I do into my physical health?*

We've been taught somewhere along the line that following God is easy. *Just let go and let God.* I've even heard a pastor suggest as much. *If you are struggling with a destructive behavior, just stop doing it.*

I promise you, though, that if your plan to deal with your pride, anger, or addiction is to *just stop*, you will fail. When I was mired in addiction to drugs, I regularly complained to God that I had *tried so hard* to stop. The truth is, I had done nothing. I had just tried *really, really hard* not to do it again. I would not confess, go to treatment, or change my life. I certainly didn't bleed for my efforts.

Luke 22:42 tells how Jesus, on the night before His torture and crucifixion, struggled with His flesh nature. He wanted out of this deal. "Father, if you are willing, remove this cup from me." It was with blood, sweat, and tears that Jesus wrestled His own will to the ground and surrendered to the Father. "Not my will, but yours, be done."

I often complain that I'm trying so hard to stop some destructive behavior. The truth is that I haven't yet resisted to the point of shedding blood (Hebrews 12:4). I may say I've tried *really hard*, but usually, that just means that I want God to magically fix me without my working for it.

Are we to *let go and let God*? No. We must find and do whatever it takes to abandon self and follow Christ. This may well mean radical effort on our part.

Day 134

FINDING GOD IN DISASTER

"Jesus, remember me when you come into your kingdom." And he said to him, "Truly, I say to you, today you will be with me in paradise."

LUKE 23:42–43

Calamity has a way of readjusting one's perspective. In times of success we have the debilitating luxury of being distracted by the unimportant. When disaster strikes, though, we're forced to focus on that which truly matters. When we're comfortable, we just don't see our need for God. In our pain, we promise that we'll follow Him forever . . . but when the storm passes, we return to the same old pursuits of self.

In today's passage, we're told the story of two men who found disaster. Both were condemned to die with Christ; but one of them, in his despair, lashed out at Christ. "Are you not the Christ? Save yourself and us!" (Luke 23:39).

His transgression wasn't simply that he mocked Christ, but that he didn't believe in Him. If anyone was in desperate need, it was this man. He just couldn't see Christ as the answer to it. He thought Jesus to be a charlatan—so in his hopelessness, he mocked Him.

The other criminal, however, knew God when he saw Him. In dreadful need, he could see that Jesus was his only hope. Thus, he did the only reasonable thing he could. He humbly threw himself on Christ's mercy. "Jesus, remember me when you come into your kingdom."

It's often not until my destruction is imminent that I turn to God. When the waters of life are smooth and the sun is shining, I captain the ship. Then, when the storm hits, I beg God to take the rudder. God then must often use pain to turn me toward Himself. The reality is, I need God constantly, but unfortunately, it's often only in my discomfort that I recognize my need.

It's only in remaining aware of our need that we can avoid returning to our own misery. Today then, we must admit our constant need, abandon self, and follow God.

Day 135
DO I NEED GOD?

*Repentance for the forgiveness of sins should be
proclaimed in his name to all nations.*

LUKE 24:47

When I worked in the emergency room, I would regularly
meet addicts, of which there were two types. The first addict still acted
like an addict. Either high or seeking a high, this addict was not *helpable*.
Enslaved to the flesh, he couldn't see any need, and thus, couldn't
seek help. I didn't spend a lot of time trying to convince this addict that
he needed help. I knew the futility of this from personal experience.

The second type of addict was the one who came seeking help. This
addict didn't have life all figured out, but he could admit disaster and thus
could start the road to recovery. Honesty alone doesn't mean recovery,
but recovery is impossible without it.

I don't enjoy working with the first type of addict, as they are blind to
their own needs. I'll go to great lengths, however, to help the addict who
wants help. I'd rather work with ten addicts who know their needs than
work with one addict who remains blind to it.

Jesus commanded, in His final words to his disciples, to carry the beautiful gospel message that all can be forgiven and restored to God through
repentance. I imagine the disciples encountered a similar experience to
the one I had in the emergency room. The world is made of two types of
people: those who know they need God, and those who are blind to
that fact.

The beautiful message of the gospel is hope and peace to those of us
who know what a mess we are. It is, however, offensive to those who see
no need for forgiveness. *I've done nothing wrong. I don't need your God or
require His forgiveness!*

We're not responsible for the one who can't see his need. We're responsible only to be honest about our own continued need, living out the
gospel daily in our own lives and then sharing that with those who need
and want it.

Day 136
BLIND AND DEAF

In the beginning was the Word. . . . And the Word became flesh and dwelt among us.

JOHN 1:1, 14

When I focus on myself, I turn my eyes and ears away from God. The more intense my focus is on self, the worse my sight and hearing become. In my drug addiction, as I was completely enslaved to my own defect, I couldn't see or hear God at all.

I shut my eyes and closed my ears to God and then had the audacity to blame Him, *if he existed at all.* In my desperation, I begged to hear His voice, but I didn't really want to hear what He had to say. I just wanted some magical reassurance.

In the opening words of John, we're told that God is the great communicator. He has spoken to us through His creation and through Jesus, who is the complete manifestation of His message to the world.

Jesus told us that God loves us and longs for each of us to live in an intimate relationship with Him. It's because of Christ that we can see and hear God if we will only open our eyes and ears to Him.

God has done and always will do His part to reach us. It's now up to us to do our part. How do we do this? We must do whatever it takes daily to abandon self and follow Him. This takes work, discipline, and effort on our part.

Just as I couldn't run a marathon without training, I can't see or hear God if I don't work at it. I don't get to feed my addiction to my pride, anger, lust, or appearance and also hear God's voice. If I pursue self, I will not miraculously find God instead.

I have, in my warped thinking, pursued self only, and then I wondered why I couldn't see or hear God. It wasn't that God was silent. It was that I wasn't listening. If we want to know God, we must open our eyes and ears.

Day 137

JUSTIFYING MY ADDICTION

> Jesus said to the servants, "Fill the jars with water."
> And they filled them up to the brim. . . . The master
> of the feast tasted the water now become wine.

JOHN 2:7, 9

Though I engaged in horrible behavior in my addiction, I do still have a conscience. Sensitive to destructive behavior, my conscience makes me feel horribly guilty when I engage in such acts. How then, did I ever get myself to the point where I could tolerate my addictive behavior?

The truth is, I simply wanted something badly enough that I figured out how to bypass my own conscience. Simply put, I made excuses. Excuses and justifications were the grease that allowed my mind to squeeze into spaces where it never should have been able to fit.

I deserve this. I need to sleep. I'm a doctor, I know what I'm doing. No one will ever know. I'll stop tomorrow. This is the last time. God will forgive me.

In my addiction, I used even today's passage as an excuse. *Jesus made wine, right?* Though it doesn't involve drugs any longer, I still justify. When I want a donut, that manipulating voice returns. *I deserve it. I'll go for a run tonight. Just one and then I'll eat broccoli.*

This might seem humorous if it were confined to just donuts, but I do this with all my destructive desires. When I want to gossip, I dress it up as concern. "Did you hear about Jack's problem?" When I want to be selfish with my time and money, I insist that I deserve what I have. *I earned this.*

The truth is, we can talk ourselves into anything if we want it badly enough. Jesus did, of course, turn water into wine. That, however, is no justification for me to get drunk. We must be honest about our destructive desires, and we must recognize our ability to make excuses. When we hear that voice trying to manipulate a toxic behavior into something acceptable, we must stop—and kill it. Because our destructive behavior begins in our minds, we must continually turn our minds toward God.

Day 138

FLESH VS. SPIRIT

That which is born of the flesh is flesh, and that which is born of the Spirit is spirit.

JOHN 3:6

In my addiction, I was in a constant state of conflict. I claimed to believe in God, but I behaved in a manner that was completely contrary to that belief. When my addiction came to light, those around me wanted to know if I was even a Christian. I couldn't blame them for asking. I didn't know either. I desperately needed an answer, so I set out to understand my own condition.

Today's passage opened my eyes to the reality that, as a Christian, I'm torn between two worlds. In the story, Jesus told Nicodemus, a Pharisee, that though he had already been born of the flesh, to know God he must be born again—of the Spirit.

Though we already have a *flesh life*, we must be born again into a new *spirit life*. Here, I think, is where we tend to get a little lost. We think that this new spirit life *replaces* our old flesh life so we're no longer affected by its defects.

This is not the case. Just as our bodies do not literally die at the moment of spiritual birth, our *flesh nature* doesn't die. Thus, we have two lives, the old flesh life and the new spirit life, which are at war with each other.

This is why Jesus taught that we must daily deny self and follow Him (Luke 9:23). This is why Paul commanded us to crucify the flesh nature. It's our daily choice to sow the seeds of our flesh, leading to destruction—or to sow the seeds of the Spirit, leading to life. The choice is ours, and the results are predictable.

This was how I came to understand my condition. Though I was a Christian, I had sown the seeds of my flesh and cultivated my own destruction. If I wanted life, I desperately needed to repent and sow the seeds of the Spirit.

Day 139

THE DARK SIDE

Everyone who does wicked things hates the light and does not come to the light, lest his works should be exposed.

JOHN 3:20

I used to see news stories revealing the secret details of some celebrity's life—and think how horrible it would be if my worst words and deeds were revealed. This is exactly what happened when my name hit the local newspaper, exposing my addiction for the world to see.

Though not everyone's dark behavior is as destructive as mine, we all have something we would rather others not see. It may be pornography, anger, resentment, hateful thoughts, envy, greed, or pride; but we all have defects that we would prefer to remain in the dark.

Jesus, in today's passage, referred to Himself as the Light that has come into the world. All who love the Light are to bring their dark deeds to Him so that He may eradicate them. We resist exposure, though. It's excruciating. The Light burns our eyes because we are accustomed to the dark. It's profoundly embarrassing and shameful to confess destructive behavior.

Our pride, which may be the darkest of defects, convinces us that we have no need for the Light. Make no mistake, Jesus insisted that when we hang on to our evil behavior, we're choosing that defect over Him. "People loved the darkness rather than the light" (John 3:19). This is the essence of pride, choosing myself over God, making myself out to be God.

I don't need to confess to the local paper, but if I want to deal with my darkness, I must drag it into the Light. I must take it to Christ, and I will likely need to confess it to someone. I must abandon my pride and admit failure.

We don't do this very well. We prefer to put on our best faces for church on Sunday. In our pride, we desperately avoid revealing our dark side. It's only in abandoning self and turning to God, though, that we can expose the darkness and embrace the Light.

Day 140

MY BROKEN APPETITE

| *My food is to do the will of him who sent me.* |
JOHN 4:34

I have an insatiable appetite for the unhealthy. I never crave broccoli. I want ice cream, pizza, and massive amounts of steak. If this defect applied only to my appetite for food, I wouldn't be writing this book. This defect permeates my entire flesh nature.

I find the most immediate gratification in those things which are most destructive to me. I do understand that there's pleasure in eating well and exercising. Those things just take too much time and effort. Why put in all that work when I can have the immediate pleasure of a donut right now?

My defect, then, is not that I desire pleasure. My defect is the direction in which I aim that desire. It's not wrong to pursue satisfaction. There is, however, a right and wrong way to go about it.

Jesus, in today's passage, used this analogy of food to teach His disciples this principle. In the story, when the disciples provided dinner, He used the opportunity to talk about their appetites. Jesus told them that His food was to do the will of His Father who had sent Him.

Jesus' greatest meaning was not to be found in filling His belly, but rather in following God. We pursue purpose and pleasure in food, sex, drugs, money, appearance, and status because they provide immediate gratification. But the route to true satisfaction is found elsewhere. Seeking God above all requires some sacrifice up front but is the only route to authentic joy.

Jesus' point was not that we're unable to enjoy any of the pleasures of life. When we become a Christian, we don't stop eating or having sex within God's boundaries. We must, however, choose not to find our purpose and meaning in food or sex. It's only in pursuing God above all that we can properly enjoy His creation. It's only when we choose to follow Him above all that we find the answer to our deepest needs and desires.

Day 141

TRUTH AND CONSEQUENCES

| *You are well! Sin no more, that nothing worse may happen to you.* |
JOHN 5:14

Over the years, I've met many patients who lament their inability to lose weight. I've felt this frustration myself. I would diet for a few days but I was still overweight, so I become discouraged. Then, I'd see a guy who could eat whatever he wanted . . . and I felt cheated.

Anyone selling a diet plan takes advantage of this frustration. To make a dollar, they promise the holy grail of dieting: *Buy my plan and you can eat whatever you want while losing weight. No more consequences to your destructive behavior!*

I know this is fantasy, but still, I long for it—not just in eating, but in life. *What if I could do whatever I wanted with no consequences?*

I tend to make Jesus out to be this kind of God. I see the God of the Old Testament as all judgment, but in the New Testament I see Jesus as all love and mercy. *Jesus forgives me and severs the connection between behavior and consequences, right?*

Jesus, in today's passage, dispelled this fantasy. In the story, He healed a man but then offered him this warning. *Sin no more, that nothing worse may happen to you.* Jesus wasn't telling the man that he had been crippled because of some previous sin. He was telling the man that there are worse things than being crippled. He loved him but told him an important truth. *There is a connection between destructive behavior and destruction.*

Following Christ means abandoning the sinful pursuits of the flesh. Jesus offers love and forgiveness, but He does not abandon truth . . . or consequences. When we consume more calories than we should, we produce fat. When we use drugs, we become addicted. When we indulge in pornography, greed, pride, or anger, we discover the consequences of those pursuits. God forgives his children for all eternity, but that doesn't mean we are free from truth and consequences now.

Day 142

THROWING STONES

> Let him who is without sin among you be
> the first to throw a stone at her.

JOHN 8:7

I've always loved today's passage, as it's a beautiful picture of how Jesus responds to our destruction. In the story, the Pharisees took a woman *caught in adultery,* to Jesus, laying a trap for Him. Would He follow God's law and condemn this woman to death, or would He, out of mercy, ignore God's rules?

The Pharisees walked right into their own trap. "Let him who is without sin among you be the first to throw a stone at her." One by one, they dropped their heads . . . and their stones. Jesus insisted that to judge, they must first declare their own perfection.

This is how Jesus comes to us in our destruction. He doesn't condemn us but provides an unconditional love—a love *not* based on performance. We don't *earn* His love with our behavior. Even in our worst disaster, He loves us and desires to save us from it.

Jesus doesn't stop with love and forgiveness, though. With His love comes truth. After the Pharisees walked away and Jesus was left alone with the woman, He addressed her destructive behavior. "Go, and from now on sin no more" (John 8:7). Jesus' love was unconditional, but He did expect it to change her. Jesus told her that as He had saved her, she needed to turn from her destructive, sinful life.

I don't do this well. I either condemn others with the truth, abandoning love, or I love them, abandoning truth. I mistakenly think that loving someone means ignoring destructive behavior. I have a hard time loving and speaking plainly about sin at the same time.

Jesus does both. He unconditionally loves but also insists that we repent. He saves us from our destruction and expects that we not return to it. He won't stop loving if we continue to fail, but neither will He stop insisting that we need to change.

Day 143

WHO IS AN ADDICT?

| *Everyone who practices sin is a slave to sin.* |
JOHN 8:34

Recently, I asked Daniel, who had just returned to jail after being out only a short time, why he came back. In jail, he prayed, read his Bible, and pursued God. When he got out, he intended to continue . . . but slowly, he drifted back to the old life.

It started by hanging out with destructive friends. Once he had made a few small but bad choices, he spiraled out of control. It ended predictably with drugs and a parole violation. Daniel's addiction wasn't just to drugs, it was to a lifestyle that revolved around self. Once he dipped his toe into the old life, he was swept away by the force of it.

My kids and I have a favorite swimming spot at the inlet of a local lake that reminds me of this. We start on one side of the current and swim *under* it, coming up on the other side. As long as we stay under the current, we remain in control. If, however, we get just a foot or hand up in the current, we're sucked in and dragged inexorably out into the lake.

The inescapable current is the source of much amusement in the water—but in life, this is disaster. Jesus described this in today's passage as *slavery*. We dip only a hand into a thing, but then it sucks us in. *When we pursue sin, we become enslaved to it.*

Though we're meant to know freedom in Christ, most of us still know some slavery. Whether it is anger, lust, greed, resentment, appearance, status, success, drugs, or pride—we all struggle with some defect.

But I don't have a problem! No one likes to admit it. The Pharisees didn't either (John 8:33).

Pride—that most devastating of defects—blinds me to the presence of my flaws, convincing me that I have no need of God. Brutal honesty is required to admit my defect. It's only in recognizing the truth of my condition that I can learn to abandon self and follow Christ daily.

Day 144

IDENTITY AND AFFIRMATION

> *Just as I have loved you, you also are to love one another.*
> *By this all people will know that you are my disciples.*

JOHN 13:34–35

Most of us find some value in the affirmation we receive from others. We much prefer that the world finds us clever, funny, attractive, and popular. A kind word can make our day but a harsh one can wreck it. We check our phones a hundred times a day to find affirmation from social media. Despite knowing that this isn't where our identity lies, we place an inappropriate amount of weight in the opinions of others.

Some of us have grown tired of living under the rule of popular opinion. With that, we have moved to the other extreme. *I am my own man!*

Jesus, in today's passage, defined an appropriate concern with the opinion of the world. He said that we should live in such a way that the world sees His love in us. Our lives must point to God and His love.

I must find my identity, then, not in the world's opinion of me, but rather in God's love. I'm to be a conduit for this love, flowing though me, into the lives of those around me. I must be shaped and defined by God's love.

What does the world think of me as a Christian? Do people know me as contentious, arrogant, condescending, and judgmental? Is my life marked by love—or am I known for my addiction, pride, lust, anger, or a need to be right?

I heard a man say once that the Church's primary job was to carry the truth. Truth is, of course, important; but the world must first see God's love in us. In putting truth above love, we give in to our own pride and the need to be right. It's only when we allow God's love to fill us that we can appropriately share His truth.

Jesus insisted that if we follow Him, others will see His love flowing out of us. This is the most important thing about us. It is our nature to continually seek purpose in our own destructive pursuits; but as followers of Christ, our identity and affirmation is to be found in God and His love.

Day 145

GOD IN THE LAMP

| *If you ask me anything in my name, I will do it.* |
JOHN 14:14

I usually read this verse with an inherent flaw that prevents me from truly understanding it. When I read that Jesus will do anything I ask in His name, I naturally begin thinking of all the stuff I want.

I can have whatever I desire if I say the magic words. Praying *in Jesus' name* becomes the enchanted phrase that I sprinkle on every prayer, hoping it will mysteriously bend God to my will. I have viewed God as my personal genie in the lamp.

This is why it's so profoundly important to be aware of my own defects. I've read this verse a hundred times, not understanding why I didn't understand it. I was blind to the fact that, in turning my gaze to myself, I was doing the very opposite of what Jesus instructed.

What then, was Jesus saying? He was insisting that I must keep my eyes on Him. I must deny self and follow Him with such intensity that I become completely aligned with His will. Then, when I pray in His name, I pray in His will.

The very idea of praying in Jesus' name suggests that I am praying with His will backing my prayer. As a physician, I know that a nurse will order a medication with my name on it only if he or she knows it to be my will. Thus, it's only in turning from my own will to pursue Christ's will that I can come to pray *in His name and authority*.

When I ask for a million dollars (in Jesus' name), God is under no obligation to comply. Jesus' purpose is not to fulfill the destructive desires of my flesh nature. His purpose is to save me from myself, restoring me to a right relationship with my Father. He came to kill those desires so that I might be saved from myself.

This doesn't mean we shouldn't ask God for anything. We can and should bring every concern to Him, but like Jesus in the garden of Gethsemane, we must bow to the will of the Father. "Not my will, but yours, be done" (Luke 22:42).

Day 146

THE CHAOS OF ADDICTION

| *Peace I leave with you; my peace I give to you.* |

JOHN 14:27

The life of addiction is one marked by chaos and turmoil, where peace is a complete stranger. Constant fear of discovery and obsession with the next high consumes the mind. Burdened with shame, the addict lies to himself constantly. *I'll never do that again . . . This is the last time!* Sleepless nights and misery are the addict's constant companions.

In this state, the addict longs for tranquility. *I just wish I could find some peace.* The only way the addict finds it, though, is in the artificial serenity of the next high. He knows there's peace to be found in God and recovery, but he's unwilling or unable to do what it takes to get there.

I was recently swimming in eight feet of water, trying to carry an anchor. I won't try to explain why. I'll just say that it reminded me of my addiction. I would dive down, grab that anchor, and then push violently off the bottom, getting my head just far enough above the waves to gasp for a breath—before gravity pulled me back beneath the surface.

I would then swim furiously toward shallower water, never getting far before I hit the bottom and again had to launch myself to the surface, gasping for another breath. Finally, exhausted and out of breath, I let go of the anchor and encountered the peace of swimming free of that cursed weight.

The problem is, in life, letting go of our anchors isn't that simple. We all have something destructive to which we desperately cling. Jesus offers us peace—which we desire—but too often, we remain unwilling to do what it takes to experience that peace.

Letting go often means significant injury to self. We want peace, but we don't want to let go of our pride, money, lust, anger, or affirmation. Jesus calls us to His peace, but we can experience it only if we're willing to do whatever it takes to let go of the anchor.

Day 147

THE MOST IMPORTANT THING

> *I am the vine; you are the branches. Whoever abides*
> *in me and I in him, he it is that bears much fruit,*
> *for apart from me you can do nothing.*
>
> **JOHN 15:5**

When I pursue that for which I hunger, whether it's a donut or some other appetite of the flesh, I often forget everything else until I satisfy that appetite. The challenge for me, then, is to focus that kind of energy into something that truly matters.

Though I live free from active addiction to drugs, I'd be a fool to think that I'm now free from all defects. My flesh nature doesn't tolerate a vacuum. Where one defect is starved, ten more take its place. I still struggle with anger, food, money, pride, and a need for affirmation.

This can be maddening until I realize that it's my need that motivates me to cling to God. Jesus said in today's passage that I must *abide*—or remain in him—as a branch remains attached to a vine. It's only when I remain attached to Christ that His life flows through me. In pursuing self and turning from Him, I abandon my source of life, purpose and meaning. My continued defects then, can be a useful thing if they motivate me to continually stay connected to God. If I had no need, I wouldn't daily make the effort to remain in Christ.

Without abiding in Christ, nothing else really matters. I could find sobriety, but if I were still following myself, then my life would still be meaningless. Abiding in God is the most important thing in life, giving purpose even to the most mundane details of my existence.

We're fulfilled only when we live in communion with God. It's our one job daily—to choose to abide in Him. Only in abiding in Him do we find the answer to all of our deepest needs.

Day 148

ETERNAL LIFE NOW

This is eternal life, that they know you, the only true God, and Jesus Christ whom you have sent.

JOHN 17:3

My desire for instant gratification pervades my entire personality, affecting more than just my appetite for drugs or food. I have a hard time waiting for pleasure later, so when I'm told that, as a Christian I'll receive some reward *after I die*, that's a tough sell. The afterlife may or may not be far off, but since it's not right now, it's difficult for me to be motivated by it.

Thus, I've found great comfort in Jesus' teaching in today's passage, where He said that eternal life isn't something we attain only after death. When we come to faith, we come to know God in the here and now. This is eternal life—to live in intimate communion with Him.

I'll never know perfection here on earth, but that doesn't mean I can't come to know God better than I do now. I'm not destined to know only the failure of following self. I can, if I desire, know eternal spiritual life, even while in this earthly flesh.

This is the purpose of my life on earth, to know and love God more and more. So often, though, I'm distracted by the immediate gratification found in the desires of my flesh. Then, pursuing self, I find destruction.

I've lived for so long thinking I had to steal my pleasure in the scandalous devices of the flesh life, when all along I could have known peace, joy, and life in God. Daily I can pursue the dead end of all-things-me, which will inevitably lead to disaster. Thankfully, the opposite is also true. I can daily choose to follow God to eternal life. I can spend the rest of my life in this flesh, realizing and knowing the greater reality of my eternal spirit life. I can come to know the joy, pleasure, and satisfaction that I had been seeking in all the wrong places.

Day 149

DID GOD MAKE BEER
AND CIGARETTES?

> *This Jesus, delivered up according to the definite plan*
> *and foreknowledge of God, you crucified and killed.*

ACTS 2:23

Joe, an inmate who participated in our jail Bible study, was once involved in an altercation. Afterwards, the other inmate required a CT scan of his brain, which revealed a life-threatening brain tumor. Suddenly, Joe saw himself as an agent of God. God had used him to save this man's life, right?

God's sovereignty versus man's free will is the stuff of which headaches are made. As a child, my brother asked me if God made everything. *Yes, of course.* He then asked, *Did God make beer and cigarettes*? I was stumped. If evil exists, is it God's will?

Someone once told my wife that my addiction was chosen for me by God. If God is in control, Scott is not accountable for his actions, right? I liked the idea.

In today's passage, Peter said that God planned for Jesus to be killed, but in the same sentence he told those gathered that *they* were responsible. How could this be? How could God choose something and then hold man accountable for it?

The story of Joseph and his brothers, who sold him into slavery, reveals a similar concept. "You [his brothers] meant evil against me, but God meant it for good" (Genesis 50:20). Somehow, God is in control *and* man is allowed to make choices. I don't understand, but the writers of the Bible seemed to have no difficulty with the concept.

God is somehow still in charge of it all. He made the world, and He allowed beer and cigarettes. It's a mind-bending mystery, but God is in control *and* man is allowed to make destructive decisions. Though it hurts my brain, I can accept the mystery that God is in control *and* that I am responsible for my own choices. According to the Bible, I must accept a God who is sovereign without absolving myself of responsibility.

Day 150

UNDER THE INFLUENCE

*They were all filled with the Holy Spirit. . . . And all were amazed
and perplexed, saying to one another, "What does this mean?"
But others mocking said, "They are filled with new wine."*

ACTS 2:4, 12–13

For those of us who have struggled with addiction, those around us will always wonder. When I have a bad day, I know others will think. *Under the influence?* We may perceive this as unfair, but because we built our reputation over time, it takes some time to turn it around. It's only when we live under the influence of something new that others will see the genuine change.

Several times a week, I have the opportunity—whether it's in clinic or in jail—to tell my story. It's a fairly simple story that always goes something like this: I came to great misery and destruction under the influence of drugs. Now I know life and peace under the influence of God. He saved me from myself, so now I try to pursue God with the same effort I once pursued drugs.

In today's passage, the disciples were first filled with the Holy Spirit. The result was apparently quite dramatic, as the disciples began speaking in languages they had not previously known. Some observers were amazed at hearing of God in their own language, but others questioned their sobriety. *That's not God. That's alcohol.*

God's effect, somewhat like alcohol, is supposed to radically change us. Where we once pursued pornography, money, status, affirmation, pride, drugs, or toys, we now must pursue God. Where we once filled ourselves with the pleasures of the flesh, we are now to fill ourselves with the Spirit.

How do we do this? Paul said we daily sow either the seeds of the Spirit, or we sow the seeds of our corruption (Galatians 6:7–8). For me, this is painfully practical. When I get up in the morning to pray, read, and meditate, I sow God's Spirit in myself, drinking deeply of Him. If I don't do this, then I don't fill myself with God; and by default I fill myself with all-things-me. If we desire to live under the influence of God, we must drink deeply of Him.

Day 151
CHEAP CHRISTIANS

> *I have no silver and gold, but what I do have I give to you. In the name of Jesus Christ of Nazareth, rise up and walk!*
>
> **ACTS 3:6**

In college I waited tables and once served a man who left me with a gospel pamphlet as my tip. He even left a nice little note explaining why the pamphlet was more valuable than money. Never mind that he was making some pretty significant assumptions about my beliefs; I just wanted a tip. I was annoyed. *Cheap Christian.*

While the pamphlet was well intended, it would have been much better received *with* a 15% gratuity. At least this man was making some effort to share his faith. At that point in my life, even though I believed in God, I had little to share with others. I was truly the cheap Christian, unwilling—or unable—to share what I had.

Many of us are cheap Christians because, spiritually speaking, we are so poor ourselves. When we give, we give out of what's inside us. If we're spiritually empty, then there's just nothing to give away.

In today's passage, Peter and John encountered a lame beggar. They had no money, but they gave what they had. Since they were filled with Christ, they naturally let that fullness flow out. They gave the lame man something worth far more than a paltry tip, healing him.

Had they not been filled with Christ, they wouldn't have been able to help the man. This is where many of us find ourselves. We encounter those in need, but because we're not abiding in Christ, we have nothing to give. We're empty and useless to the world.

We must continually abide in Christ, allowing His life to flow into us and out again. We're called to give of what we have—money, time, food, or simply love—to those around us who need it. If we find ourselves with nothing to give, we must fill ourselves with Christ. He didn't save us just so we could be cheap Christians.

Day 152
SORRY, NOT SORRY

| *Repent therefore, and turn back, that your sins may be blotted out.* |
ACTS 3:19

I'm not a very tidy person. In fact, I'm a bit of a slob. My wife, on the other hand, is not. I tend to leave a mess, only later to apologize. The thing is, my apologies, to date, have not been followed by much actual change. I say *I'm sorry* for making the mess, and though I *intend* to do better next time . . . I don't. This makes my apology insincere and, ultimately, empty.

Many of us apologize this way. We pretend that just saying the words *I'm sorry* is repentance. We may *feel* sorry and we may *want* to change, but if our apology isn't accompanied by actual change, it's not repentance.

In today's passage, Peter insisted that, to be forgiven by God, we must repent. A verbal *I'm sorry* is useless. If we desire forgiveness, our words must be accompanied by some change in behavior, or *it's not real.*

If my defect is gluttony and my sin is overeating, then saying *I'm sorry* doesn't make me skinny. If I want to be different, and if I want the peace that accompanies absolution, then I must do whatever it takes to stop overeating.

In my addiction, I begged for forgiveness with every pill I took. I wanted to change but remained unwilling to confess, go to treatment, or change my life. I only said I was sorry because I longed to feel forgiven. Since my words were accompanied by no action, however, they were empty and meaningless. God is not fooled by a fake apology.

If we're addicted to pornography, drugs, money, work, affirmation, pride, anger, or toys, then we must continually do whatever it takes to repent and abandon our destructive behavior. We will not do it perfectly. We will fail. There's always grace for that, but we don't fool God into bestowing His grace upon us when we say *we're sorry* with no intention of ever changing.

Day 153

ON ALCOHOLICS, HIGHER POWERS, AND DOORKNOBS

*There is salvation in no one else, for there is no
other name . . . by which we must be saved.*

ACTS 4:12

When I first attended Alcoholics Anonymous, I discovered that there is significant division between the church and AA. Passages like today's expose some of the substance behind this rift. As AA espouses a generic *higher power*, Christians feel that the organization has abandoned God.

I get this. In AA, I heard that my higher power could be a doorknob if I wanted. This is nonsense, of course. Any higher power that I manufacture is neither higher nor a power.

Still, the twelve steps are taken straight from the Bible. *I am helpless on my own. I must surrender to God.* I found great truth in AA despite their ambiguity in naming God. I knew His name.

This division exposed a greater conflict for me—that is, the exclusivity of claiming Jesus as *the only way* to God. This is the same conflict that Peter and John found themselves in after healing a lame man. The religious leaders found the exclusivity of Christ offensive and demanded they stop. Peter and John pointed to the healed man and insisted on preaching the name of the One who had healed him, no matter who was offended by it.

I still go to AA meetings. Despite their ambiguity in naming God, they teach a biblical truth that addresses my greatest defects in life. When I go, I freely share what Christ has done for me. If some are offended that I don't follow a doorknob, I don't worry about that. Because Christ saved me from myself, I must tell others of Him.

The world will always find the gospel to be offensive. How are we to respond to this as followers of Christ? We can learn something from Peter and John's response. We don't need to fight with those who disagree with us, but neither must we abandon truth. We should merely point to what Christ has done for us and insist that He is the only way to God.

Day 154

ONCE AN ALCOHOLIC ALWAYS AN ALCOHOLIC?

> *But Peter said to him, "May your silver perish with you, because you thought you could obtain the gift of God with money!"*
>
> **ACTS 8:20**

Most of us have gone to God begging for transformation. *God, take away my desire for donuts. Help me to like broccoli.* We know those passages that seem to say that we are miraculously fixed when we come to Christ. "Our old self was crucified . . . so that we would no longer be enslaved to sin" (Romans 6:6).

When we still struggle, we wonder why. *Why has God not fixed me? Does my ongoing struggle mean I'm not a Christian?* Does the alcoholic's continued struggle mean that he cannot be a Christian? Does God deliver me from my struggles . . . or not?

In the book of Acts, we're told the strange story of Simon, a con man who made his living with his ruse of the dark arts. Then he met Christ and believed. When temptation came, though, Simon went back to his old tricks. He saw a miracle—and tried to buy the power that had produced that miracle from the disciples. His old patterns of behavior were not miraculously removed; and when tempted, he went back to the old life.

Just as Simon's flaws were not immediately removed, our flaws are not all removed when we come to know God. Though God may miraculously transform us in some areas, we're not delivered from everything. We all still wrestle with something.

God, in His infinite wisdom, allows some flaws to remain so that we continually need Him. It's because of our ongoing failings that Jesus commanded us to daily deny self and follow Him. In doing so, we are delivered daily.

So, does God deliver . . . or is an alcoholic always an alcoholic? Yes. We may be continually delivered from bondage to a thing, but our flesh remains. If we stop denying self and following God, we will return to the destruction of self.

Day 155
PAIN OF THE PAST

> *When he had come to Jerusalem, he attempted to*
> *join the disciples. And they were all afraid of him,*
> *for they did not believe that he was a disciple.*

ACTS 9:26

I have an oddly persistent memory of a sucker I stole from the neighbors when I was five or six years old. Though there were no direct consequences, I knew that they knew. Forty years later, I could not tell you their names, but the fact that they know me as a thief still bothers my conscience.

As an adult, I graduated to significantly more destructive behavior. Though I know that I am forgiven by God, earthly consequences are not erased. I have regular reminders of the destruction of my addiction. At times this still afflicts my conscience. Some will say I need to forgive myself, but that doesn't eliminate the very real results of my actions.

Paul, in today's passage, also found that his past behavior had ongoing consequences. Though he changed his name when he came to know Christ, everyone still knew him as the one who had arrested and killed Christians. Jesus' disciples thought he was faking devotion to Christ, and the Jewish religious leaders felt betrayed and sought to kill him. His former behavior and subsequent conversion made him enemies on both sides. God forgave him, but the consequences of his former life persisted.

Whether or not this afflicted Paul's conscience, we don't know. What we do know is that Paul didn't allow the pain of the past to paralyze him. God told him to spread the gospel and he obeyed. Paul accepted God's grace and lived a radically new life.

As Paul rested comfortably in the grace and mercy of God, we also find significant comfort in His absolution. It seems that God's capacity to forgive cannot be outdone by our ability to sin. Paul committed horrible crimes against God and man; yet God wiped his account clean, forgiving him of all he had ever done. As Paul reckoned this to be true, we too must accept and live in this reality.

Day 156

ATTITUDE

> *About midnight Paul and Silas were praying*
> *and singing hymns to God.*
>
> **ACTS 16:25**

One Sunday, I found myself irritated that I had to go to work. It was a beautiful summer day and I was going to miss it. When life fell apart due to my addiction, I promised God that if He would put my career back together, I would never complain about work again. My promise failed on that lovely Sunday.

Before work, I stopped at the jail for Sunday morning Bible study, where Kent greeted me with a big smile and a hug. He said he was thankful—that his cold was getting better, and for Bible study. His joy irritated me. *What was wrong with him? Did he not realize he was in jail?*

Fortunately, his attitude was infectious, and I quickly realized I was being a baby. Though I was going to miss out on a sunny day, I had so much for which to be thankful.

The book of Acts tells the story of Paul and Silas, who were imprisoned for their faith. In jail, they didn't whine about their misfortune. Rather, they sang and praised God. I can't imagine how much this would irritate me. *What is wrong with you? Do you not know you're in jail?*

In treatment I learned this lesson over and over. *My attitude does not need to be a slave to my circumstances.* Though I needed treatment, it was a constant exercise to not obsess about the disaster of my life. It was only in choosing the right attitude that I could get what I needed out of treatment.

It's no different today. Daily, I have this choice to focus on the misery of self and circumstance, or I can choose to know the freedom and joy that God has given me in focusing on Him. Like Kent—and like Paul, even in prison—I can find a joy and freedom that no one can take away. My attitude is my choice. I can live enslaved to the misery of self, or I can enjoy freedom in God, no matter my circumstances.

Day 157

NEMESIS

He made . . . every nation of mankind . . . that they should seek God . . . and find him. Yet he is actually not far from each one of us.

ACTS 17:26–30

A few years ago, I signed up for an endurance race that would require months of training. On race day, I was nowhere to be seen. I wasn't there because I didn't train for it. At all. I wasn't there because I had a knee injury. I wasn't there most of all, though, because I was in treatment. I hadn't spent months pursuing the race. Instead, I had spent months pursuing my addiction.

On the day of the race, I could have blamed someone or something else: *my knee, work, no one to train with.* Only a fool would have believed those excuses.

What or who was to blame? The only answer was *me.* I was and remain my own greatest nemesis. I alone get to choose misery or joy. No one else can choose for me unless I allow it. Life may bring trials, but only I can choose my response to them. If I'm not living the life I was meant to live, it's because I'm following self. If I don't know God, it's because I choose not to know Him.

Paul, in today's passage, told the Athenians that God is near to each one of us, but that He desires for us to pursue Him. It's in seeking God that we find life, joy, and meaning. Why then, do so many of us limp along without Him? Why, as Christians, do we still live enslaved to our own defects? Why does God remain a stranger?

We must look no further than Christ's words to find the answer. "If anyone would come after me, let him deny himself and take up his cross daily and follow me" (Luke 9:23). The first step in following God is getting past ourselves.

Day 158

DRY DRUNK

| *I do not account my life of any value nor as precious to myself.* |
ACTS 20:24

The greatest defect over the first four decades of my life was not my drug addiction, but rather that I pursued self above all. This wasn't always obviously destructive.

The American dream (nice job, a house, and plenty of money) doesn't necessarily look evil, and it's not wrong in itself. When the pursuit of the good life consumes me, though, I'm lost. The worst sin is the one that appears so innocent that it steals my gaze from God while blinding me to its existence.

I didn't set out to become an addict. When I got to treatment, however, I could clearly see the steps I had taken to get there. It started simply with following my *normal* desires.

Even in recovery, it's still easy to turn my path toward self. In treatment, I learned the term *Dry Drunk* used to describe the person who has stopped drinking but is still indulging in other defects. Quitting the alcohol is necessary for recovery, but one doesn't necessarily recover when the drinking stops. A man may stop drinking, only to reveal that he is a colossal jerk—even without alcohol. If I refrain from one addiction, but continue to follow self, I'm not living as God intended.

It's only in following God above "the good life" that I am able to enjoy it appropriately. It's only in losing ourselves in God that we find ourselves. We may continue to pursue purpose and meaning in everything-me, but it will only lead us to misery and emptiness. If we desire to know true joy, then, like Paul, we must follow God above all, surrendering not just my drug addiction, but also my pursuit of all-things-me.

In today's passage, Paul revealed that his life's goal was not the pursuit of self. His life purpose was simply to pursue God and His will. Paul realized this profound truth: *We were created to love God and do His will. Doing anything else leads to destruction.* It's only on His path that we discover our ultimate joy, purpose, and meaning. If we are not following God, we are still living as the dry drunk.

Day 159

THE DEFINITION OF INSANITY

| *It is hard for you to kick against the goads.* |

ACTS 26:14

I've often read passages that I felt applied to others—only to realize yet another defect of mine. So it was one day when I read about *kicking against the goads*. Paul, in describing his conversion, quoted Jesus, "Saul, why are you persecuting me? It is hard for you to kick against the goads" (Acts 26:14).

The goad, a long sharp stick, was used to prod a farmer's oxen along in the field. When oxen stubbornly refused to move, the farmer used pain to *goad* them along. To kick against the goads, then, would be foolish—it would only increase the pain. To kick against the goads repeatedly would constitute stupidity or insanity.

When I read this passage, I immediately thought of those who have an inherent need to rebel against authority. To me, this is miserable. I'm thankful I don't suffer from this defect. I *never* kick against the goads, right?

The verse stuck in my head, though. I've started to learn that when I see a defect that I think only others have, I probably haven't thought long enough about it. Rethinking that verse, I realized that all my self-inflicted pain has come from kicking against the goads. Every time I took pills—thinking it would bring me pleasure—I knew the pain that would follow. Every time I overeat, increasing my weight, I display a profound inability to learn from my past destructive behavior. Every time I go my own way, pursuing the defective desires of my flesh, I kick against the goads.

To this, Jesus seems to have sympathy. He didn't ask Paul why he was so stupid. He just acknowledged that this was a tough way to live. *"It must be hard for you. Follow me. Stop your self-destruction."*

It's insanity to do the same thing over and over, expecting different results. If we have become weary of our grief, we must learn to stop causing ourselves pain. In our ruin, Jesus says to us, *"Why not follow me instead? Stop kicking against the goads."*

Day 160
DON'T JUDGE ME

> *In passing judgment on another you condemn yourself,*
> *because you, the judge, practice the very same things.*

ROMANS 2:1

I was broken when I hit the doors of chemical dependency treatment. My public fall had humbled me, and I thought my pride was dead. I went to an urban treatment facility, where a physician was a little out of place; so, when I found myself among *real addicts*, my pride found new life. When I met heroin and meth addicts, I scrounged together enough arrogance to be judgmental. *I don't belong here. These are criminals. I'm a doctor, after all.*

Fortunately, I quickly realized that though the details were different, my addiction was the same. I was able to accept that my behavior was as toxic as that of those around me.

Paul, in the opening chapter of Romans, identified numerous transgressions but then turned around in the second chapter (today's passage) to say that we cannot judge our neighbor's offense because we are all guilty ourselves. How is it that we are to *identify* destructive behavior without *judging*?

The error I make is in the question. Identifying destructive behavior and judging are not the same. My daughter pointed this out by taking the idea to its extreme. *I'm not supposed to judge, but if I see a murder being committed, I'm not being judgmental if I call the police.*

She's right. Identifying destructive behavior isn't the same as judging. Judgment grows from a prideful attitude. *I'm the judge. I'm better than you. You deserve punishment but I don't.*

When I lovingly address the struggle of a friend, that is very different, as I am genuinely concerned about what is good for that friend. The judge claims to be carrying the banner of truth but is just using the truth as a facade for his own pride. Compare this to the one who admits his own struggle and tells another what Christ has done for him.

This isn't easy, but if we want to follow Christ, we must work to focus on God and identify sin without being prideful and judgmental.

Day 161

ON NUTRITION AND FAITH

> *Do you presume on the riches of his kindness and forbearance and patience, not knowing that God's kindness is meant to lead you to repentance?*

ROMANS 2:4

At a recent discussion on nutrition at our gym, the dialogue turned to the question of whether poor nutrition was a knowledge problem or a behavioral problem. Some said it was a knowledge issue. *We do not eat well because we do not know what to eat.*

That's not me. I know what I shouldn't eat. I just eat it anyway. This is a life pattern. I know what right is, I just want wrong more. Mine isn't a knowledge problem, it's a behavioral problem.

Paul taught that we are saved by faith, not by works (Ephesians 2:8–9). God's grace is a free gift that we can't earn by our good behavior. Paul's point in today's passage seems to be in response to a shallow knowledge of God that never led to repentance.

I am tempted to think that if I can come to know God by simply accepting a *thought* in my mind, then I really don't have to *change* anything. I can have all the benefits of knowing God and I can behave however I want.

However, this is a *brain-deep faith*, consisting only of an intellectual knowledge of a thing. This isn't actually faith. It's a mirage. In today's passage, Paul explained that God's kindness must change you. It's not the change that saves you; but if your life never changes after you come to faith, then that faith is not real.

So, which is it? Is knowledge or behavior more important? Both are necessary. Knowing what I should eat is a necessary step to proper nutrition, but knowledge alone does not make me healthy. Knowledge must translate to changed behavior.

Likewise, faith must always start with the right knowledge of God. We can't come to know God if we don't know the truth about Him. Repentance, though, is necessary to complete faith. Authentic change must grow from our belief, or that belief is just empty knowledge.

Day 162

THE WEIGHT OF ME

> *The righteousness of God has been manifested apart from the law, . . . the righteousness of God through faith in Jesus Christ for all who believe.*
>
> **ROMANS 3:22**

It's not essential that people fail radically to understand their need for God . . . but it helps. Those who haven't made many obvious mistakes in life—or the ones who think they haven't—will not likely appreciate the importance of today's passage. In a culture where self-esteem, self-actualization, and identity are worshipped as gods, it's an affront to claim that we are all broken. *Who are you to tell me that I'm defective?*

Yet this is Paul's message. We're all a mess. "None is righteous, no, not one" (Romans 3:10). "For all have sinned and fall short of the glory of God" (Romans 3:23). Contrary to our culture, Paul taught that we're defective and self-destructive. We don't all go to treatment, but we all pursue self instead of God. Though not all see it, we all suffer from the same need. We're all being crushed by the weight of ourselves.

To this, Paul taught this blessed hope, that the righteousness of God is available to you. You are now made spiritually alive and perfect. Christ offers absolution and restoration to those of us crushed by the weight of our own failures.

Paul's message was that our defects vary greatly, but our predicament does not. If we're honest, we can see that we have all chosen self over God. We've all sinned and fallen short. We don't have to go out and make disasters of our lives to appreciate this, but the disaster does help us see what God has done for us. God has saved us from the crushing weight of all-things-me.

As not everyone sees their own need, not everyone appreciates the profound gift of Christ's forgiveness. This righteousness offered to us doesn't just mean life after death, it means life *now*. Through Christ, we can now live in intimate communion with the God who made us.

Day 163
FALLING DOWN

> *We rejoice in our sufferings, knowing that*
> *suffering produces endurance.*

ROMANS 5:3

I spent a day one summer driving the boat, teaching a group of newbies how to wakeboard. From my seat, I watched the inevitable process of fall after fall with gradual improvement. I did my best to provide instruction ... but as we all eventually realized, there's no substitute for just trying and failing. A lot. After many falls, each rookie succeeded. Though they didn't enjoy those falls, in the end it was worth the struggle.

I can identify. I have fallen. A lot. For better or worse, though, falling down is part of learning. Pain and suffering are the tools God often uses to provoke transformation. Most of us can look back and see that our times of suffering have coincided with our most intense pursuit of God. Likewise, we can also look back and see the apathy and laziness that has come from success. When we feel a need for God, we seek Him. When we're comfortable, we often seek ourselves.

It would be a tragedy for pain to come and go . . . and for us to learn nothing from it. This would be like *attempting to wakeboard*, falling again and again, never improving, never growing, and never getting any closer to *actually wakeboarding*.

According to today's passage, the difference between growth and futility is in my attitude. Do I look to God for guidance? Do I seek change? The right attitude doesn't mean that suffering is pleasant, but it does give me a new perspective. I can now look back at my devastation with sorrow but still be thankful for how God has used it. I can truly say that I'm better off now than I ever would have been without my addiction. I know God better because of my falls.

Because we won't be perfect in this life, we can still expect that trials are ahead. In life, though, as in wakeboarding, falls are part of the experience. Because none of us want to learn the same painful lesson over and over—daily we must turn our gaze from self to God.

Day 164
LICENSE TO SIN

> *Where sin increased, grace abounded all the more. . . . What shall*
> *we say then? Are we to continue in sin that grace may abound?*

ROMANS 5:20–6:1

What would you do if you knew you could get away with anything? If you knew there were no consequences attached to your behavior, what would you eat? How would you live? This was the problem in my addiction. I had convinced myself that *I could get away with it.*

Many of us find ourselves in this position spiritually. Paul rightly taught that we are saved by grace through faith. Our restoration to God isn't earned by works. But here's where we go wrong: *If I'm forgiven, why not just do whatever I want? If God's grace increases with sin, I'm actually growing God's grace the more I sin, right?*

This is absurd, but it reveals how our flesh nature twists grace. God's kindness is meant to lead us to repentance (Romans 2:4). We tend to look at God's grace, though, and see it as a license to sin. God saves us so we can follow him, but we pervert this into permission to follow self.

This *license to sin* is a cheap grace, revealing that I don't really understand grace at all. Grace always lies in tension with repentance. Yes, I'm forgiven for all eternity, but forgiveness means that I've been *saved to follow God.* When I fail, God forgives, but this doesn't mean that I can do whatever I want.

When we abuse grace, it's possible we're fooling ourselves into thinking we know God when we don't. Even if we do know God, we're still sowing the seeds of our own pain and misery. Grace isn't a shield to protect us from the consequences of deliberate sin. If we want to know life, joy, and peace, we must continually choose to abandon self and follow Christ. There's always forgiveness when we fail, but grace isn't a license to do whatever we want.

Day 165
WHEN GOD FAILED

> *We know that our old self was crucified with him in order that the body of sin might be brought to nothing, so that we would no longer be enslaved to sin.*
>
> **ROMANS 6:6**

In my addiction, I turned to the Bible to understand my condition. I knew I had followed my flesh to disaster, but I didn't understand why. I remember reading today's passage about how my old self was crucified so that I can live a new life.

I didn't feel as if I had a new life, though. I still had a ravenous appetite for destruction. What did that mean? If being a Christian meant that the old self was gone, then either I was not a Christian, or God had failed me. I had believed . . . but God had not delivered. *Where was God? Why had He failed me?*

Some Christians told me that I had just not believed hard enough. Freedom lay in *believing really hard.* That turned out to be a joke. I prayed and strained my brain, but I couldn't mentally defeat my addiction.

God had failed me. Paul had lied to me. My flesh nature wasn't dead. *What gives? Why do I still have destructive desires?* Though an addict, my mind was working well enough to realize that if it came down to *God failing me* or *me failing God,* God was probably not the problem. I accepted that I must have gone wrong somewhere.

As I studied the Bible, I began to understand this continual tension between the *flesh life* and the *spirit life.* Jesus taught that I was born once of the flesh and then born *again* through the Holy Spirit (John 3). I now have this daily choice to invest in my flesh life or my spirit life. Whichever one I choose, the consequences are predictable. In my addiction, God never failed me. I failed myself when I chose to indulge in my flesh life.

Paul's death and resurrection then, referred to a rebirth in our *spirit lives.* We don't die *physically* when we come to know God. The death, resurrection, and new life Paul described is in the *spirit life.* We must daily choose to live in that spirit life.

Day 166

CHEAT DAY

> *Let not sin therefore reign in your mortal body, to make you*
> *obey its passions. . . . For sin will have no dominion over you.*

ROMANS 6:12, 14

At the coffee shop, I once asked if there was sugar in a certain drink. The question turned into a discussion on the evils of sugar. I indicated that yes, I was trying to cut such wickedness out of my life. The barista then asked, "Do you have a cheat day?"

The answer just popped out of my mouth, "Well, I'm an addict . . . so, no, a cheat day isn't an option. It would turn into a cheat month." Apparently, that was a conversation killer. I got my sugarless coffee without any further questions.

Still, the concept is intriguing. *Is cheating helpful?* For addicts, though, the concept of a *planned relapse* is horrific. One doesn't avoid addictive behavior by allowing small indulgences in that behavior. This would be like an alcoholic having just a few beers so he can stay sober.

Paul, in Romans 6, explains that in Christ, we've been given this perfect spirit life as an option to our flesh life. With that, there is only one appropriate response: "Let not sin therefore reign in your mortal body, . . . present yourselves to God" (verses 12–13). Because we have this new life in God, we must pursue Him above all, abandoning the pursuit of self.

As Christ freed us from ourselves, now we are to avoid a return to slavery. Indulging in our destructive desires must never be an option. When it comes to the destructive defects of our flesh nature, cheat day is a fantasy.

In pursuit of my addiction, I told myself the most outrageous lies. *I can indulge just a little. I deserve a cheat day.* A cheat day may be fine for the casual dieter. But the concept—when considered in light of the defects of my flesh nature—is disastrous. I don't enhance my pursuit of God by sinning just *a little.*

If we want to follow God, we must not tolerate anything that distracts from Him, no matter how small it may seem.

Day 167

WHAT GOD DOES FOR ME

*Do you not know you are slaves of the one whom
you obey, either of sin, which leads to death, or of
obedience, which leads to righteousness?*

ROMANS 6:16

The addict, in his misery, ironically knows only one way to feel better. He finds respite in that which made him miserable in the first place. The one enslaved to self will pursue sex, drink, money, toys, or status because those things do provide some momentary pleasure. The pleasure doesn't last, though, and then the misery sets in. In his pain, the addict repeats the cycle.

As it turns out, Paul knew quite a bit about addiction, insisting that we're slaves to that which we obey. Most of us can identify with being enslaved to some defect. This addiction is a compelling need to do something despite harmful consequences. It may be anger, gluttony, sex, greed, or pride. We all have different defects, but we have all promised never to do a thing again—only to break that promise. This is addiction.

Paul said that we always follow something. We are either slaves to our own flesh nature, leading to ruin—or we follow God, leading to life. In following our own desires, we think we're free, but we're not. We are slaves to self.

To this, God simply offers Himself as the only adequate alternative. Sin and self always enslave, but God never enslaves. In Christ, we are free to pursue the one thing that will provide the joy, purpose, and meaning we were seeking in the empty pursuits of self in the first place. It's our broken nature to pursue pleasure in our own desires. We're only complete, however, when we find those things in God.

We may abandon drink or drug without finding God. Many do. Something will always fill that vacuum, though. Many have found the futility of replacing one destructive pursuit with a slightly less destructive one. God, however, offers the only perfect alternative to us. We can continue to wallow in our self-addiction, or, we can find freedom in Christ.

Day 168

WHY CAN'T I STOP?

> *I do not do the good I want, but the evil I do*
> *not want is what I keep on doing.*

ROMANS 7:19

Why can't the alcoholic put down the bottle? Why does the heroin addict keep inserting the needle? Is it just a lack of self-control? Why does the angry father continue to scream at his wife and children? Why can't the food addict stop overeating?

We all know that our defective desires will lead to painful consequences. Ours is not a knowledge problem. It's a behavioral problem. Something in us is broken. It can be nothing short of pathological for the one suffering from diabetes, hypertension, and obesity to continue to eat donuts. It can only be described as diseased behavior to continue to pop pills, knowing the destructive consequences to self, family, and career.

Though it has different manifestations in all of us, we all have a *disease* called the *flesh nature*, which comes with a full complement of flaws. To be sure, we have constructive traits as well, but that's not what I'm referring to here. I'm addressing the fact that we can all identify with Paul. *I do not understand my own actions, I keep doing the things I do not want to do. What is wrong with me?* The only answer is that I am sick.

This is no excuse for bad behavior. The fact that I have this diseased flesh does not relieve me of liability. I may not have chosen a predisposition to use pills, but I alone bear the responsibility for indulging in my defect—or seeking recovery. Acknowledging my disease isn't justification, it's merely an indictment of my nature.

We can seek treatment for our sicknesses only after we acknowledge their existence. Sticking our heads in the sand does us no good, it only makes us ill *and* ignorant. When we admit our problem, though, we can begin to accept the solution found in Christ.

Day 169

THE ANSWER

*The law of the Spirit of life has set you free in
Christ Jesus from the law of sin and death.*

ROMANS 8:2

It's not uncommon for a patient to seek my help with an ailment for which there is no pill. I'll insist that the answer lies in weight loss or some lifestyle modification, but the patient invariably repeats the question, *Can't I just take a pill?* I can identify. If, in the throes of my addiction, you told me that a pill could fix me, I would have been interested. I didn't want to do anything. I just wanted the easy answer.

Paul, in today's passage, offers the answer to my greatest need. It's no pill. It's simply *Jesus Christ.* Through His death on the cross, Christ gave us a new spirit life as an alternative to our flesh life. When we come to know God, our flesh nature isn't removed; but we are spiritually reborn through the Holy Spirit.

We are then flesh and spirit with the freedom to choose. This new life offers to us the profound transition from *condemnation, misery, and sin* to *life, joy, forgiveness, and freedom.*

How do I attain this freedom? Paul said we are simply saved by faith. We don't earn this new life by good behavior. Walking by faith, though, is turning from the pursuit of self to the radical pursuit of God. Therein lies the problem for many of us. We see our need and would like it fixed . . . but we long for an easier option. *Can't I just take a pill for that?* Radical commitment to God seems a little extreme.

Not everyone is ready for profound change. There are, after all, other ways to get sober. Paul insisted, however, that God is the only answer to the underlying disease of our flesh nature.

When we come to know God, our flesh nature isn't made perfect—but we are given the solution to the problem. Christ doesn't offer a magical pill, but He does offer the answer to our disease of self.

Day 170

I CAN'T BE AN ADDICT— I'M A CHRISTIAN

> *To set the mind on the flesh is death, but to set the mind on the Spirit is life and peace. For the mind that is set on the flesh is hostile to God, for it does not submit to God's law; indeed, it cannot. Those who are in the flesh cannot please God.*
>
> **ROMANS 8:6–8**

When my life fell apart due to my addiction, those around me quoted this passage, asking if I was a Christian. I couldn't blame them. I had to examine myself. *What did my behavior mean about my spiritual condition?* I was obviously an addict. Did that mean I wasn't a Christian?

In my black-and-white thinking, I have thought that today's passage referred to being a Christian or not. It seems to say that the one pursuing self is hostile to God and cannot please Him. This certainly sounds like someone who doesn't know God.

The danger in seeing the passage only this way is that I may begin to think that, as a Christ follower, I'm incapable of pursuing the flesh. If I'm a Christian, then I can't be in opposition to God, right? *I'm a Christian so I cannot be an addict.* In this mindset, to admit failure is to admit that I'm not a Christian.

This, of course, is ludicrous and dangerous. Christians obviously can and do pursue the flesh nature to painful consequences. Though God gives us an alternative to pursuing self, we sometimes still fail.

Admission of my addiction didn't solve it, but I would never have found recovery if I hadn't admitted it. In the wreckage of my addiction, I was right to question my condition. I desperately needed to understand it. It would have been tragic to refuse to admit that I was an addict because I thought that Christians couldn't be addicts. My misguided faith would actually have become a hindrance to my recovery.

It also would have been tragic, though, to decide that I wasn't a Christian because I had failed. I was a Christian who had failed . . . *spectacularly.* Thankfully, God's grace is always spectacular enough to cover our failures.

Day 171

I KILL MY ADDICTION OR MY ADDICTION KILLS ME

If you live according to the flesh you will die, but if by the Spirit you put to death the deeds of the body, you will live.

ROMANS 8:13

I once met a man in his mid-twenties who had dealt with uncontrolled diabetes since childhood. He was nearly blind, had suffered several heart attacks, and was in kidney failure. His disease was treatable, but because of his failure to control it, it was killing him. For him, apathy was destruction.

I can identify. When I first went through outpatient treatment, I knew that I was fine. *I'll never be stupid enough to do that again.* Like the diabetic, I ignored my problem. *I don't need to work at recovery.* The problem was that I have a persistent disease called the flesh nature, which feeds on apathy.

Paul, in today's passage, insists that I have two choices. I either pursue the desires of my flesh, leading to destruction, or I put those desires to death and find life in God. *I daily kill my destructive desires or they kill me. Not to choose is to choose death.*

Some will die young, but some will die long, slow deaths. The cruelest disease is perhaps the one which allows its host to live a long life, separating him from God, while never being quite miserable enough to seek attention. *Sure, I look at porn, but I'm not hurting anyone. Sure, I'm a little prideful, but I am pretty amazing.*

How do I put to death the deeds of the flesh? If I'm a drug addict, it means going to treatment and continuing in regular recovery activities. If I'm addicted to food, pride, money, or pornography, I must likewise commit to radical, permanent lifestyle changes. Though I kill a defect today, it may rise again tomorrow. This isn't a once-and-for-all choice. This is a daily effort.

If we want to know life instead of destruction, we must daily choose to abandon self and follow God. Not choosing is to have already chosen destruction.

Day 172

THE HOPE OF AN ADDICT

> For those who love God all things work together for good
> for those who are called according to his purpose.
>
> **ROMANS 8:28**

It's natural for my faith to be warped by my own defective desires. It's natural, but not often helpful. When I was a child, I wanted God to give me asthma or some other *not-too-bad* illness that might make me special. I'd like to say that I have grown out of my stupidity, but sometimes I still seek things that later seem absurd. I continue to have an inherent addiction to self, which distorts my expectations of God.

In treatment, I read this passage and found great comfort in Paul's words that all things work together for good for those who love God. *Sure, God, I made a mess—but you promised to fix it all, right?* After a couple days of treatment, I was reformed and ready to have my life back. *Okay, God, lesson learned! Put it all back now.* Months later, when life wasn't perfect, I began to suspect that God wasn't working on my timeline.

Paul did indeed say that all things will work out for good for those who love God. It would be ridiculous, though, to say that God works everything out for *my* version of good. My plan is so nearsighted and self-serving that I have many times had to thank God for protecting me from myself. Thankfully, God works out *His* plan, not mine.

Paul insisted that nothing "will be able to ever separate us from the love of God" (Romans 8:39). Though I may cause and experience horrific pain, and though the world may kill my body, nothing in all of creation can steal me away from God's love. I may lose my flesh, but nothing can rob me of my spirit. No matter what happens in this life, all things, in the end, come to good for those who love God. We find our hope and security then, not in our plans, but in God's promise that we will never be separated from Him.

Day 173

WE KEEP WHAT WE HAVE BY GIVING IT AWAY

> *"Everyone who calls on the name of the Lord will be saved."*
> *How then will they call on him in whom they have not believed?*
> *And how are they to believe in him of whom they have never*
> *heard? And how are they to hear without someone preaching?*
>
> **ROMANS 10:13–14**

When I first found recovery, my participation was underwhelming. I didn't want to attend recovery meetings, and I certainly didn't want to share my recovery story with other addicts. I wasn't committed to recovery, and thus, I didn't keep it very long.

This lack of commitment mirrored my attitude about my faith as well. I had what I wanted from God. I was saved, but I really didn't want to get too crazy with my faith. I went to church, but the only desire I had to share my faith was out of a sense of guilt. *I guess God said I should tell others about Him.*

Both Christianity and the 12 steps of AA insist that what we have been given must be shared with others. The twelfth step says, "Having had a spiritual awakening, . . . we . . . carry this message to alcoholics." Likewise, Jesus commanded us to "make disciples of all nations" (Matthew 28:19). Reaching out to those in need and sharing what God has done for us is necessary if we wish to participate in recovery or faith. It isn't optional. If we want to keep what God has given us, we must also give it to those who need it.

If I say that I don't know anyone in need, I have probably insulated or blinded myself to the world. Need is all around me. When I got out of treatment, I began volunteering at a jail and a transitional house where I began to meet weekly with those who, like me, knew how desperately they needed God. In doing so, I have never had to look far to find those who want God desperately.

If we refuse to share our faith and recovery, we'll likely lose them, finding that we never really had them in the first place. We keep the most important things in life (faith, love, joy, recovery, and peace) only by sharing them with those around us.

Day 174

THE ADDICT'S HALF-GOD

| *Note then the kindness and the severity of God.* |
ROMANS 11:22

Early in our marriage, my wife and I had a significant disagreement over the color of tape I had used a few weeks prior in painting the trim on our house. I had used green tape, but she claimed it was blue.

Because I was the one who had done the job, I was more than a little irritated with her. She was equally convinced of her rightness. In our mutual frustration, we headed off to the hardware store to settle the dispute.

We were both shocked and a little embarrassed to find both blue and green tape. I had forgotten that I started with blue tape, run out, and then finished with green. We each possessed half a truth, which led us both to believe that we individually knew the whole truth. Our half-truths had led us to a whole lot of conflict.

This is a common error of mine. I take a truth I like about God . . . and I run with it. My theology becomes tainted by my own biases and defects. I go to the Bible with a concept in mind, find all the verses that support it, and then explain away all the verses that don't. Thus, I build a half-truth based on my preconceived ideas of God.

Many of us do this without realizing it. The addict, for example, prefers to focus on God's mercy and grace while ignoring His holiness. Thus, the addict knows a half-god, who will never say no and will never allow consequences. This is, of course, disastrous to the addict. To deny consequences is to reject reality and to court death.

Paul, in today's passage, insists that we must recognize both the kindness *and* severity of God. God is love, but one does not need to read far to find that God is also just. To know God then, we must embrace the whole. Embracing only half a truth may be as destructive as a lie. Just as our tape was green *and* blue, God is both kind *and* severe. Paul says we must strive to know the *whole* God.

Day 175

CHANGE IS HARD

> *Present your bodies as a living sacrifice. . . . Do not be conformed*
> *to this world, but be transformed by the renewal of your mind,*
> *that by testing you may discern what is the will of God.*

ROMANS 12:1–2

Many times I've read this passage and begged God for transformation. *Help me to like broccoli instead of donuts.* Nothing. My efforts have come up empty. To call them *efforts*, though, would be to miss Paul's point here.

In retrospect I can see that, though I desired transformation, I remained unwilling to *do anything about it.* I wanted God to change my desires . . . and then my behavior would follow, right? *If you would just make me hate donuts, drugs, and pride, then I'll be good. I promise.* However, this isn't how transformation works.

So how do we change? In today's passage, Paul reveals the *how:* We must do whatever it takes to offer ourselves as sacrifices—not in death, but in life. We are to consciously take every day and give it to God, continually abandoning self and following Him.

In the struggle, I've often prayed for God's will, but then spent hours watching television. I say I want His will to be done, but then I do my will. This isn't biblical and it isn't faith.

I don't have it all figured out, but I will testify that taking the time every morning to read, pray, and meditate, has radically transformed my mind. In the idle moments of the day, I now try to take the day's passage and meditate on it instead of spending my imagination on the pursuit of self. This has had a profound transformational effect on my mind and desires.

We often want God to change our minds so our behavior will change. The reality, though, is that God often doesn't move until we obey. It's in drawing near to God that He draws near to us.

If we spend all our energies pursuing self, we cannot complain that we're not experiencing transformation. We get to know the spirit life only as much as we participate in it. Daily, each of us must abandon self and follow God as a living sacrifice.

Day 176
STILL AN ADDICT?

I say to everyone among you not to think of himself more highly than he ought to think, but to think with sober judgment.

ROMANS 12:3

I am occasionally chastised by other Christians—for referring to myself as an addict. They feel it's wrong to use such disparaging language to define myself. As a Christian, I must identify as a Christian. *If you say you are an addict, you will continue to act as an addict.*

While I know that I have a perfect spirit life, I still have a flesh life. To deny this isn't helpful. The most destructive flaw would be to remain blind to the fact that I still have defects. I carry the perfect spirit life, but I carry it in an earthen vessel, full of cracks and flaws.

Looking back, I can't deny that I'm an addict. There's little other explanation for my pathological behavior. I have a disease, which—when indulged—breeds disaster. I'm not using drugs now, but the underlying appetites remain. If I stopped pursuing God daily and started following self again, I could easily return to active use. To deny this fact is to flirt with disaster.

This is what Paul was saying in today's passage. *Reflect on yourselves in sober judgment. Don't be blinded by your pride. Know your struggles. Continually acknowledge and crucify whatever distracts you from God.*

If I insist that my only identity is perfection in God, I'll be blind to my sin. Ignoring my failures isn't constructive. Being a disciple of Christ involves two steps. First, I must daily deny self *and* second, I must follow Christ (Luke 9:23). If I refuse to acknowledge that which distracts me from God, I'll never take the first step and thus, will never be able to take the second step.

Denying the reality of our struggles doesn't make them go away, it only makes us ignorant. The only way to crucify our destructive tendencies is to daily acknowledge them, abandon them, and follow Christ.

Day 177
PAUL'S GUIDE TO CONFLICT

> *Repay no one evil for evil. . . . If possible, so far as it depends on you, live peaceably with all. . . . Do not be overcome by evil, but overcome evil with good.*
>
> **ROMANS 12:17–18, 21**

In treatment I learned a key phrase. Do the next right thing. For addicts, impulsive behavior is a profound problem. In most situations, our first impulse is the wrong one. This concept, then, of pausing to make a thoughtful, conscious choice, to *do the next right thing,* is an important one to the addict.

This impulsive behavior isn't just about drug addiction. It's about self-addiction. The self-addict always demands his way, caring more about winning than behaving right. Unconcerned with the one with whom he's in conflict, he cares only about getting his way. Unfortunately, it's usually family and friends who bear the brunt of the one addicted to self.

The thinking of a self-addict is distorted by his addiction; If I'm right, then it doesn't matter how wrong I act. Toxic behavior, anger, and ridicule become suitable tactics when I'm justified by being right. *I'm right, so I'm justified in acting wrong.*

Paul, in today's passage, said there's something more important than winning, though. He said it's far more important to behave right than to be *declared* right. Evil from others doesn't justify an evil response. As much as it depends on us, we are to live in right relationship with others.

This is the opposite of my first impulse. My first impulse when confronted is to use whatever tactic it takes to prove my viewpoint. *I'm going to hammer you with my opinion until you see it my way.* Paul didn't say that I could never disagree. He just insisted that my right conduct is more important than my victory.

Paul insisted that we must not allow others to cause us to do evil. We're always to *do the next right thing,* denying our impulse for the wrong thing. Because our conduct is more important than our victory, we must continually deny self, keeping our eyes on God.

Day 178

THE HARD WORK OF FAITH AND RECOVERY

Put on the Lord Jesus Christ, and make no provision for the flesh, to gratify its desires.

ROMANS 13:14

In active addiction, I worked constantly to find the next pill. From the time I woke up, I started planning. Family, career, and faith all took a back seat to my appetite. Using required effort . . . I planned and schemed, spending my energies on that which I craved.

An inmate once told me that, as hard as I used to work at my addiction—that's how hard I must work at the new life. Paul said the same in today's passage. Just as we get dressed every morning, we must purposefully put on Jesus Christ, or we will, by default, put on self.

But we are saved by faith and not by our works! It's true that we are saved only by faith, through which we inherit the gift of the new, perfect spirit life. While we're in this flesh, though, we carry that perfect gift in an imperfect vessel. For now, we know two realities—the flesh life and the spirit life.

This is why a two-step process was so often repeated in the New Testament. Paul used the imagery of clothing. *Take off the old and put on Christ.* Christ said we must deny self and follow him. Always, it's this two-step process of abandoning self and pursuing God. Though we are saved by faith, we must daily choose—and work—to live in the spirit life.

It's the disastrous error of many Christians to think that because we are saved by faith, we need to do nothing. *I'm saved, so I can continue to pursue porn, money, power, status, toys, affirmation, or drugs. I don't have to change anything because that would be work. No work for me!*

Daily, though, we must choose to put on Christ and cast off the old. If we want God—and if we want recovery—we get there only by working at it.

Day 179

PRETENDER

Watch out for those who cause divisions; . . . avoid them. For such persons do not serve our Lord Christ, but their own appetites.

ROMANS 16:17–18

I've picked fights with others over issues like predestination or the age of the earth, pretending to defend *God's truth* while really just flexing my own opinion. I told myself I was defending logic, reason, and God; but really, I was just addicted to being right. To feel good about winning, I had to prove someone wrong.

How many of us have done the same, dividing and fighting while masquerading as disciples? We make bitter enemies, not because we follow Christ, but because we need to be right. We become convinced that our side of some disputable matter is God's truth, and we can't tolerate any dissension.

Paul warned against such dividers and pretenders. He insisted that we practice grace in these matters where there is room for genuine disagreement. Some issues, such as what foods are acceptable, do not need to be settled. Not every dispute requires a winner and a loser.

This doesn't mean that we don't take a stand on anything. There are disputable matters, and then there are basic tenets of faith which are indisputable. The problem is that we have difficulty distinguishing between the two. In our persistent defective flesh, we attribute every personal opinion to God's will . . . and then force that opinion on those around us.

It's then a good exercise for me to ask myself an important question. *Whose will am I serving? Do I care about this person, or am I just arguing to be right? Will this discussion move us closer to God or farther away?*

God rarely asks me to fight with others. He never asks me to be hateful in my pursuit of Him. If I'm producing conflict, I must ask myself if I'm pursuing God or just pursuing self under the guise of following God. Am I a disciple, pointing others to Christ; or am I just a pretender, still addicted to everything-me?

Day 180

AM I WEAK ENOUGH FOR GOD?

But God chose what is foolish in the world to shame the wise;
God chose what is weak in the world to shame the strong.

1 CORINTHIANS 1:27

I stood on the porch of our lakeside home one night, watching the storm and pondering this passage. As the lightening flashed and the waves beat upon the shore, I asked God to speak and explain the passage. I should know better. Even though I knew what was coming when I saw the lightning strike the water, I still jumped as the crack of thunder hit me a split second after. It was impossible, in the power of the storm, not to see how small I was.

In the storm it was easy to see my profound need for God. If only I could always live in that place. My greatest failure in life has not been my drug addiction, but my pride and dependence on myself.

It was only in the pain of following everything-me that I finally accepted my neediness. I was always in need of being saved from myself. I just didn't see it until life came crashing down. Only in my misery and desperate need did I finally turn to God.

Paul pointed out this truth in today's passage. God draws near not to the strong and capable, but to the lowly and weak. Those who are self-sufficient don't feel a need for God and thus will never find Him.

The strong will see me as weak. I wholeheartedly agree. I'm a mess and I need God. I don't know where I'd be without Him, and I don't care to find out. Left to my own pursuits, I'd be lost. God has provided for me the only adequate answer to my deepest needs, and I don't want to live life without Him.

As the storm passes, it's easy to slip once again back into the lie of self-sufficiency. *Thanks for your help back there, God. I'm good now.* As that's the kind of thinking that led me into treatment, though, I must daily remember my weakness. I *always* need God.

Day 181

ADDICTED TO THE FLESH

I, brothers, could not address you as spiritual people,
but as people of the flesh, as infants in Christ.

1 CORINTHIANS 3:1

In today's passage, Paul referred to his audience, who were consumed with jealousy and conflict, as *people of the flesh.* The term *flesh* referred not just to the body, but also to the fallen human nature attached to the body. Just as we each have a physical body that is imperfect, we also have a flesh nature that's broken and flawed. The Christians to whom Paul wrote were living in addiction to their destructive appetites.

We're tempted, then, to divide Christians into two groups: those who follow the flesh and those who follow Christ. The reality is that we all struggle with some defect of the flesh. This doesn't mean, though, that we must live our lives addicted to our defects.

Recently I was reminded of my persistent flesh nature. For a few weeks I had cut sugar out of my diet and had enjoyed some success in weight loss. I started feeling as if maybe I was finally getting ahead of my flesh nature. *Not much left to work on, God.* Reality came crashing back as my family informed me that, in my dietary change, I had become pretty cranky. Apparently, I was jollier when fatter. I worked on one defect, only to reveal another.

The temptation, then, was to throw my hands up in frustration. *I'll never be free, so why keep trying?* However, Christ insisted that the normal life of a disciple is a continual process of abandoning self to follow Him. Though we live in the broken flesh, we're not to live enslaved to it. We were made to walk in the Spirit, not the flesh.

If I ever feel that I don't need to daily abandon myself, then I've embraced a blinding pride. I'll always feel the gravity of my flesh nature pulling at me, but because of Christ's work, I don't need to live addicted to my flesh.

Day 182

NORMALIZING ADDICTION

> *It is actually reported that there is sexual immorality among you, and of a kind that is not tolerated even among pagans.*
>
> **1 CORINTHIANS 5:1**

It's unbelievable to me, looking back, to see the conduct I had come to consider as normal when I was engaged in active addiction. It's embarrassing to write of how I once left church just so I could go find some pills. I didn't start out pursuing drugs on day one. It was an incremental process that led me to behavior that I now consider unfathomable.

Paradoxically, I remember being offended by the sin of others even while I was using. Once I switched off a certain television show because it offended my faith. *Never mind that I'm using drugs—that show is just offensive.* I came to accept my own caustic behavior as normal, even while remaining judgmental of others.

This is the condition Paul addressed in today's passage. Writing to the church in Corinth, Paul chastised them for tolerating a leader in the church who was engaged in an incestuous relationship. Because the man was a church leader, his debauchery had been tolerated.

To this Paul objected. I can imagine him saying, "What on earth are you thinking?" As a church, they were claiming to follow God while tolerating horrific sin among themselves.

This is the height of Christian hypocrisy. To presume to be a spiritual leader, while refusing to acknowledge my own addiction, is profound duplicity. It's not that I must be perfect to serve God. Paul insisted, though, that I must not normalize my destructive behavior.

This is, inherently, part of my defect—to grow tolerant of my own garbage. It requires brutal honesty and introspection to continually ask myself what toxic behavior I'm tolerating today. The normal life of a disciple, as described by Christ, is to daily deny self to follow Him. I must not choose blindness to a defect just because it's my own struggle.

Day 183

WHAT IF I STILL DO THE BAD STUFF?

> *Do you not know that the unrighteous will not*
> *inherit the kingdom of God? . . . But you were . . .*
> *justified in the name of the Lord Jesus Christ.*

1 CORINTHIANS 6:9, 11

There are those who feel that their destructive life choices stand as evidence that they don't know God. They've prayed time and again for transformation, but they continue to struggle. *A real Christian cannot act like this.*

Reading all of verses 9 through 11 reveals that Paul certainly did list a bunch of bad stuff in today's passage, insisting that those known for drunkenness, greed, and sexual immorality will not inherit the kingdom of God. At first glance, it seems that Paul is saying that anyone who struggles with any defect is not even a Christian. This is a little terrifying.

Paul went on to say that those who have faith in Christ have been justified. Though our flesh is not made perfect, God sees us as righteous. He's not blind to our failures, but in an eternal perspective, He sees us in the perfection of Christ.

Still, faith must lead to some transformation. If I use grace as license to continue in sin, then it may be that I don't actually have faith. The problem is that we like to use Paul's list to judge others. *If you engage in this one sin, you are not a Christian.*

In using the passage this way, we miss out on Paul's point: When we pursue the desires of our flesh, we are, by definition, not pursuing the kingdom of God. We can't pursue both at the same time. We may be saved but still make a mess of life. If we want joy and peace, we must pursue God. We don't lose our faith when we fail, but we absolutely produce pain when we pursue ourselves.

God allows us to pursue either Him or ourselves. When we follow ourselves, we manufacture our own misery. If we want life, we must be willing to do whatever it takes to abandon self and pursue Him—every day.

Day 184
THE POWER OF SEX

> *Flee from sexual immorality. Every other sin a*
> *person commits is outside the body, but the sexually*
> *immoral person sins against his own body.*

1 CORINTHIANS 6:18

A few years ago, during hunting season, my father and I sat in my pickup at dawn, watching a buck in rut, chasing a doe. That buck acted like no deer I had ever seen, jumping and prancing around the doe, as she ignored him. Driven by the stupefying need to reproduce, he was out of his mind.

I imagine our behavior looks similar from above. Though I most often use food as an example of our destructive flesh nature, sex may be a better example because it often leads to much more obvious disaster. In our pursuit of sexual gratification, we must appear mentally ill to anyone watching from the outside.

In today's passage, Paul exposed our defective sexual desires. It's not that sex is inherently wrong. God is the author of sex, and He intended it for both reproduction and pleasure, within the confines of His boundaries. If we want to know God as we should, though, we can't live enslaved to destructive sexual behavior. When we pursue anything above God, that thing becomes our god.

Paul insisted that if we want to know God, we must flee sexual immorality. This includes sex outside of marriage, pornography, and lustful fantasies (Matthew 5:28). Sex outside of God's boundaries, by definition, distracts us from God. In our pursuit of it, we often participate in toxic behaviors, betraying trust and destroying relationships. Sex can be as destructive as any drug, causing us to sacrifice all that is most important to us.

The truth is, we can't push God out of our lives in one area and then demand His help with another. If we turn our backs on God, He allows it. If we are pursuing sexual immorality, lust, or pornography, we shouldn't wonder where God went when we beg for help with some other problem. God wants every part of us.

Day 185
THE COST OF GOD

| *You are not your own, for you were bought with a price.* |
1 CORINTHIANS 6:19–20

In medical school I went on a mission trip to Venezuela. Perhaps the group did some good, but I came to realize that my job was pretty useless, spending my days handing out children's vitamins. Though the people were eager to see us, I realized what my efforts were worth when I later saw the kids throwing vitamins at each other. That which I had freely given had little value to them.

This isn't uncommon. We don't necessarily care about something for which we pay nothing. *If it's free, it's not valuable.* As Christians, we speak of salvation as a free gift. Because salvation is free, I have often treated it as those kids treated my vitamins. *I didn't earn this, so I don't have to do anything.* I've treated my relationship with God like a cheap trinket.

Paul, in today's passage, insisted paradoxically that, though salvation is free, it costs us everything. He said that as Christ died for us, we must live for Him. We're not saved to pursue ourselves, but to follow God.

I have this attitude that, because I'm forgiven, I'm free to pursue everything-me. *I should just follow my heart!* The problem, though, is that my desires lead me to disaster. Though I think I'm free when I follow myself, the quickest route to slavery is to do whatever I want.

I don't do it perfectly, but in abandoning self and following God, I've found infinitely more joy and peace than I ever found in pursuing self. When I give the desires of my heart over to God, He refines them and returns them to me so that I can be who I was meant to be.

Though we may revolt at the idea of giving up our hearts' desires, it's in the pursuit of our desires that we become enslaved. It's from ourselves that we must be saved. We only come to know true freedom when we surrender everything to God.

Day 186

HOW TO KNOW THE WILL OF GOD

Keeping God's commands is what counts. Each person should remain in the situation they were in when God called them.

1 CORINTHIANS 7:19–20, NIV

A few years ago, my family was contemplating a considerable geographic change. Since I claimed to follow God, I asked His opinion on the matter. I desired the confidence of knowing that I was following God's plan for my life. Never mind that I was living a secret life of addiction at the time. I wanted to know God's will.

Though I wanted God's opinion in what I considered to be an important thing, I remained unwilling to follow His will in the day-to-day decisions. I thought I was being obedient by giving Him the big choices, not realizing that my life was made of a thousand little choices.

As it turned out, God was much more concerned with *how I lived* than *where I lived.* Paul said as much in today's passage. "Each person should remain in the situation they were in when God called them." Paul said that where I live or what I do for an occupation isn't nearly as important as how I follow God. "Keeping God's commands is what counts."

We often pray for God's guidance only when we get to the *big decisions. Where should I go to college? What job should I take?* We pretend to follow God in the *big picture,* while still following ourselves. We're unwilling to consider that God wants us to abandon our pride, gluttony, greed, drugs, toys, and pornography—here and now.

God's will for us is no mystery. If we truly want to know God, here's what we must do: Put our relationship with Him above all—loving Him fully, with heart, soul, and mind. We must abandon ourselves and love our neighbors. We must tell others what He has done for us. This is not complicated, and it's no secret. It is, however, difficult—which is why we often prefer to pretend to follow God.

Day 187
DANGEROUS KNOWLEDGE

| *This "knowledge" puffs up, but love builds up.* |
1 CORINTHIANS 8:1

The universal question in the admission interview for medical school seems to be, *why do you want to be a physician?* We all gave similar answers, blathering on about caring for our fellow man. Most of us meant it, but very few of us were honest enough to admit that we also wanted to be physicians for the prestige that accompanies the title.

We all want to be smart. Knowledge, as Paul said, inflates the ego. If we want to insult others, we don't call them unkind. We truly insult by calling them stupid. Most of us are much more fearful of appearing unintelligent than we are of being seen as uncaring.

However, Paul said that there's something far more important than how much I know. In today's passage, he insists that love is beyond knowledge. Knowledge elevates and points to me, while love elevates God and others. Pride in my intellect always distracts from God as it focuses on me.

Abandoning self to love God and neighbor is what it means to be a disciple. As Christians, we often get this wrong. We think that being a disciple means possessing great knowledge. In church, the teaching of right doctrine is sometimes accidentally elevated above obedience and love. We find ourselves saying things to this effect. *The most loving thing I can do is tell someone the truth. I don't have to do anything except tell him he's going to hell.*

We come to equate truth with love, absolving us from ever actually practicing love. *I do not have to feed the poor, visit those in prison, or clothe the needy. I just need to speak the truth and I'm good.* Knowledge and truth aren't the same as love, though.

Knowledge is but a stepping stone to obedience and love. It's not the end in itself. Anything, no matter how good it is, can become destructive if it replaces God. If we use intellect to elevate ourselves, we're just addicted to one more thing that's not God.

Day 188

DRINK OF CHOICE

*These things took place as examples for us, that
we might not desire evil as they did.*

1 CORINTHIANS 10:6

It's painful to watch those who cycle in and out of jail. They come to Bible study with good intentions while in jail, but upon being released—sometimes within minutes—they're back at the same behavior that got them locked up in the first place. It's truly maddening to watch.

Paul said the same of the Jewish nation in today's passage. Having been set free from slavery in Egypt, they wandered. They drank deeply of God when in distress, but in success they repeatedly turned their backs on Him. It's exasperating to read their cyclical history.

Why would the Israelites turn from God over and over? Why would released prisoners return to jail? *What is wrong with them?*

I only have to look inward to find the answer. I too have tasted of God's goodness only to turn my back on Him. I've done this and continue to do it because it's in my nature to do so. I do it because—though I have a new spirit life—I still live in this fallen flesh.

The truth is, I'm always going to seek satisfaction for my thirst. The question is, am I going to find my satisfaction in Christ—or drown in the pleasures of my flesh?

I don't say this flippantly to those I've hurt, but I'm thankful for my addiction. It was only in my addiction that I came to understand how badly I needed God. The pleasure, peace, and joy I've found in God is immeasurable compared to the temporary pleasure (and subsequent misery) I found in the pursuit of everything-me.

We know that we should abandon instant gratification for that which truly lasts; but still, we bristle at giving up our desires. We believe in God intellectually, but we don't know Him experientially because we continue to pursue self above all. It's only in drinking deeply of God that we are most deeply satisfied.

Day 189
WITHDRAWAL AND ADDICTION

> *God is faithful, and he will not let you be tempted beyond*
> *your ability, but with the temptation he will also provide*
> *the way of escape, that you may be able to endure it.*

1 CORINTHIANS 10:13

Over the years working in the ER, I met many alcoholics who, when drunk, begged for help—only to recant when sobriety and withdrawal set in. As their blood alcohol levels dropped, their misery drove them back into the bottle.

I too have known the maddening hunger of withdrawal. When the mind and body become accustomed to a drug, dependency becomes an irresistible force. Many times I swore to God and man that I would stop. When the sweating, agitation, insomnia, and hunger returned, though, my promises meant little.

In my futility, I looked at this verse and laughed cynically. Paul promised that God wouldn't allow me to be tempted beyond what I could endure. This didn't feel possible. My inability to resist temptation stood as evidence that Paul had lied to me. I became bitter at God for this lie.

My logic was, of course, as sick as my drug-polluted mind. I had taken a thousand steps in one direction and then demanded that God undo all my habit-forming behavior in one magical act. God did provide a way out, telling me to confess and go to treatment. However, I didn't view that as an option. *I'll lose my marriage and my job. I don't want this to cost me anything. Please help me!*

To my cry, God says, *"Yes, I'll help you, but it won't be easy. This will require a daily denial of self and a pursuit of me. However, it won't be as painful as continuing down the road you're on now. You don't need to live in misery any longer. Accept the joy and peace of following me instead of self. Yes, you will still go through the pain of withdrawal, but it won't last forever. It will get better, if you want it to. There is a way out."*

Day 190
GOD'S DIET PLAN

So, whether you eat or drink, or whatever
you do, do all to the glory of God.

1 CORINTHIANS 10:31

For most of my life I've rarely asked *what I should eat.* I've simply pursued *what I want to eat.* Likewise, with the rest of my life, I often act without even considering what's good for me. I just do what I want. I may have made a mess of life . . . but I want what I want.

Food, one of my favorite metaphors for sin, is one of Paul's favorites as well. In today's passage he used it as an example of how we must approach our daily decision making. Some in the church in Corinth were accustomed to eating meat that had been offered to pagan idols, while others believed this practice to be sinful. To this, Paul said, "Whether you eat or drink, or whatever you do, do all to the glory of God."

No matter what I do, I must keep my eyes on God and His will. If I cannot do a thing without being distracted from God, then I need to change my behavior. There are some activities that I'm unable to do while maintaining my focus on God.

With food, there are harmful things that I eat just to satisfy the destructive appetite of my flesh nature. I don't want to over-spiritualize eating; but for many of us, food is an addiction that robs God of our attention. Paul insisted that I must continually discipline my body so I control it—and not the other way around.

Whatever we do, we must do it for God. What does this look like? This isn't just about food. This is about all of life. This is about running everything we do through the filter of God's will. When we live enslaved to our own appetites, our spiritual lives are paralyzed.

Paul said that whatever we eat or do, we must do it for God—with eyes on Him. This is God's diet plan.

Day 191

LOVE, LUST, AND INFATUATION

> *Love is patient and kind; love does not envy or boast; it is not arrogant or rude. It does not insist on its own way.*

1 CORINTHIANS 13:4–5

When I met my wife, it was *love at first sight*—for me anyway. (She didn't share the feeling for some time.) I must admit, though, that what I felt on that day, so many years ago, was not really love, but rather lust—or infatuation. My wife is a wonderful person, but my 18-year-old hormones were not smitten with her fantastic personality.

We often mistake infatuation for love, "loving" someone in the same way we love pizza. We love how that person makes us feel. Because we understand love to be an emotion, we equate it with *being smitten.*

Paul said, though, that love isn't just a feeling. Love is being consumed with concern for another. Love doesn't look primarily to my own interests. Love is pointing the energies of my life at someone else. When I love, I don't insist on doing everything my way, seeking my needs above all.

Compare Paul's definition of love to infatuation or lust, which, like a drug, we need more and more of to satisfy ourselves. When we find the high of infatuation or lust, we want it to last. *True love lasts forever, right?* Since emotions are fleeting, however, when the feeling fades and a relationship becomes difficult, we feel cheated.

True love, though, is a conscious *choice.* Lust is natural and involuntary. True love is not. True love is choosing selflessness, which is completely unnatural. We think love should be easy, but it certainly isn't.

Love endures *if we choose.* Love is kind and caring *because we make it so.* My wife and I do have an intense feeling of love for each other, but our marriage would have not survived tough times if our love had been only as deep as a warm, fuzzy feeling.

Day 192

SHAME OF THE PAST

I am the least of the apostles, unworthy to be called an apostle, because I persecuted the church of God.

1 CORINTHIANS 15:9

In my addiction I caused others significant misery, which has left me with painful memories. As much as I would love to be able to forget, sometimes I need to remember. Though I'm unable to change the past, I can choose whether or not I continue in recovery. In this, my memory can be useful.

Paul too, must have been haunted by memories, as evidenced in today's passage. He lamented his past. Paul didn't seem to wallow in his guilt, but neither did he dismiss it. These seem to be the two extremes in which we err in addressing our shame. Either we choose to pretend the past didn't happen, or we find ourselves crushed by its weight.

In treatment, I saw others just dismiss their past with a wave of the Bible. *God has forgiven me!* This carefree attitude bothered me. What about those whom they had hurt? Forgiveness, for them, meant forgetting. *I may have robbed someone yesterday, but I found Jesus. No worries now!*

This self-imposed amnesia is just a convenient manipulation to avoid facing my own evil. Forgiveness doesn't undo the pain I caused, and it doesn't change my destructive behavior patterns. If I ignore the past, I will likely repeat it.

The other error I make is to wallow in my guilt, being paralyzed by it. Some of you have seen me in this place and have told me so. If I allow it, the past can become a destructive force, preventing me from growing in faith and recovery.

Paul didn't seem to take either extreme and thus is a model for how I should handle my own past. Paul acknowledged the evil he had done and he clung to God's grace.

It's appropriate to be sorrowful for my addiction while still being thankful for what God has done with it. It's appropriate to remember my misdeeds—as long as they motivate me to continue my pursuit of Christ.

Day 193

WHY WE RELAPSE

| *I die every day.* |

1 CORINTHIANS 15:31

I've lost a thousand pounds—and found almost all of them. Similarly, in my drug addiction, I quit using hundreds of times . . . just to relapse every day. With food and drugs, I could resist for days or weeks; but eventually, I always found my way back. Why did I fail repeatedly?

Why is the addict able to stay clean while in treatment? Why do so many fail when they leave? In treatment, as with a diet, a person changes radically—for a short period of time. In doing so, one finds short-term success and short-term sobriety. Like going off the diet, though, when addicts leave treatment, they often return to the same defects. Neither the addict in short-term recovery nor the short-term dieter have actually committed to life-long change.

Paul understood what it took to change. He understood that to truly follow Christ, he needed to die to himself daily. Paul taught that, because the flesh life was continually at war with the spirit life, he had to commit to killing it continually.

What does this mean, *to put to death* the flesh nature? With my addiction, it meant leaving my job, going to treatment, and committing to a new life. I didn't just go on a short-term diet from pills. I committed to a life without drugs. Now, I must get up early every day, point my life at God, and do my best to follow Him instead of myself. I go to meetings to remind myself that this change must be permanent. Because my flesh nature won't be gone until my flesh is, I don't get to let up sometimes. If I want to follow Christ, I must die daily.

This process won't look the same for everyone. We don't need to go to treatment for every defect. We may commit to a new way of eating without going to treatment for overeating. Make no mistake, if we want radical change, we must make life-long commitment to change, continually dying to self so we can follow Christ.

Day 194

MY TWO LIVES

What is sown is perishable; what is raised is imperishable. . . .
If there is a natural body, there is also a spiritual body.

1 CORINTHIANS 15:42, 44

As children in Sunday school, we sang a song that used bullfrogs and butterflies as a metaphor for the Christian life. Just as the tadpole and caterpillar underwent radical transformation, so too, was the Christian to be radically transformed in coming to Christ.

As a teen, when I began to struggle with lust, pride, and food, I became frustrated. *If I'm a butterfly, why do I still feel like a worm?* I thought something was wrong with me. Much later, when I went to treatment for my addiction, I again experienced this identity crisis. *If I'm a new creation in Christ, why am I an addict?*

Today's passage was one of those that eventually helped me to understand my condition as a Christian who still struggles. In the passage, Paul speaks about our physical flesh, which, like a seed, must eventually die so we may truly live.

Though we are born again into a new spirit life when we come to know God, we still live in the flesh and retain our defects. One day, the flesh will die and we'll become like the butterfly. For now, though, we are like the lowly caterpillar with the spirit of the butterfly inside. Are we then doomed to live enslaved to our defects while in this life? No. Christ died so that we can live free from slavery to ourselves.

Though we still live under the influence of the flesh life, because we now have the alternative of the spirit life, we can know freedom. This, however, isn't an automatic process. Paul insisted that we must spend the rest of our lives abandoning the flesh so we can walk in the Spirit. For now, we may be stuck in the worm's body; but because of Christ in us, we don't have to live enslaved to it.

Day 195

THE DEFECT OF ISOLATION

> *Blessed be the . . . God of all comfort, who comforts*
> *us in all our affliction, so that we may be able to*
> *comfort those who are in any affliction.*
>
> **2 CORINTHIANS 1:3, 4**

When those around me first became aware of my drug addiction, I wanted to hide. Nearly a year later, when the news hit the local paper . . . again, I wanted to disappear.

It was my pride that pushed me away from others. Just when I needed more help than ever before, I wanted to isolate. I slipped in and out of church and was afraid of the grocery store.

It's the fear of what others think of us that isolates us. In our fear, we hide our problems, thereby avoiding the solutions. In avoiding, we perpetuate our destructive behavior. If we can keep our messes secret, we never have to deal with them.

In today's passage, Paul said we must not live in isolation. We must go to God with our defects, and we must share our life struggles with others. Just as God comforts us, we are to comfort each other. We're meant to live in community so we don't suffer alone.

I don't have to tell everyone all of my problems. I do, however, need to find a small community where I can be honest. For me, this is a group of just a few guys, meeting for coffee once a week. For others, this will be AA or a small group from church.

When I'm honest about my own mess, several things happen. First, it's only in exposing my defects that I can begin addressing them. Second, my honesty encourages others that they are not alone. Third, and probably most importantly, my honesty reveals my continual need for Jesus Christ.

If we attempt a facade of perfection, then when we do fail, we'll attempt to bury it, living in secret shame. It's only in humbly admitting our persistent need that we continually rely on Christ.

Day 196
MY PERPETUAL MESS

> *We were so utterly burdened beyond our strength ... But that was to make us rely not on ourselves but on God.*
>
> **2 CORINTHIANS 1:8–9**

In church we love the story of the one who used to be a sinner but then came to Christ ... and lived happily ever after. We rarely celebrate the sufferer who prayed for healing—only to be told *no*. Even though that individual grew closer to God through the pain, we don't like that story. We dislike persistent suffering. We want deliverance. And we want it now.

Paul spoke of a much different reality, though. In today's passage, he told of his suffering and the reason behind it. He said that it was only in his suffering that he understood his desperate need for God.

It's the same for us. It's often only in our affliction that we become aware of our need. We were created to live in dependence on God, but it's usually only in our trials that we embrace that dependence.

We don't like to admit defect. We want to be fine. We want others to recognize our successes and ignore our failures. In doing so, we create a ridiculous facade of perfection that actually repels those who are seeking God and prevents us from depending on Him.

I write then, not just as one who has failed some time ago. I may have stopped using pills, only to find gratification in food. I may have had some success with food, only to become judgmental of those who still struggle. I'm always going to seek satisfaction, purpose, and meaning— either in the defective appetites of my flesh nature, or in God.

Our ever-present defects aren't cause for despair, though. They're the assurance that we won't run out of need. It will be when we no longer feel the need for God that we'll stop pursuing Him. When we stop needing Him, in our self-sufficiency, we'll become horrifically prideful. As long as we can see our need for God, we'll live in dependency on Him.

Day 197

WHO AM I SELLING?

We are not, like so many, peddlers of God's word,
but as men of sincerity, as commissioned by God,
in the sight of God we speak in Christ.

2 CORINTHIANS 2:17

In treatment I once tried to convince an atheist that he needed God. I meant well, but if I'm honest, I was doing it to soothe my own conscience. My life was a mess, and I thought that leading him to Christ would give purpose to my disaster. *Look what I did!* Unfortunately, my flesh nature can pervert almost anything—even the gospel—into self-promotion.

Paul, in today's passage, insisted that the gospel be shared out of sincere obedience to God. Those who share their faith out of self-promotion are, by nature, salesmen. They may truly believe, but their need to convince others is, at its root, not the cause of Christ, but the cause of self.

God doesn't ask me to sell Him or myself. He asks that I honestly tell what He has done for me. I must be watchful then, of my motive in all things. *Are my eyes on God or on myself?* I require constant course correction. I'm afraid it will always be my nature to turn everything to self.

I started out writing a blog—and then this book—to share my struggle with other strugglers. However, it's easy to be seduced by affirmation—not writing what God is telling me, but what I think will sell. *The more readers I get, the more good I do for you, God!* A blog or a book can easily become an ego trip. *Sure, I was an addict . . . but look at how well I've recovered.*

This natural bent toward self can be frustrating, but it's not useful to deny it. When driving, it doesn't help me get where I'm going by insisting that my steering wheel stay in a fixed position. If I want to stay on the road, I must accept constant course corrections. This is, after all, what Jesus described as the normal Christian life, to daily—and many times a day—turn from self to follow Him.

Day 198

WHEN I CAN'T SEE GOD

> *A veil lies over their hearts. But when one*
> *turns to the Lord, the veil is removed.*

2 CORINTHIANS 3:15–16

It may sound silly, but I have a place in my head where I go to talk to God. In my mind, I sit at the beach where I find that God is in the sky, the sand, the air, and the water. Every day before the sun comes up in this world, I go to sit in that sun-drenched place, communing with my Creator.

Imagine what would happen to my time with God if I relapsed. Actually, I don't have to imagine. I've been there. I told myself once that I could indulge in my addiction and return to God the next day . . . but the next day, I couldn't face Him because I had dropped a sin-bomb in my mind, damaging our relationship.

Though the consequences aren't always quite so obvious, when we follow self we always drive a wedge between God and ourselves. In today's passage, Paul described this as a veil. Though the temple veil between God and man was torn at Christ's death, Paul said we reconstruct it in our pursuit of ourselves.

If I find that God is distant, it's not that He has left me. I can walk a thousand miles away from God only to find that He's right there, if I will but turn around. That, of course, is the hard part. Turning around and gazing upon the blazing Light of God is painful to eyes darkened by the pursuit of self. For me, turning back to God meant confessing, getting help, and facing my mess. Though I wanted God, I remained unwilling to do what it took to repent because I knew the turn-around would be excruciating.

If we want to know God, and if we want freedom from the destruction of self, then we must daily do what it takes to remove the veil. Daily I must sit on my beach, accept forgiveness for my failures, and bask in the warmth of His presence and His grace.

Day 199

GODS OF INSANITY AND ADDICTION

The god of this world has blinded the minds of the unbelievers, to keep them from seeing the light.

2 CORINTHIANS 4:4

I've met alcoholics who, though dying from alcohol, still found it impossible to stop. Though yellow from liver failure, they still consumed the bathroom hand sanitizer for its alcohol content. They loathed the drink that was killing them, but still they remained desperately thirsty for it. This is insanity—to hate something while sacrificing everything for it, pursuing it as a god.

This is the nature of addiction, though, for the drug or drink to become a god that dictates every choice. No one sets out to worship a chemical; but incrementally, the chemical replaces faith, family, and career.

Anything we follow above God becomes our god as we become addicted to that thing. This can be pornography, identity, money, power, career—even good things. Even family and friends can become destructive if we place them above God.

In today's passage, Paul said that those who don't see God have been blinded by the god of this world. He was speaking of Satan, but Satan uses what we desire to distract us from God. Even exercise, work, family, and church can become addictions if we put them before God.

I'm not suggesting that the one who struggles doesn't know God. This would disqualify all of us. I am saying that if we spend our lives serving something other than God, we must ask ourselves if we truly have faith in God—or if we're just deceiving ourselves. Many claim faith in God in theory, while in practice serving some other god. This is the insanity of addiction—to follow as god something that we know is not God.

If we want to live free from the insanity of addiction, we must daily do what it takes to turn from those false gods that would demand our attention. We must turn to the one God who deserves it.

Day 200
JARS OF CLAY

| *We have this treasure in jars of clay.* |
2 CORINTHIANS 4:7

I always cringe a little when another Christian tells me that I have been delivered from my addiction. I do believe that it's only in coming to Christ that I can know freedom from slavery, but that's only half of the truth—and to teach it as the whole truth isn't helpful.

Paul insisted that, though we have this tremendous treasure of God in us, we carry it in jars of clay. To teach only the treasure part is to teach only half the truth. The other side is the persistently defective jar of clay. We live in both realities, and to acknowledge only one is to live in maddening frustration.

We struggle with this concept because we prefer to believe that we're either one thing or the other, either A *or* B. We think that we cannot be both at the same time. However, Paul dispelled this belief by insisting that we have both a faultless spirit life *and* a defective flesh life.

If I cling only to the first truth—that God saves me from myself—but I refuse to accept my ongoing need, then I'll falsely believe myself to be made perfect. In that condition, I'll either refuse to accept my failure when it inevitably occurs, or my faith will be revealed as a sham.

There are few things more maddening than a prideful Christian who thinks himself perfect while behaving horribly. There are few things sadder than one who loses his faith, returning to addiction, because he thought he was incapable of failure.

If I embrace only the second truth—my ongoing defectiveness—I will never find freedom. If my only identity is that of an addict, then I will never know the joy, freedom, and hope of a life in Christ.

To live as a disciple, I must accept that I have a perfect spirit life but carry it in a cracked pot. I don't need to live enslaved to my defects, but neither are they gone. I'm daily delivered from my addiction as long as I keep my eyes on Christ.

Day 201
WASTED

> *Though our outer self is wasting away, our inner self is being renewed day by day. For this light momentary affliction is preparing for us an eternal weight of glory beyond all comparison, as we look not to the things that are seen but to the things that are unseen. For the things that are seen are transient, but the things that are unseen are eternal.*
>
> **2 CORINTHIANS 4:16–18**

As I played football with my 15-year-old son one day, I realized that the narrow window of time, when I was his equal, has closed. As I gasped for breath to keep up, I realized that as he gets bigger, faster, and stronger, I'm in decline. The ache in my legs the next morning confirmed this. I'm in a state of decay. Even if I live to see my life expectancy, I'm over halfway there.

As I contemplate this painful, beautiful passage, I can't help but look back on my life and ask if I have lived for that which truly matters—or if I've spent my life on vain pursuits. Paul insisted on this perspective: This life is wasting away. What is seen . . . is temporary. It's only my spirit life that is eternal, and only the unseen that will last forever.

Frankly, I have regrets. I have memories stained with drug use and the pursuit of all-things-me. Sure, I've done some good things. I've never regretted a moment spent with my wife and children. Still, when I look back, I can see that I don't want the remaining decades of my life to continue like the first four.

Paul insisted that if I want to live for what truly matters, I must make a conscious choice to live for the eternal. This is unnatural. My focus, by nature, is distracted by the temporary. I don't instinctively want to give my time to someone struggling with addiction. I want to sit on my couch watching football.

Our bodies are in decay. Each of us will come to an end. At the end, will we lament a wasted life? Or will we be able to look back and see that we loved God and lived for the eternal?

Day 202

BOUNDARIES

| *Do not be unequally yoked with unbelievers.* |
2 CORINTHIANS 6:14

One of the necessities of recovery is to have a strong support group of family and friends. I know this to be true from my own experience, but I also know it to be true in observing those who don't have such support. I've seen many leave jail or treatment with good intentions, only to relapse as they returned to a using environment.

I'm unsure how it works with women, but when I used to go out with the guys, we rarely spurred each other on to good works. We weren't purposefully destructive, but we very much encouraged each other in the pursuit of tobacco and alcohol. As we pursued the desires of our flesh, we encouraged each other to do likewise.

We don't like to struggle alone, and we don't like to see the success of others while we ourselves are struggling. If our addictive behavior makes us feel guilty, we soothe the conscience with company.

In recovery and life, then, I must be careful in my choice of company. I can't choose my relatives, but I *must* choose those with whom I spend my time. Paul, in today's passage, insisted on this, instructing that I must not attach myself to those headed in a different direction than I am.

When I got out of treatment, I was blessed with a family who strongly supported my faith and recovery. I did, however, need to construct a supportive network of friends. I have friends in my Saturday morning coffee group, jail Bible study, AA, and church—all of whom encourage me in my pursuit of God.

If I want to stay sober—and if I want to continue my pursuit of God—I must be ruthless in choosing friends. Though I don't ignore the rest of the world, it's completely appropriate that I maintain boundaries with those who would influence me toward destruction. I must daily do whatever it takes to keep my life pointed at God.

Day 203

USE THE PAIN

> *Godly grief produces a repentance that leads to salvation*
> *without regret, whereas worldly grief produces death.*
>
> **2 CORINTHIANS 7:10**

When I was in treatment, I came to hate the place. It felt like prison. Those around me who had been to prison assured me that I was a cupcake—and that treatment was not prison. Still, as I was accustomed to doing whatever I wanted, it seemed like a prison.

It was in the confines of treatment that I started to use my imagination to escape and talk to God. One day I told a fellow addict of my habit of using my imagination to get away. He wisely suggested that, just as I used my imagination to escape treatment, once I got out, I needed to use my imagination to bring me back.

His point was that, as the pain of my mistakes lessens with time, so too may the impetus to change. It was the painful consequences of my addiction that forced me to seek transformation. Without the pain, I would never have been desperate enough to change.

My grief or shame, Paul said, should move me toward God; but unfortunately, it can also paralyze me. The choice of what to do with my pain is mine. Treatment wasn't the first time I felt grief over my addiction. I was grieved every time I used. Instead of using that pain to drive myself to God, though, I used it as an excuse to use more, finding perverse comfort in the very thing that was killing me.

My grief and shame, then, can push me in either direction, motivating me toward God . . . or farther into destruction. In my worst disaster, I used it to find repentance.

Even so, that repentance was not once and for all. Following God is a choice that I must continually make. I don't wallow in the grief of the past; but if I completely forget it, I risk returning to it. I will choose to use my memory and imagination to take me back to that place so I can be continually motivated to abandon self and pursue Christ.

Day 204

CAPTAIN OBVIOUS AND THE LAWS OF THERMODYNAMICS

Whoever sows sparingly will also reap sparingly, and whoever sows bountifully will also reap bountifully.

2 CORINTHIANS 9:6

I once met a patient who was convinced that he had bent the laws of physics. Massively overweight, he insisted that he *ate nothing* and still gained weight. Knowing the first law of thermodynamics, I didn't believe that he could create mass out of nothing, so we set out to determine his calorie intake. Though he wasn't *eating* anything, he was *drinking* thousands of calories a day. We had our answer, and the laws of the universe remained intact.

We are what we eat (or drink), and we get out of a thing what we put into it. This is the universal principle that Paul explained in today's passage. When we seek God, we find Him. If we seek Him little, we will know Him little. Thank you, Captain Obvious.

This principle, however, is often lost on Christians, who live by grace. We're taught, correctly, that because of Jesus' death on the cross, we're forgiven for all time. The strings connecting our sin from its eternal consequences have been severed.

This is true in my eternal, spiritual life. I often think, however, that this is also true in my temporary flesh life. I've often pursued the desires of my flesh and then begged God to deliver me from the consequences. I used to think that faith was just an intellectual acceptance of God . . . so grace meant that I could live however I wanted.

I think Paul would have looked at me as I looked at that patient with his supersized milkshake in hand. *Accepting Christ does not mean you can circumnavigate God's laws. If you pursue yourself, you will find destruction. If you pursue God, you will find Him.*

If I rob a bank this afternoon and then accept Christ this evening, I may be forgiven by God; but I'm still going to prison. When I pursue self, I reap the consequences. I may be forgiven for all eternity, but I still reap what I sow in this world.

Day 205
DESTRUCTIVE THOUGHTS

| *We . . . take every thought captive to obey Christ.* |
2 CORINTHIANS 10:5

I have destructive thoughts. In the privacy of my own mind, I have impulsive, angry, lustful, prideful, and hurtful thoughts. Maddeningly, they just naturally pop into my head.

A young man once asked me when he would stop struggling with impulsive thoughts of sex. I'm afraid I choked a little, as I knew the futility of the question. Donuts are always going to taste good, and sex will always feel good. Becoming a Christian doesn't make my appetites magically disappear.

This wouldn't be such a problem, of course, if my destructive thoughts never led to destructive behavior. My thoughts matter, though. All of my destructive behavior began with thought.

I was told once by a well-meaning Christian that lustful fantasies are a healthy alternative to adultery because they appease lust. This is nonsense. If I practice eating donuts in my mind, when I meet a real donut, I will not suddenly gain self-control.

If I want to have right behavior, I must learn to have right thoughts. What do I do, then, with these impulsive thoughts? Paul, in today's passage, insists that I must interrogate every thought, running it through the filter of Christ. *Does this push me more toward God or self?*

This is a discipline that will take a lifetime, as some thoughts never die. God allows us to need Him continually so we can pursue Him continually. Though engaging in destructive fantasy injures me, the opposite is true as well. I can use every toxic thought to turn me toward God.

I don't have to be a monk to do this. I always have some thought running in the background of my mind. I can, if I'm willing, discipline myself to apply this verse to my thought life without ever abandoning my daily responsibilities. This is how I learn to live in continual relationship with God. Since my defective thoughts never seem to take a break, I can continually use them to turn my mind to God.

Day 206

THE BEAUTY OF EVIL

| *Satan disguises himself as an angel of light.* |
2 CORINTHIANS 11:14

Why is evil so attractive? Though I know exercise, broccoli, and prayer are good for me, what I want right now is to sit on my couch, eating donuts while watching TV. What I want to be someday is unattainable by pursuing what I want right now. In my addiction, I desperately wanted to be sober *tomorrow* . . . but at the same moment I just wanted a pill.

One doesn't have to be an addict to find our predicament unfair. We live in a world full of forbidden fruit, for which God has allowed us an insatiable appetite. *Why don't you just make me a robot, God?*

This is His plan after all, right? If I truly believe in a God who is in control, then He has allowed my anguish over broccoli and donuts. He allows me to chase sobriety or addiction. He allows me to pursue Him or myself. It's not enough that He allows a choice, though. He allows the alternative to Him to be profoundly attractive. Evil tastes fantastic. Why would God allow such a thing?

The answer lies in the purpose for which we were made. Our primary purpose in life is to love God above all (Matthew 22:37). God loves us and longs to be loved back. For true love to exist, though, there must be a choice. God created us in His own image—with preferences, appetites, and the capacity for choice. God allowed us to know an appetite for something not-God so that we could make a choice. It would be no choice if God offered broccoli as the only alternative. God allows evil to appear delicious.

This doesn't mean that we must give up everything pleasurable in this life. In fact, the greatest pleasures we can know come through enjoying this life while in right relation to God. We do, however, need to be brutally honest with ourselves. Are we pursuing God . . . or are we pursuing destruction—dressed up as something beautiful?

Day 207

I AM WEAK

If I must boast, I will boast of the things that show my weakness.

2 CORINTHIANS 11:30

A reader once told me that he could see a lot of healing going on in my writing. His words implied that I was writing for the purpose of recovering from past wounds. This offended me. I had a visceral response (which I didn't say aloud). *I'm fine. Don't you see that I'm writing this for all of you sinners, still trapped in your addiction?*

Now, that wasn't true—but it's what I wanted to say. Though I tell myself that I'm always growing, it offended me when someone else said it. I've had to learn and relearn an important truth. *I will always have need.* It's my continual need that keeps me pointed at God. The day I refuse to see my weakness is the day I'll begin to relapse.

Sometime after the reader's comment, when a friend pointed out that visible growth is still taking place in my writing, I was able to embrace it as an obvious truth. I'm still growing up. It's when I begin to think I have it all figured out that I turn my gaze from God. *Pride is the faith killer.*

Paul emphasized this in today's passage. He had been whipped, beaten, stoned, and even shipwrecked. Often he was thirsty, hungry, and cold. He was a failure in the eyes of the world, yet he found that his weakness kept him dependent on God. Though he had reason to boast, Paul refused to succumb to the seduction of pride.

Choosing humility, while unnatural, is the only cure for my deadly pride. When I turn my gaze to God, I assume my only proper position before Him. If I find myself in that dangerous place where everyone else in the world is wrong and I'm the only one who has it figured out, I'm in trouble. If I can't see that God has much work yet to do in me, then I'm lost. It's only in admitting my continual weakness that I continue to depend on God.

Day 208

THORNS OF THE FLESH

> *A thorn was given me in the flesh, a messenger of Satan to harass me, to keep me from becoming conceited. . . . I pleaded with the Lord about this. . . . But he said to me, "My grace is sufficient for you, for my power is made perfect in weakness."*
>
> **2 CORINTHIANS 12:7–9**

In today's passage, Paul honestly admitted that he too had some defect (thorn) for which he asked God for deliverance. He prayed, but God refused, for it was in Paul's weakness that he remained dependent on God's strength.

We all have thorns in our flesh. We all know defect, whether we like it or not. For some, the greatest challenge in life is some physical insult. For others, it's past physical or emotional trauma, depression, or anxiety. Still others have a predisposition for addiction, pride, anger, lust, greed, or a need for affirmation. The defect or thorn isn't necessarily a sin in itself, but rather some imperfection that causes misery.

Paul was familiar with struggles. Whether his thorn was a physical defect or a struggle with his flesh nature, it ultimately doesn't matter. There are lessons to be learned from Paul's condition.

First, while our defects may not be sinful in themselves, they remain a source of suffering and misery. In my defective predisposition for drugs, I can do horrible things. Though depression isn't a sin, it can lead me to self-destructive behavior.

Second, it's appropriate that we ask God for healing. Paul prayed three times and had some expectation that God would deliver him. In our suffering it's always appropriate to ask God for help. We need to realize, however, that we are not faithless if God's response is *no*.

Paul insisted that God uses our thorns for good. It's often only in our weakness and need that we turn to Him, relying on and revealing His strength. If we were perfect, we wouldn't need God. Paradoxically, Paul said, it's only when I am weak that I am strong. We may not like our weaknesses, but if we assume Paul's attitude, we can use them for good.

Day 209

PEOPLE PLEASER

| *Am I now seeking the approval of man, or of God?* |

GALATIANS 1:10

You might think that getting my name in the newspaper for my addiction would diminish my concern over what the world thinks. If I'm honest, though, I have to admit that deep down, I still seek affirmation from others. Though I still dislike it, I'm often motivated by the affirmation I derive from those around me.

This defect manifests itself in various ways, masquerading often as positive personality traits. Going to the gym can be about discipline . . . or about wanting to look like I go to the gym. Being kind can be about loving others . . . or it can be about appearing likeable. Writing a blog or a book can be about the desire to help others . . . or it can be about showing off my recovery.

When I'm obviously selfish, I'm at least honest about serving myself. In my people-pleasing defect, I pretend that others' interests are important, but really, I'm just trying to feel good about myself.

Make no mistake, affirmation is a drug. When I get it, I feel good; but when I don't, I feel awful. Praise from those around me produces a high. My brain feeds on it. Like a drug, the need for affirmation can dominate my behavior, distracting me from God. Since following God will never be popular in the eyes of the world, when faced with pleasing God or pleasing man, I'll choose poorly if I'm focused on my own affirmation.

Paul, in today's passage, said that we must choose to find our meaning in God alone. We were made to be fulfilled not by the world, but by our relationship with God. Only He is adequate to meet our deepest needs. When we pursue meaning and purpose in the world, we'll always come to disappointment and pain because the world is incapable of filling God's role. We must daily ask if we are living for the approval of God or man.

Day 210
THE TWO SCOTTS

> *I have been crucified with Christ. It is no longer I who live, but Christ who lives in me. And the life I now live in the flesh I live by faith in the Son of God.*
>
> **GALATIANS 2:20**

There are two of me. One wants those things that are best for me in the long run. The other me wants gratification now, forgetting the consequences. In following the one, I automatically neglect the other.

Scott One gets up early every day to point his life to God. This me wants to exercise and eat right for all the right reasons. He takes the time to share his life with others. Scott One can put off the desire for immediate gratification, instead finding joy and purpose in God.

Scott Two, on the other hand, is an impulsive, reckless creature, bent on immediate gratification. He would rather wake up late and eat donuts. Selfish with his time, he has nothing to give others because he hasn't filled himself with Christ. Sure, he believes in God, but he follows self. Scott Two is a walking disaster.

These two versions of me represent the conflict between my spirit life and my flesh life, which are at war with each other. Paul acknowledged this conflict but insisted that my greatest reality lies in my perfect spirit life. This life, though, doesn't manifest automatically. Because I'm still in this body, I don't just naturally live the perfect life.

I used to take this verse to mean that I was already made perfect in the flesh; but when I looked at my life, I saw addiction. How could Christ be living in me if I was still such a mess?

Though Christ's work was done at the cross, the manifestation of His work depends on our daily decision to follow our spirit or our flesh. Living in faith isn't passive. Living in faith means we must continually deny the pursuit of ourselves for the pursuit of God.

Day 211

FREEDOM FROM ADDICTION

> *When you did not know God, you were enslaved. . . . For freedom Christ has set us free; stand firm therefore, and do not submit again to a yoke of slavery.*
>
> **GALATIANS 4:8, 5:1**

In my addiction, those around me wanted to know why. *Why would you do this?* There really is no answer that makes sense, other than this: *It's my broken nature to do so.* Therein lies the only route to understanding. We can understand the defects of others only in light of the defects we struggle with ourselves. The truth is, we all struggle with something.

When looking at those with different defects, though, we like to point to today's passage and insist that they should be free in Christ. We believe in God's Word and we want it to be true, so . . . we apply it to others. *You can be set free in Christ.* We believe others should be free, but we don't feel free ourselves. Why do we not know freedom in Christ?

I had assumed that this freedom was a forcible takeover of my free will. I misunderstood freedom as the absence of choice, but it's rather the opposite. Before I came to know God, I was spiritually dead, only capable of following myself. In coming to faith, I received a new spirit life and only now am I able to choose between my spirit life and my flesh life.

There are those who interpret this verse to mean that a Christian cannot be addicted to drugs. This verse means rather the opposite, though, and serves as a dire warning. *Christ died so you could follow God. Do not return to the slavery of your defects.* Paul wouldn't have warned against a return to slavery if it were not possible.

If, as Christians, we find ourselves enslaved, it's not because Christ hasn't set us free. It's because we've made countless poor choices, leading to slavery. No amount of begging God to set us free will make us freer than He already made us. If we want freedom, we must make radical changes to live in the freedom Christ has already bought with His life.

Day 212
THE WAR INSIDE

> *Walk by the Spirit, and you will not gratify the desires of the flesh. For the desires of the flesh are against the Spirit.*
>
> **GALATIANS 5:16–17**

Recently, I asked a group of recovering addicts if Christ sets us free from addiction. They agreed that He does. When I asked them how that works, I got blank looks. They truly believe themselves to be free, but I know that a year from now, many of them will have relapsed.

Lest we think this is an issue just with addicts, we're all in the same situation. Though we believe we should be set free from our defects when we come to God, we don't experience it. If being a Christian means our defects are miraculously removed, then Christians should be perfect; but we seem to struggle with as much pride, anger, lust, and greed as the rest of the world. This discrepancy exposes a serious flaw in our understanding.

We cling to a faulty belief. *When I came to Christ, I was delivered once and for all from my old self. I don't have any more struggles.*

We desperately want freedom from our defects to be instantaneous, but it's not. To be sure, when we first come to Christ and receive the new spirit life, we may experience radical changes. None of us, though, is made completely perfect.

Paul, in today's passage, dismissed the illusion of the perfect Christian life. He said that inside each of us there is a continual war. Though our eternal spirit life in Christ will outlive our flesh life, for now the two occupy the same body in anything but a peaceful coexistence.

Paul insisted the only way to battle the flesh nature is to walk in the Spirit. We can't pursue both lives simultaneously, so daily we must do whatever it takes to pursue God—instead of ourselves. This isn't a passive process. If we want to walk the spirit life, we must pursue God like we mean it. As we do what it takes to follow Him, He daily sets us free.

Day 213

THIS IS US

> Now the works of the flesh are evident: sexual immorality, impurity,
> sensuality, idolatry, sorcery, enmity, strife, jealousy, fits of anger,
> rivalries, dissensions, divisions, envy, drunkenness, orgies, and
> things like these. I warn you, as I warned you before, that those
> who do such things will not inherit the kingdom of God.

GALATIANS 5:19–21

Occasionally, I find myself getting pulled into this argument: *If God created me this way, it can't be wrong. God doesn't make junk.* It works its way into different discussions, but the theory is that if I was born with it, it can't be defective because God made me this way.

Paul rejected such thinking, insisting that the nature (flesh) into which we are born is inherently opposed to God and terminally self-absorbed. He went on to list the defects to which we're prone. These are defects, as they inherently turn us toward self and away from God. Anything that distracts us from God is a destructive idol when we place it above God.

Born this way, doesn't save us from fault, as it's the very nature we had at birth that is opposed to God. This is who we are; and the sooner we accept it, the sooner we'll be able to turn from self to find God.

Anything not-God that I pursue above God is destructive because it robs me of Him. *Those who do such things will not inherit the kingdom of God.* I used to understand this to mean that those who engage in such behavior won't go to heaven. Paul's meaning may also be understood with a much more immediate consequence; that is, when I pursue the works of my flesh, I'm not pursuing God. The two endeavors are mutually exclusive, and I pursue one at the expense of the other.

Our highest purpose in life is to abandon ourselves to embrace God. Paul insisted, though, that we ourselves stand in our own way. We're our own greatest distraction from God. Only in accepting that can we turn from ourselves to find God.

Day 214

THE FRUIT OF MY ADDICTION

> *The fruit of the Spirit is love, joy, peace, patience, kindness,*
> *goodness, faithfulness, gentleness, self-control.*
> **GALATIANS 5:22–23**

In today's passage, Paul speaks of self-control as a fruit—a result—of the Spirit-filled life. In my addiction, I saw my hunger for drugs as my greatest problem; and thus, self-control was my greatest need.

I begged for God to take away my hunger and give me self-control. He did not. It took a disaster for me to understand why. Only after I stopped using and began making a genuine, daily attempt to deny self and follow God did I begin to understand. My hunger for drugs was but a symptom of the greater disease of self. Self-control is a result of living the Spirit-filled life.

In seeking only relief from a symptom and in pursuing only the fruit, I wasn't addressing my disease . . . and I wasn't seeking the cure. I wanted the benefits of abandoning self without doing the work of abandoning self. I wanted the fruit of the Spirit without growing the tree. As always, I just wanted the easy route.

Paul, in today's passage, described the effects of living the Spirit-filled life. When I pursue God, I grow the fruits of love, joy, peace, and self-control. If I lack self-control, the cure is to do whatever it takes to abandon self to follow God. In that process of growing God's Spirit life (the tree) in me, I'll develop self-control (the fruit). I don't get the fruit without growing the tree.

In my addiction, I remained unwilling to do what it took to abandon everything-me. In this state, I couldn't be filled with the Spirit—and thus, I couldn't develop self-control.

Though we'll always feel the influence of our defects, we don't need to live addicted to them. If we're willing, we may daily do what it takes to abandon self and follow Christ. In doing so, we daily treat the disease of our own nature, embracing the cure of Christ.

Day 215
KILLING MY DEFECTS

*Those who belong to Christ Jesus have crucified
the flesh with its passions and desires.*
GALATIANS 5:24

Around age 10, I found myself overweight the day before a wrestling tournament. I hoped to wrestle in a specific weight class, but I was a half-pound heavy. I knew if I ate light that day, I would be fine. That night, my family attended an event where several bakery boxes filled with dozens of donuts sat on a table, tempting me. I fought the good fight for perhaps 10 minutes . . . but eventually I caved, eating no fewer than four donuts. I didn't make my weight class.

Fast forward three decades. I'd like to claim that I've grown up, but donuts still tempt me. Though I eat pretty clean, that box of donuts at work still seems to call my name. I've begun to learn, though, through my addictions, what it means to crucify the desires of the flesh.

Paul said in today's passage that we must crucify the flesh nature. This phrase, used several times by Paul, is similar to Christ's call to take up our crosses daily.

What does this mean? All I can tell you is how it has looked in my life. With my thought life, I've learned that I must continually work at not putting garbage into my brain. I don't do it perfectly, but picking a Bible verse a day to meditate on has radically changed my thought patterns.

With my drug addiction, I couldn't stop until it was dragged into the Light. I had to go to treatment, leave my job, and radically change my life. Years later, I continue to work at killing my addiction, meeting with others who have the same defect.

As Christians we tend to think that change comes about miraculously, just by praying for it. *We are Christians so God does it for us, right?* While some may be miraculously delivered from specific destructive appetites, most of us find that Christ's command to crucify self means sacrifice and hard work. Our responsibility is to always do whatever it takes to abandon our destructive behavior and follow God.

Day 216

I NEED HELP

> *If anyone is caught in any transgression . . . restore him in*
> *a spirit of gentleness. . . . Bear one another's burdens.*
>
> **GALATIANS 6:1–2**

Though we all struggle with something, we'd much prefer to struggle in secrecy. If we're physically ill, we may not mind if others know. However, if we wrestle with addiction, lust, an eating disorder, or depression, we'd rather keep it quiet. Often we don't get the help we need because we're afraid to admit that need.

In my addiction, I was completely unwilling to get help because I couldn't bear the thought of discovery. Then, when it finally came to light, I just wanted it buried. I insisted I didn't need or want help. I'd love to say that my openness now is completely voluntary, but my defects were dragged—kicking and screaming—into the Light. Now that my addiction has been exposed, though, it's easy to meet regularly with others who are struggling.

This was Paul's message in today's passage. He insisted that, as a Christian, I must help carry my brother's burdens. When another is wrestling with a destructive behavior, I must be honest enough about my own defects that he can tell me about his.

This works both ways. When I'm struggling, I must humbly acknowledge that I need help. It's easy to speak of how I *used to struggle*. It's a much greater challenge to admit how I'm struggling today. I must bear my brother's burdens—and allow him to help me with mine.

Why is it a struggle to be honest? It's our pride, that faith killer, that keeps us more concerned about our reputation than our faith. We find it easier to remain in our defects than to go through the discomfort of confession and change.

If we want freedom from slavery, though, we must continually choose to do whatever it takes to get there. Are we willing to acknowledge and confess our need? If we desire to know freedom, we would do well to ask for help in getting there.

Day 217

GRAVITY, DONUTS, AND DRUGS

> Do not be deceived: God is not mocked, for whatever one
> sows, that will he also reap. For the one who sows to his own
> flesh will from the flesh reap corruption, but the one who
> sows to the Spirit will from the Spirit reap eternal life.

GALATIANS 6:7–8

Several years ago during a long winter, I had to shovel the snow off our roof. As the piles on the ground grew, so did a fantastic idea. *We should jump off the roof! What could go wrong?*

We had grand fun . . . until someone broke a wrist. That's when my wife gave me the look. *What did you think was going to happen?* It's often only after such an incident that I remember my actions always have consequences.

Paul, in today's passage, shared this universal principle. Just as I cannot cheat gravity, I cannot cheat God. I reap what I sow. If I spend my life chasing lust, money, anger, affirmation, and all-things-me, I'll breed spiritual destruction. If, however, I pursue God, I'll grow life, joy, and peace.

I used to deny this principle because it sounded too much like karma, a decidedly un-Christian concept. I was saved by faith, not by works, so life wasn't about my behavior—or so I thought. I was forgiven, I could do whatever I wanted, right?

Then, in my disaster, I had the audacity to blame God. *How could you allow this?* To this kind of thinking, I believe Paul would have vehemently responded. *"What did you think was going to happen? If you eat too many donuts, you'll get fat. If you use drugs, you'll be an addict. If you jump off the roof . . ."* You get the idea.

Though I am forgiven by God for all eternity, faith doesn't turn the pursuits of my flesh into the life of God. I can't walk a thousand miles in one direction and then expect that God will simply transport me a thousand miles—or more—in the other direction. I reap what I sow. If I pursue self, I'll find disaster. If I pursue God, I'll find life.

Day 218

COMFORTABLY MISERABLE

> *I do not cease to give thanks for you, remembering you in my prayers, that the God of our Lord Jesus Christ, the Father of glory, may give you the Spirit of wisdom and of revelation in the knowledge of him, having the eyes of your hearts enlightened, that you may know what is the hope to which he has called you.*
>
> **EPHESIANS 1:16–18**

Before my marriage, I lived on my own for the better part of a decade. During that time, unwashed dishes and dirty bathrooms became normal to me. I gradually grew desensitized to living conditions that I now look back on with some disgust. It was only after getting married that I returned to normal cleanliness, regaining my sensitivity to squalor.

The same was true with my addiction. I didn't start out enslaved to a pill; but gradually, with one bad decision after another, I descended into darkness and became comfortable with behavior that I now find revolting. Corruption became normal—and the idea of living free was a hopeless dream. I couldn't imagine climbing over the mountain of misery that it would take to break free.

In my recovery I became aware of my desperate condition and thus learned to seek God desperately. In seeking Him, I've become much more aware of those things that come between us. Where I was once comfortable in my misery, I now feel significant discomfort in the absence of God's hope and joy.

I regularly meet others who think they want to be free. Living in misery, they have some idea that they want God, but they remain unwilling to do what it takes to get there. They see the mountain of discomfort they must climb to be free, and they decide that it would just be easier to remain in the mess at the bottom. I understand. I've been there.

However, if we want to know the peace, hope, and joy of God, then we must daily be willing to do whatever it takes to get there. Often, though, we remain in our squalor because it's just too much work to leave behind what is making us miserable. If we want to know God, we must continually abandon the misery of ourselves.

Day 219

MY OWN PRISON

We all once lived in the passions of our flesh, carrying out the desires of the body. . . . But God, being rich in mercy, . . . even when we were dead in our trespasses, made us alive together with Christ.

EPHESIANS 2:3–5

Every Sunday morning, a friend and I attend a Bible study at our county jail. On our way in, we pick up a hand-held radio so we can notify the guards when we are done. Occasionally, we forget to take a radio and then we're trapped until someone checks on us. Though it's never been more than half an hour, it's maddening to have no way out. When the door is finally opened, we don't linger.

There are those, however, who find strange comfort in prison. Freedom at times seems daunting, and perversely, they want to go back. This may sound ridiculous, but we've all chosen, at times, to remain in our own prisons.

Paul, in today's passage, reminded the Ephesians that, before Christ brought them to life, they were dead in the desires of their own flesh. He wrote to remind them—and us—of this, as he knew it was their nature to return to the pursuits of the flesh.

I must admit, I have completely misunderstood what Christ does for me. I once thought that when I came to Christ, He forced me out of my prison and locked the door behind me. I now see that Christ opens the door and beckons me to live free, pursuing Him. It's my nature, however, to return to the desires of my flesh. When I choose to indulge in lust, drugs, anger, pride, greed, and all-things-me, I return to incarceration.

Christ has set us free, but we must *choose* to live free. If we find ourselves in prison, it's because we have *chosen* prison. Christ opens the door, but it's up to us to walk with Him. If we don't continually choose Him, we will—by default—return to our own prisons.

Day 220

HOPE

> *Now to him who is able to do far more abundantly*
> *than all that we ask or think, according to the*
> *power at work within us, to him be glory.*
>
> **EPHESIANS 3:20-21**

In my addiction I laughed bitterly at this verse. I prayed for God to fix me and became cynical when He didn't. I grew hopeless as I questioned His power and His existence. In the middle of my disaster, my mother told me something I'll never forget. She insisted that my life was not over—and that God could make something of my mess.

I hesitated to tell her my true feelings. *While I appreciate your faith, you have no idea how many times I've begged God for help. My career is gone. My wife is leaving. God cannot—or will not—fix this.*

In my despair, I was unable to see any hope. All I knew was that recovery would be a mountain of misery. I had to leave my job and go to treatment. If and when I got clean, my life would still be a disaster. Getting clean just meant I had to face my problems sober.

In treatment I recognized the error in praying for a magical fix, so I changed my prayer. *God, tell me what I must do to change.* He insisted that I must do whatever it takes to deny self and follow Him daily.

Though I don't do it perfectly, life has radically changed in pursuing God daily. This life isn't about things or money. I didn't get my job back, but I do have my family. Circumstances didn't return to what they were before, but then . . . they couldn't have.

My life needed to change radically, but it's grown into something far better. The life that God has grown in me, is now peace, joy, and hope in Him. Where I once couldn't stand to look in the mirror . . . I now enjoy my life, my time with God, and my family. As it turns out, Mom was right. God's power was beyond what I could imagine in the disaster.

Day 221

HOW TO DEAL WITH DESTRUCTIVE BEHAVIOR

| *Speaking the truth in love, we are to grow up in every way into him.* |
EPHESIANS 4:15

It's not uncommon for a family member of an addict to ask me how to help him. *Do I simply love him? Do I kick him out of the house? How can I make him get help?*

When confronted with an addict, most of us err in one of two ways. Either we sweep truth under the rug, attempting to love the addict into sobriety, or we beat him over the head with the truth. We don't naturally strike the right balance of truth and love.

In today's passage, Paul said that we must always strive for this balance of truth and love. They are two sides of the same coin, each requiring the other to be whole. One without the other is inadequate at best—and harmful at worst.

While loving an addict often means I must tell him the truth, this doesn't mean that truth equals love. It does little good if I tell a brother of his need but remain unwilling to help him. Truth without love is usually just judgment. The opposite is unhelpful as well. Love without truth enables the addict, simply encouraging him to continue in the toxic behavior.

How then, do I interact with the addict? Paul's words are the best advice I can give. In dealing with the addict, I must always speak the truth in love. When confronted with toxic behavior of the addict, I must choose to respond like Christ. *I love you, but I will not allow you to remain in my home when you are using. I will not tolerate your abuse. I will help you get the help you need, but I will not enable you. I love you, but I will not participate in your addiction.*

This *love and truth* approach will not be appreciated by the addict who desires only to be enabled. We must realize, though, that we're not responsible for the behavior of the addict. We are responsible only for our own behavior. We must leave the rest up to God.

Day 222
SLOW LEARNER

> *You were taught, with regard to your former way of life, to put off your old self, which is being corrupted by its deceitful desires; to be made new in the attitude of your minds; and to put on the new self, created to be like God in true righteousness and holiness.*
>
> **EPHESIANS 4:22–24, NIV**

In today's passage, Paul used the imagery of clothing, insisting that we must continually take off the old and put on the new. This echoes Jesus' command to deny self and follow Him—and Paul's previous commands to crucify the flesh.

In writing this book, I don't wish to be repetitive, but as I progress through the New Testament, I feel compelled to emphasize those concepts that God repeats frequently. Besides, there are some lessons I must hear over and over.

In recovery from my addiction, I realized that this command—take off the old and put on the new—is one that I never really learned. Yes, I *knew* it . . . but I failed to *live* it.

Most of us can identify. We know that we must deny self and follow Christ, but we have no idea what that looks like. We have struggles . . . but if they're not too destructive, we never deal with them. We limp along, handicapped by anger, food, pride, lust, greed, or the need for affirmation, not realizing that we are spiritually paralyzed.

A friend once called my addiction a painful gift. He saw me as the fortunate one, as it was only in my profound need that I came to desperately seek God. My friend was right. Though I'm not thankful for the pain I caused, I wouldn't give up the lessons I've learned through my addiction.

I used to see this passage as something I would do *when I was a better Christian.* Abandoning self to follow God, though, isn't something we do to attain a better Christian life. This *is* the Christian life. If we're not daily denying self to pursue God, we're not living as disciples. It isn't optional.

If we call ourselves Christians, yet remain enslaved, then we must do whatever it takes to abandon self and follow God. He will likely repeat this lesson until it sinks in.

Day 223

ANGRY

"In your anger do not sin": Do not let the sun go down while you are still angry, and do not give the devil a foothold.

EPHESIANS 4:26–27, NIV

When a patient in the ER once threatened my family, I exploded with a rage I've never felt before or since. I regained control before I laid hands on him; but in my anger, I spent much of the next week obsessing about what I wanted to do to him. My anger derailed my thought life for days.

Though I may have been right to be offended, I was wrong in my reaction. This is often the case with my anger. My offense may be warranted . . . but as with many of my defects, it's in my response that I go wrong.

Not all my anger is righteous. When I snap at my kids out of my own frustration, I'm wrong from the start. The problem is that, in my anger, I always feel justified. Like a drug, anger clouds my mind.

In anger, I've said many things that I later wished I could have back. Initially I felt my response to be justified, but my thinking was impaired. It usually takes me a day or two to sober up to the point where I can think clearly enough to reply appropriately. Thus, the right response to my anger is often to bite my tongue until I cool down. It takes only a second of uncontrolled rage to do a spectacular amount of damage.

As with any other defect, the more we feed our anger, the more it grows. We may use Jesus overturning the tables in the temple as justification for anger . . . but the truth is, anger is a weapon that few of us are mature enough to wield without sinning. Most of us should not even try.

The *I can't help it* of my anger sounds a lot like the *I can't help it* of my drug addiction. I may not be responsible for the initial defect, but only I am responsible for my behavior. I can act badly—growing the defect— or I can learn to kill each destructive impulse, diminishing its control over me.

Day 224

FAITH AND MARRIAGE

| *Do not grieve the Holy Spirit of God.* |
EPHESIANS 4:30

In my addiction, I severely injured my relationship with my wife. My lies and toxic behavior destroyed trust and communication. I followed my appetite above all, and in doing so I radically distanced myself from her.

What I did to my relationship with my wife illustrates what I do to God when I pursue self above Him. While my wife and I remained married, my addiction eviscerated our intimacy. Similarly, when I pursue myself above God—though I don't *lose* my relationship with Him—I severely damage it. I may be forgiven for all eternity, but the practical manifestation of God's Spirit can be great or small in me, depending on whether I grow God's Spirit—or grieve Him.

I've lived most of my life as if spiritual growth is a passive process for which I'm not responsible. But Paul insisted that I must walk in the Spirit (Romans 8:4). This is anything but a passive process. I can't pursue self while being filled with God.

How do I grieve God's Spirit? In pursuing anything above God, I distance myself from Him. I can't draw close to God while indulging in drugs, pornography, pride, anger, or greed. Even good things can be destructive if I put them above God.

How do I grow God's Spirit? In keeping with the marriage metaphor, I must pursue Him in the same way I pursue my relationship with my wife. If I want to grow my marriage, I must spend time with my wife, communicating with and loving her.

Just as we can't ignore our spouses and expect intimacy, we can't ignore God and expect to know Him. If we want to know His presence and power in our lives, we must seek Him. We must daily read His Word, talk to Him, listen to Him. We can't neglect God and then wonder why we don't know His presence. We find God when we seek Him.

Day 225

INTOXICATED

> *Do not get drunk with wine, for that is debauchery, but be filled with the Spirit.*
>
> **EPHESIANS 5:18**

Under the influence of pills, my mind was altered. As the drug acted on receptors in my brain, my thoughts and actions changed. As I grew physically and emotionally dependent on the drug, my life came to revolve around acquiring and consuming it. In the end, I pursued the pill above all else.

Substance abuse and dependency was apparently a problem in Paul's time as well. Several times, Paul addressed the destructive effects of intoxication and insisted that, just as we once filled ourselves with wine, we now must be filled with the Spirit of God.

It's a compelling juxtaposition of two apparent opposites: a mind-altering chemical . . . and the Spirit of God. Paul said that just as I once chose to get high, I must now habitually fill myself with God. Where once my behavior was under the influence of a drug, it must now be under His influence. As I became dependent on a pill, now I must remain dependent on Him for my strength, purpose, and meaning.

An inmate at the local county jail once told me that, just as he had once spent all his energies in pursuit of drugs, money, and women, he had started to expend that same energy in pursuit of God instead. Likewise, as I once spent all my efforts on my addiction, I must now do the same with God. Recovery and faith don't mean that I sit back and do nothing. It's my responsibility to drink deeply of God if I desire His influence in my life.

Our lives will be defined by whatever we pursue and consume. If we fill ourselves with drugs or wine, the effects will be obvious. If instead we daily read, pray, and meditate, then our lives will be marked by God. When we pursue Him instead of ourselves, where we once wrought destruction we will grow life instead.

Day 226

I DO

Husbands, love your wives, as Christ loved the church and gave himself up for her. . . . Let each one of you love his wife as himself.

EPHESIANS 5:25, 33

The nature of addiction is to pursue the drug above everyone and everything. I once chose to take a vow to love my wife . . . but in my addiction, I chose and loved the drug. She was heartbroken, "You don't love me, you love the drug." I insisted it wasn't true, but my behavior betrayed the reality that she knew. I can take all the vows I want. If my behavior doesn't follow, my words are meaningless.

I'd like to say that this problem evaporated in my recovery; but if I'm honest, I must admit that it's simply not my nature to put another's needs above my own. In today's passage, Paul insisted, though, that this is what marriage means.

Paul said I must value my wife's needs as my own, and I must love her *as Christ loved the church.* This means that my desires are not to be my primary pursuit. I often love my wife for how she meets my needs, but Paul insisted that my responsibility is to meet *her* needs. Again, this just isn't natural.

I have a difficult time sacrificing my way of doing things. I may not be addicted to a pill anymore, but I'm still addicted to everything-me. With my time, money, relationships, and appetites, it's my default setting to look to my own needs first.

Though I'm not good at it, it's a good exercise for me to ask how I would feel if my wife acted as I do. *How would I feel if my wife sacrificed our relationship for a drug? How would I like to be treated?*

If we truly want to love our spouses, we must choose to act in a manner consistent with that love. We can't just *speak* the words, we must *live* them.

Day 227

POWERLESS

| *Be strong in the Lord and in the strength of his might.* |
EPHESIANS 6:10

In my addiction to both food and drugs, I promised myself again and again that I would quit. Every indulgence was the last time. *I'll quit tomorrow, I swear! I mean it this time.* I wanted to mean it . . . but as I was enslaved to my defects, I did not control them. They controlled me.

The first step of Alcoholics Anonymous is this: "We admitted that we were powerless over our addiction—that our lives had become unmanageable." Honesty didn't make me sober, but to find recovery I had to admit that I wasn't able to do this on my own. I shudder to think of where I would be if consequences had not forced me to accept this reality.

Many dislike step one, as it seems to say that there is absolutely nothing I can do about my predicament. I will insist, though, that the only way to deal with my addictions has been to admit that, on my own, I am powerless. *I cannot do this alone.*

This was Paul's message in today's passage. "Be strong in the Lord." Paul insisted that I wasn't made to live on my own. I must constantly choose to find my strength in the God who made me.

Without God, all I have is me. And I am a disaster. I've proven this. God gives me the only adequate alternative to my problem of myself because He made me to be complete only in Him. The puzzle of my life comes together only when I find my strength in God—because that's how he made the puzzle to fit.

We may find sobriety or weight loss in other avenues. We can move to a desert island where there are no drugs or donuts, but our problems will still be there. We may be skinny and sober on the island, but we'll still be stuck with ourselves. Only in God can we find the strength, joy, purpose, and life that we were pursuing in the desires of our flesh.

Day 228

THE BIG PICTURE

> *He who began a good work in you will bring it*
> *to completion at the day of Jesus Christ.*
>
> **PHILIPPIANS 1:6**

The week before my addiction came to light and my life fell apart, I had the opportunity to be involved in a *save-a-life* kind of event in the emergency room. I remember desperately wanting to be known as that guy, *the hero*. At the time, though, my life was crumbling. Hints and suspicions told me that my secret would soon be exposed. The heroic image I coveted was about to evaporate, and I shuddered at the approaching calamity.

When it hit, it was as horrible as I had feared. Life came apart. Naively, I hoped that my good works would balance out my toxic behavior. *Maybe people will see all the good I've done and view this as a minor setback.* It wasn't just a little fall, though. It was spectacularly bad. At that moment, addiction defined my life.

When someone fails epically, we're quick to define that person only by the fall. When an addict relapses, we declare him a failure. Likewise, when he recovers for a month and finds God, we often declare him *recovered*. We're terminally short-sighted and can't see beyond the moment.

In my addiction and subsequent destruction, I saw only the disaster. As it turned out, it was a defining point in my life—just not the way I imagined at the time.

Paul, in today's passage, said that God works from a different perspective than we do. While we're trapped in time, living moment to moment, God sees the big picture. Where we see momentary successes and failures, He sees the final outcome. He knows that His children will have ups and downs but will one day be made perfect in Him.

God can see that, though we may fail spectacularly, we'll one day be made complete. Whatever seems to define us now . . . in a thousand years won't matter. In a hundred years, only our eternal spirit lives will exist. We'll one day be made perfect in God.

Day 229

DID GOD DO THIS?

*I want you to know, brothers, that what has happened
to me has really served to advance the gospel.*

PHILIPPIANS 1:12

As miserable as my addiction was for me, it was that much worse for my wife. In her despair, several well-meaning Christians told her this was God's will. *God chose this for a reason.* What she heard was that Scott could not be blamed. This wasn't consoling. She was angry and had a right to be. *Scott did this, not God.*

Paul, in today's passage, spoke of his imprisonment and insisted that God had used it for good. In prison he shared the gospel with the entire guard. Did God put Paul in prison? Did God make me an addict?

Paul's words echo the words of Joseph to his brothers (Genesis 50:20), "You meant evil against me, but God meant it for good." Joseph's brothers, jealous of him, had sold him into slavery. God used this event for his own purposes. Joseph's brothers did evil, but God meant it for good.

Was God in control or did Joseph's brothers choose? Yes. On both counts. Though I can't grasp how both can be true . . . these stories both reveal a world in which people make choices while God remains in control.

Knowing that God is in control doesn't make painful things . . . not painful. My wife was miserable, and telling her that God wanted her to be miserable was certainly not comforting. It just made God the cause of her pain. Pain still hurts, no matter the source. Having a husband lose his job and go to treatment is awful. Hearing others insist that God did it is not comforting.

Looking back, both my wife and I can see that God's hand was working in our misery. During the disaster it was impossible to take this view. Now, through time and growth, we have gained perspective. We can see that, though we don't wish to go through it again, we wouldn't give up the work He did in our lives. I chose evil, but God purposed it for good.

Day 230

WHERE ARE YOU, GOD?

| *Work out your own salvation with fear and trembling.* |

PHILIPPIANS 2:12

God, why won't you help me? I've asked you again and again to fix me, but you remain silent. Where are you? Do you not care . . . or am I not your child?

It was my own defects that led me to question my faith. In my toxic behavior, I came to hate what I was doing, as it was so contrary to the faith I claimed. I blamed God for this bitter internal struggle. I begged Him a thousand times to change me. He didn't.

In my destructive behavior, I desperately needed to understand whether I knew God or not. I knew Jesus' words about those who thought they knew Him but did not. "Depart from me, you cursed" (Matthew 25:41).

In my crisis of faith, I remembered today's verse and finally came to understand its meaning. Faith isn't automatic, and a right relationship with God isn't assumed. There are those who think they know God . . . who actually do not. In retrospect, I believe that I did know God—but in my wandering, I was right to question the nature of the relationship.

In working out my own salvation *with fear and trembling*, I came to see the faithlessness of my previous prayers. In my addiction, I had told God that I would have faith in Him if He did what I wanted. I studied for a C and prayed for an A. To this, God responded, *"Get up and obey. Then, and only then, will you see what I can do in you."* I thought faith meant that I asked God to do for me, but in reality, faith is believing in and obeying God.

It wasn't until I confessed, faced my consequences, went to treatment, and pursued God that He began to change me. No one else could do this for me. I had to decide for myself if I wanted a relationship with God. I didn't feel Him draw near to me until I began to take steps toward Him.

Day 231
ADDICTED TO DISCONTENT

Do all things without grumbling or disputing, that you may be blameless and innocent, children of God without blemish in the midst of a crooked and twisted generation, among whom you shine as lights in the world.

PHILIPPIANS 2:14–15

When my addiction came to light, I had to leave my work in the emergency room, and for months I could not practice medicine. Appropriately, I had to go to treatment if I ever wanted to get back to work. After treatment there were numerous hurdles to overcome, and for some time I didn't know if I was going to ever practice medicine again.

During that time, I prayed and promised God that I would never again complain about going to work. I was eventually blessed with a fantastic job, but a few years later I now find myself complaining. I love my job, but I'm lazy at heart. I've forgotten the misery of being unemployed, and some days I just don't want to work.

It's my nature to focus not on the privilege of working, but on what I want to do at any given moment. *It's so nice outside. Why do I have to go to work? I know I need a paycheck tomorrow, but today . . .* It's my nature to be discontent with what God has given me because I have an insatiable appetite for what I want—immediately.

Paul, in today's passage, insisted that I deny my destructive nature. Knowing our propensity for self-focus and immediate gratification, Paul said that we must consciously choose gratitude over discontent.

This is, after all, the only cure for chronic discontent. As with any destructive thought, we must take it captive and kill it. *Does this thought point me at God or at self?* If we find we're complaining about our jobs, we must consciously choose gratitude instead. In doing so, we point ourselves—and others—to God.

In our grumbling and complaining, we focus on ourselves. In our gratitude, we turn to God. Daily we must choose to be thankful for the good God has given us. Daily we must refuse to give in to the destructive self-focus of discontent.

Day 232

I WOULD DO ANYTHING TO LOSE WEIGHT

Whatever gain I had, I counted as loss for . . . the surpassing worth of knowing Christ. . . . I have suffered the loss of all things . . . that I may gain Christ.

PHILIPPIANS 3:7–8

In my addiction to food and drugs, I told myself that I would do anything to change. That was a lie. I wanted transformation, but I remained unwilling to *do anything* about it. I thought that change happened by asking God to magically alter my desires. In my pursuit of *change by thought*, I *did* nothing . . . and nothing changed.

Though Paul was not talking about diet or drugs in today's passage, his story does reveal what transformation looks like. This was no mental exercise. Paul insisted that in comparison to life in Christ, everything else was worthless. He gladly gave up everything he had to follow Christ. He considered it all garbage in comparison anyway.

Paul lived out his belief. He didn't just have a thought about God's will and pray for it to be done. He went out and did God's will. He believed and obeyed.

Likewise, if I want radical change, I must be willing to do whatever it takes to abandon the garbage of my life and follow Christ. This isn't just a mental exercise. *I intend to eat better tomorrow.* This is cleaning out the cupboard, getting rid of the junk, and changing the structure of my life.

Frankly, most of us want change but remain unwilling to do what it takes to get there. We want skinny without the exercise or dietary change. We want God, but we remain unwilling to abandon our garbage and pursue Him. We'd rather say a thousand prayers, begging for change, than to do one thing to change ourselves.

A thought or desire for change is not the same as change. Faith is not positive thinking. Faith is a belief coupled with action. We change our lives and come to know God only by doing whatever it takes to abandon our garbage in exchange for the surpassing worth of knowing Christ.

Day 233

AM I AN ADDICT OR A CHRISTIAN?

Not that I . . . am already perfect, but I press on. . . . One thing I do: forgetting what lies behind and straining forward to what lies ahead.

PHILIPPIANS 3:12–13

One of the most common conflicts between those in church and those in recovery revolves around identity. Am I a Christian or an addict? The extreme position on one side says that, as an addict, I'll always wallow in addictive behaviors. To claim freedom from addiction is to deny reality. The other extreme says that, since I'm forgiven, I'm delivered and will never struggle again. Any evidence of a struggle betrays my lack of faith.

Both views are equally unhelpful. The two most destructive things to tell an addict are that he is either *destined for addictive behavior* or that he is *fixed and will never struggle again*. Both lead inexorably back to active addiction.

In today's passage, Paul strikes the correct posture between the extremes. *My name is Paul. I still struggle. I'm not perfect, but I continually press on to a better life.*

When I go to a recovery meeting and say, "My name is Scott. I'm an addict," I'm not claiming a primary identity as an addict. I'm just acknowledging a defect that I must continue to abandon if I want to follow Christ. Likewise, when I identify as a Christian, I'm not claiming that I am perfect. I'm simply acknowledging my ongoing need for Christ. I may not be struggling with drugs today, but I still wrestle with other defects. I need God every day.

Frankly, I don't meet many in recovery who insist that I'll always act like an addict. I do, however, occasionally meet condescending Christians who believe themselves perfected because they're forgiven.

The world doesn't need more condescending Christians. The world needs honest Christians, willing to admit their own continual need, who will share the love that Christ has shown them.

So . . . am I a Christian, or an addict? Yes. I've been forgiven, but I'm not perfect.

Day 234
DAILY STEPS TO A NEW LIFE

I press on toward the goal for the prize of the
upward call of God in Christ Jesus.

PHILIPPIANS 3:14

In Alcoholics Anonymous, we celebrate *clean time*. On the anniversary of your sobriety date, you're recognized for the months or years that you've been clean. The brief celebration culminates in the entire group asking, "How did you do it?" This is your opportunity to tell those still struggling how you got where you are.

The clean life isn't something that happens accidentally. It's attained only by a purposeful, continual pursuit. So too, Paul insisted, is the Christian life. In both recovery and faith, success is not automatic or assumed. The road to destruction is broader and better populated than the road to life. The road to life is narrow and difficult. Not everyone makes it. In fact, most don't.

In today's passage, Paul insisted the *how* of his life could be defined by this: abandoning the old life and pursuing the new life in Christ. This is anything but a passive process. Paul used words like *strain, press on*, and *by any means possible*. His language here reveals that the Christian life is to be an all-consuming, life-defining, profound pursuit of Christ.

This takes purposeful time and effort. Christ has done the work to provide the new life, but He doesn't force our behavior. If we want to dwell in the new life, we must seek it. When we're forgiven, we're not made perfect, but neither are we destined to wallow in the misery of the old life. If we will, *by any means possible*, abandon the old life, we can continually pursue the new life in Christ. That's how we do faith—and recovery.

Day 235

ANXIOUS AGAIN

> *Do not be anxious about anything, but in everything*
> *by prayer and supplication with thanksgiving let*
> *your requests be made known to God.*

PHILIPPIANS 4:6

Some Christians will use this verse to say that anxiety is a sin. While anxiety can lead to constructive or destructive behavior, anxiety is an involuntary emotional response, which in itself is not wrong. I do refer to anxiety as defect, in the sense that we all have painful traits that we wish we didn't have. Paul himself admitted to anxiety in Philippians 2:28.

In today's passage, He didn't explicitly teach that it's wrong to feel anxiety, but rather that there's a right response to it. When we're anxious, Paul said we must learn to give it to God. Like any other defect, as often as I'm tempted to indulge in it, I must drag it before God. In my anxiety, I focus on myself. In faith, I look to Him.

I may not be accountable for an anxious impulse, but my behavior is my responsibility. In my anxiety, I can reach for a drink or reach out to a friend. How I respond may grow or diminish my anxiety. If I had diabetes, I wouldn't necessarily be responsible for its presence, but my behavior could exacerbate or improve my condition. If I pursued donuts, I would worsen my diabetes. If I ate right and took my insulin, I would improve it.

Giving my anxiety to God must involve prayer, but that may not be my only response. In giving up my anxiety, I may need to talk with friends, seek counseling, or even take medications. Though medications can be a problem in themselves, it's not faithless to do whatever it takes to give something to God.

As with all our defects, we want our anxiety to be gone forever. As with our other defects, this is rarely the case. Our imperfections remain, but we can diminish them or grow them. We can focus on ourselves, causing further destruction—or in faith we can turn to God.

Day 236

THE PEACE OF GOD

The peace of God, which surpasses all understanding, will guard your hearts and your minds in Christ Jesus.

PHILIPPIANS 4:7

I have, with heart pounding and mind racing, begged God for His peace. In my self-inflicted disaster, I have sought comfort and calm in Him. *God, I have made a mess of life. I am a wreck. Please fill me with your peace.*

Paul, in today's passage, tells me the peace of God is there for the taking. I just need to do what it takes to dwell in it. I only recently realized that I often ask God for a magical peace, just as I asked for magical deliverance from addiction. I didn't want to do anything to attain it. I just wanted Him to supernaturally do all the heavy lifting.

When I ask for peace, though, God asks me if I'm willing to let go of that which is causing me angst. *Are you willing to leave that pursuit? Are you willing to abandon yourself and dwell in me?* I didn't plan on this. I just wanted peace of mind. I wasn't ready to change my behavior.

However, to know the peace of God, I must dwell in God, not in self. It's in my focus on everything-me and my own pursuits that I cause myself anxiety. It's only in doing whatever it takes to abandon myself that I can rest in the peace and joy of God.

If I find myself twisted in knots, I must examine the unhealthy pursuits I'm clinging to. Do I need to abandon my resentment, anger, social media, relationships, behavioral patterns, pornography, alcohol, or even my job?

We don't get to continue in our angst-inducing pursuits of self while asking God for His peace. That isn't how the peace of God works. We attain His peace only when we abandon self and abide in Him. The peace of God is a consequence of our behavior, not a magical charm for which we pray.

Day 237
THE GOD FILTER

> *Whatever is true, whatever is honorable, whatever is just, whatever is pure, whatever is lovely, whatever is commendable, if there is any excellence, if there is anything worthy of praise, think about these things.*

PHILIPPIANS 4:8

I'd very much like to think of myself as having recovered from addiction to become a spiritual giant. *I have a blog and I've written a book about recovery, after all. I must be pretty fantastic.* Such thoughts reveal that I'm still completely full of pride. Though I am in recovery from my drug addiction, my pride betrays that I still struggle with the gravity of my flesh with its defective thoughts, desires, and behaviors.

In today's passage, Paul insisted that I must continually run every thought through the filter of God. I must interrogate every impulse and desire that I have—to see if they are right, pure, true, and honorable. If they're not, I must abandon them, turning my mind to something of God. I can't just think of nothing. I must replace each defective thought with a pure one.

As long as I'm in this flesh, I'm going to be affected by its defective thinking. Just as the schizophrenic's mind is not automatically healed when he comes to Christ, my defective thought patterns have not dissolved. Though I have a new spirit life, my brain isn't automatically transformed. I must still choose what I do with my mind.

There are those who insist that right knowledge leads to right behavior. Right knowledge, though, isn't the same as right thinking. I can know pornography is wrong and still indulge in it. I can know what I should eat to be healthy and still indulge in junk food.

Paul said that to live right, we must start in our thoughts. We must daily choose to focus our minds on God. When we find ourselves dwelling on destruction, we must do whatever it takes to filter those thoughts, turning our minds to Him.

Day 238
THE SECRET TO CONTENTMENT

I have learned in whatever situation I am to be content. . . . I have learned the secret of facing plenty and hunger, abundance and need. I can do all things through him who strengthens me.

PHILIPPIANS 4:11–13

If there were a pill that would allow me to eat or do whatever I wanted and still be healthy and content, I would be interested. Never mind that the pill itself would prevent any positive change in behavior, if it were the secret to happiness and health, I might take it. Who doesn't want the guaranteed route to the good life?

When Paul offered the secret to contentment in today's passage, my ears perked up. I knew the passage, but upon first read I didn't completely understand. What was the secret to Paul's contentment? His was a miserable life. Beatings, imprisonment, homelessness, cold, and hunger were common to him. If he could endure such things and proclaim contentment, I figured that maybe I should listen.

Paul insisted that the secret to his contentment was to continually dwell in Christ, being strengthened by Him. This was no simple trick of the mind. Paul's contentment wasn't just a mental exercise where he chose not to dwell on his misery. He purposefully lived in such a way that he continually pursued God and not self or circumstances. In pursuing God, he found all of his affirmation, meaning, joy, and purpose in the one source that never fails.

We can't live in pursuit of affirmation, status, money, sex, drugs, success, or pride and expect to miraculously find our contentment in God. We don't get to pursue ourselves and expect God's joy. If we want—like Paul—to be content, we must choose not to rely on circumstances, but rather to find our contentment in God alone.

Day 239

WHEN GOD DISAPPOINTS

God will supply every need of yours according to his riches in glory in Christ Jesus.

PHILIPPIANS 4:19

Life doesn't always go according to my plan, and God doesn't always answer prayer exactly as I had hoped. Sometimes, God disappoints. What do I do with my faith when I feel that God has let me down?

My response depends largely on my perspective and level of maturity. In my immaturity and lack of faith, I have used today's passage to prosecute God. *You promised you would give me everything I need. You've failed me. Why? Do you not care? Are you even real? Why should I follow you?*

In my continued addiction to self, my perspective is still sometimes limited to a world that revolves around everything-me. I can still often see my temporal preferences as my absolute needs. God, though, has a radically different perspective regarding my ultimate eternal needs.

The Bible describes how some Christians "were stoned, they were sawn in two, they were killed with the sword" (Hebrews 11:37). Was God's promise from today's passage not for them? Or does this passage mean something other than my immature faith takes it to mean? Did God abandon those who met with violent ends, or did they—in eternity—receive exactly what they needed?

This is a difficult perspective for me, as it requires a faith that looks beyond my temporal, fleshly desires. This perspective requires me to look to the greater reality of my spirit life. What I may need according to God may have very little to do with what I want—or think I need.

It's only in choosing the perspective of faith, keeping our eyes on God, that we're able to accept that God always gives us exactly what we need. It's only in faith that we can know contentment and joy despite life's disappointments. Faith is not expecting that God will execute *our* plans. Faith is following God, particularly when life *doesn't* go according to our plans.

Day 240
DELIVERANCE

> *He has delivered us from the domain of darkness and*
> *transferred us to the kingdom of his beloved Son, in*
> *whom we have redemption, the forgiveness of sins.*

COLOSSIANS 1:13-14

I have mistakenly thought this passage meant that I was delivered from my addiction when I came to Christ. I paid a painful price for my error. As an addict, it's disastrous to accept the belief that I no longer struggle.

Though some are miraculously delivered from a defect, miracles by definition are not the normal experience. The normal experience is that we all have defects that we wish were gone but are not. Everyone has some struggle.

Jesus insisted that "the spirit indeed is willing, but the flesh is weak" (Mark 14:38). Paul taught that we are to continually "put to death . . . what is earthly in you" (Colossians 3:5). Why would they warn us of the flesh nature if we were already delivered from it? What does today's passage mean?

It means that, in my eternal spirit life, I am forgiven and delivered. This passage doesn't say that the destructive defects of my flesh life are all magically removed. As long as I dwell in this flesh, I'll have some destructive appetites for donuts, sex, and drugs. I have a perfect spirit life, but I carry it in this defective vessel.

Deliverance from my flesh defects is not a once-and-for-all experience. Neither is it some exercise of the mind where I simply convince myself to accept a thing. I experience deliverance only when I follow Christ's command to daily deny self and follow Him. I don't experience deliverance by pursuing myself, changing nothing, and then whispering this verse as a mystical phrase.

If we want to live free from our destructive behavior, we must continually do whatever it takes to abandon that behavior to follow Christ. He transforms us as we follow Him, but we won't be made perfect in this life. As we follow Christ, He daily delivers us from ourselves.

Day 241
A DEADLY PLAN

And you, who once were alienated and hostile in mind, doing evil deeds, he has now reconciled in his body of flesh by his death, in order to present you holy and blameless and above reproach before him.

COLOSSIANS 1:21–22

As an addict, my opinion regarding my need for pain medications should be suspect. If I arrived at the clinic with a subjective complaint and no objective findings, no physician should even consider giving me pain medications. I have proven, in my addiction, that my defective and subjective perception of my pain cannot be trusted.

Likewise, my will is so warped by my own self-centeredness that it's not reliable. In my self-addiction, I continually gravitate toward Scott's plan, not God's. It's not that God isn't interested in my well-being. He very much is. It's just that His plan looks very little like mine.

In today's passage, Paul describes how God's grand design was that Christ come to earth, suffer, and die to restore me to a right relationship with Him. It's God's will that I become like Christ in His death so that I can also participate in His life. Seen in this light, it's apparent that God's plan is not about my earthly comfort. It's about what's ultimately best for me.

His plan is always deadly to my will. It's only through continual death to self that I continually know life. This isn't a once-and-for-all decision of the past. I must daily die to self if I want to continually embrace true life. I find His life only through the death of my old life.

In our perpetual self-addiction, we worry that God's plan will cause us to miss out on the life we desire. The only thing we miss out on in self-sacrifice, though, is our own destruction. In dying to self, we abandon death and misery, trading it in for true life in Christ. God's plan is always deadly to self, but it's more than a fair trade.

Day 242

LIFE AND DEATH

You, who were dead in your trespasses . . . God made alive
together with him, having forgiven us all our trespasses, by
canceling the record of debt . . . nailing it to the cross.

COLOSSIANS 2:13–14

The predicament of the drug addict is similar to that of others. The drug addict wants sobriety . . . sometime. Right now, though, he just wants the drug. Likewise, the food addict doesn't want to be overweight, but right now he just wants to eat.

We seem to be of two minds, one desiring life and the other bent on destruction. Unfortunately, the destructive pursuit delivers immediate pleasure and often calls in a louder voice.

In today's passage, Paul explained that, as Christians, we've undergone a spiritual transformation from death to life. We were restored to God when our sins were nailed to the cross with Christ.

This isn't some far-off truth that I'll appreciate only after death. This is a blessed reality for here and now. My sins have been nailed to the cross, and I bear the burden of their debt no more. I can and should live in this spiritual reality, investing my time and effort into a very real relationship with the Father. This is my life purpose.

My problem is the immediacy of my defective flesh nature. Though I should live with my mind focused on my spirit life, my flesh life is profoundly distracting. I want sobriety, health, purity, and love; but my flesh distracts with drugs, food, lust, and resentment.

Because of Christ's sacrificial death, we are free to live in our spirit life, but God allows us to continue to pursue our flesh. He doesn't choose for us, and He doesn't force us to spend time with Him.

When we feel the weight and shame of our addictive, destructive behaviors, we must blame no one but ourselves. Then we must do whatever it takes to abandon our flesh and desperately pursue life in the Spirit where we're forgiven and free. This is life or death.

Day 243

DEATH BY DISTRACTION

Let no one disqualify you, insisting on asceticism and worship of angels.

COLOSSIANS 2:18

As we practice driving with our kids, we frequently attempt to impress upon them that little distractions can have drastic consequences. *No phone. Don't mess with the radio. Eyes on the road. Don't get distracted, even for a second.*

I am, of course, reminded of my own hypocrisy. I know the purpose of my life is to focus continually on God, but my attention is easily diverted. It's not always an obvious evil that sidetracks me. It's often the good things in life that rob from the best.

I can, in my pursuit of sobriety, elevate AA to my religion. I can, in my attempt to help others, put my blog's success (and the success of this book) above my walk with God. My family can rise above my faith. Even church activities can consume my energies, robbing from my actual pursuit of God.

Paul said in today's passage that we must not allow ourselves to be distracted by anything. He said that even religion can become evil if we elevate the rules above all, following "a self-made religion. . . of no value in stopping the indulgence of the flesh" (Colossians 2:23). We must keep our eyes on the Creator, not the creation. As with driving, anything that distracts is potentially deadly.

If I were the devil, I'd find profound success in keeping Christians distracted from the pursuit of God while thinking they were living the Christian life. The more harmless the distraction the better, as long as it would paralyze the Christian from a vibrant relationship with the Father. If I could get a disciple to pursue something good above God, my job would be done.

As in driving, we must continually focus on what truly matters. Even seemingly harmless pursuits can be destructive if we allow them to seduce our gaze from the Father.

Day 244

YOU ARE FREE. LIVE LIKE IT.

*If then you have been raised with Christ, seek the things
that are above . . . not on things that are on earth. For you
have died, and your life is hidden with Christ in God.*

COLOSSIANS 3:1–3

If I've been set free, why do I not always feel like it? In my addiction, I didn't understand how I could struggle so badly if I was a Christian. I knew my old self was supposed to have died and been raised again with Christ. So why was I such a mess? Why was I hopelessly addicted to pills if I was *free*?

The Christian life is a paradox. Because of Christ's death and resurrection, I have—in my spirit life—been set free. I've died and risen again with Christ, *in my spirit life*. This is a reality that I should experience daily, but it's not necessarily the reality that I know in the here and now. Though I have this perfect spirit life, God still allows me to dwell in the defective flesh life.

Paul, in today's passage, explained the duality of this life. He insisted that I've been set free *and* I must choose to live in that freedom. This is not automatic. I *want* to live as a disciple, but the life of the flesh still pulls with a gravity that grows as I feed it.

I didn't set out to be addicted to pills. I started with smaller indulgences—ones I considered harmless at first. As I followed the things of earth, I ignored the things above. Then, as my appetite grew and came to control me, I felt betrayed. *But God, I'm a Christian. I thought you set me free from this kind of thing!*

If we find ourselves addicted to the earthly things, it's because we haven't been willing to do what it takes to abandon them and pursue God. God has set me free. I must choose to live like it.

Day 245

THE 12 STEPS OF ST. PAUL

*Put to death therefore what is earthly in you: sexual
immorality, impurity, passion, evil desire, and covetousness,
which is idolatry. . . . You must put them all away:
anger, wrath, malice, slander, and obscene talk.*

COLOSSIANS 3:5, 8

In my quest to understand my flesh nature, I've found today's passage to be profoundly important. In it, Paul again insisted that I must kill my old nature. I have long been frustrated with him for insisting that I must do a thing while omitting the details of how to do it. In my addiction, I very much wanted to understand what it meant to put to death my defects. I would have found it quite helpful if Paul would have just recorded his *12 Steps to Holiness.*

If Paul had given me a detailed set of steps, though, I would likely have become legalistic, elevating the rules above the ruler. Christ set me free from a performance-based salvation, yet I desire specific rules to follow.

Still, I have longed to know what it means to crucify my flesh nature. How do I do this thing? My answer is still in progress, but I've come to realize that putting to death any one defect means doing whatever it takes to cut it out of my life. Depending on the person and the defect, this may mean treatment, leaving a job, abandoning destructive relationships, getting rid of social media or a cell phone, or going to meetings.

Paul couldn't give us specific steps because for each of our defects the process looks different. In my own experience, I've had to commit to radical structural change in my life when I've needed to kill a behavior. When I change nothing, nothing changes.

If I've been unable to stop a behavior, it's because I've been unwilling to do what it takes to crucify that behavior. Faith isn't doing nothing and praying for change. Faith is doing whatever it takes to abandon self and follow God.

Day 246

THE THREE-DAY DIET

> *Put on then, as God's chosen ones, . . . compassionate*
> *hearts, kindness, humility, meekness, and patience. . . . And*
> *above all these put on love.*
>
> **COLOSSIANS 3:12–14**

Because I'm prone to extremes, I have—many times—gorged myself and then promised that I'd starve to make up for it. *If I don't eat for three days, I can lose 10 pounds.* My many failures didn't stop me from trying the next time, but always with the same result. After a few hours of starvation, I'd lose control and binge again, ending up worse off than before.

Many times, struggling with some destructive behavior, I've promised to *stop for real this time.* My only plan, though, was *just never do it again.* As with my crash dieting, I didn't replace my destructive behavior with constructive behavior. My appetite doesn't tolerate a vacuum, so I always go back to the destructive behavior in a state of starvation, more addicted than ever.

Paul, in today's passage, insists that we put off the old . . . but then we must *put on the new.* It's not enough to just crucify the old life. We must embrace the new one. We'll always fill ourselves with something—satisfaction and meaning in the flesh life . . . or the spirit life. If we deny the old without pursuing the new, we'll inevitably return to the flesh life. It's our natural state.

With a diet, it's not helpful to stop eating. That's the plan of someone who wants to change only temporarily. If we truly want to change, we must work at eating *differently.*

The same is true with the rest of life. If we truly want change, we don't just abandon the old; we must put on the new. As Christ said, we must deny self *and* follow Him.

Day 247

PAGING DR. SELFISH

Whatever you do, work heartily, as for the Lord and not for men. . . . You are serving the Lord Christ.

COLOSSIANS 3:23–24

I can have two very different experiences at work—based completely on my attitude. The events may be the same, but my perspective makes all the difference. In my selfishness, I'm preoccupied with what I want. I focus on myself and become easily frustrated by everyone and everything that doesn't meet my expectations. I can be irritable and condescending with patients and coworkers. In my me-focus, I'm discontent and frustrated by everything. In this state—the whole world annoys me.

The opposite occurs when I turn my focus from myself to God. When I see that it's my purpose to serve others instead of myself, I realize that I've been blessed with the opportunity to help those in need. In turning my gaze from everything-me, I see the hurt of others and I allow God's love to pour out of me into them. When I focus on God and not self, I live the kind of day that has true purpose and meaning. Irritations and trials are much fewer; and when they do occur, I can handle them with grace and patience. I much prefer this kind of day, but it takes discipline to get there.

Daily we must choose to turn our gaze to God, realizing that we live for Him, not ourselves. If we want to live a life of purpose and meaning, we must continually pursue it. This isn't automatic. To live the life of self, we don't need to make an effort. It's just our natural state.

We can discipline ourselves to live every day for God, living every day in the purpose and meaning for which we were made.

Day 248

HOW DO I LOVE ME? LET ME COUNT THE WAYS.

We speak, not to please man, but to please God. . . . For we never came with words of flattery. . . . Nor did we seek glory from people.

1 THESSALONIANS 2:6

In the disaster of my addiction, one of the most painful consequences was that everyone knew. My reputation was the last thing I should have been worried about; but still, I desperately desired to protect my ego. That was futile, of course. My name showed up in the newspaper. I had to leave my job as an ER physician. I went to treatment and for months was unable to practice medicine. Everyone knew what I was and what I had done.

In that pain, I realized the profound purpose and meaning that I had found in others' opinions of me. I derived great affirmation from being a well-liked, upstanding physician. When the curtain was pulled back to reveal what a disaster my life was, my first concern was not that I needed help, it was for my ruined reputation.

I needed to be humbled. I needed to abandon my pursuit of myself.

I thought I had learned my lesson, but my pride isn't so easily dismissed. Like a horror movie villain, it just keeps coming back. I've recently realized (again) that all my activities must be suspect. I can do good things out of good or bad motives. Do I enjoy being a physician so I can help others—or because it massages my ego? Do I go to the gym to discipline my flesh—or for my appearance? Do I dress up for church out of respect for God—or so I look shiny on the outside?

All of our behaviors and motives must be filtered through this question. *Are we doing this to point to ourselves, or to God?* We must continually accept that this life is *not about us.* Our wills and our reputations are not at the center of it all. This life is about loving God and doing His will. In our self-focus, we make a mess of life. In turning to God, we find authentic life.

Day 249

WATCHING MY OWN BOBBER

But we urge you, brothers, . . . to aspire to live
quietly, and to mind your own affairs.

1 THESSALONIANS 4:10–11

As painful as it is to admit, in my drug addiction, I became condescending toward those who struggled differently from me. If I could find cause to be critical of another, it made me feel better about myself. My preoccupation with the defects of those around me was a fantastic distraction from my own mess. In watching another's bobber, I could conveniently ignore mine.

Though we are severely self-centered, when it comes to destructive behaviors, we prefer to focus on anyone but ourselves. Like a child during a Sunday school prayer, we keep our eyes open so we can police those who are . . . keeping their eyes open.

Anyone can fall victim to the obsession with the defects of others, but Christians are particularly prone to it. We carry a profound truth, and thus, we see ourselves as keepers of that sacred flame. Avoiding the big, obvious sins, we pat ourselves on the back. *I don't drink, smoke, or gamble—so I'm kind of a big deal . . .*

Then, we often condescend to those who struggle in ways we don't. Our obsession with the lives of others protects our own egos from self-examination. If we can continually point out the defects in those around us, we never have to examine those to which we're enslaved.

In today's passage, Paul said that we must mind our own affairs. It's our responsibility every day to deny our own defects and follow Christ. We must first maintain a right relationship to God. Doing so should also mean that we deny the temptation to obsess with the flaws of others. We're responsible for our own defects, not our neighbor's. We may well encourage our neighbor to pursue God, but this doesn't justify an obsession with his affairs. We must always watch our own bobbers.

Day 250

A CONVERSATION WITH GOD

| *Pray without ceasing.* |

1 THESSALONIANS 5:17

During Bible study at the local jail one day, we were discussing prayer when Ron told me that he was uncomfortable praying in front of others because he didn't know how to pray. He said his only experience with prayer was simply talking to God all day, carrying on a continual conversation about whatever was on his mind. I felt that was a pretty fantastic way to commune with God and told him so. Emboldened, he went on to pray the most honest prayer I have ever heard, simply pouring out his concerns to God.

When Paul in today's passage told me to pray continually, I like to think he was not just using hyperbole—and that he actually meant my life is to be in perpetual communion with God. Though I'm miserable at it, I set out each morning to carry on a running conversation. It's not that I have that much to say, it's simply that I desire to keep my focus continually on God instead of myself.

I used to envision *unceasing prayer* as something only a mountain-top monk could do, abandoning the world to maintain a singular focus on God. It's much closer to Paul's intent, though, not for me to abandon my daily responsibilities, but rather to learn to focus on God within those responsibilities.

I know that I can get through my day with my focus on everything-me. It's natural to perform my duties while looking to my own interests. I have to believe that, through discipline, I can accomplish the same tasks while looking at God instead of self.

Praying without ceasing isn't yet one more step we must perform in the Christian life. *This is the Christian life.* This is how we fulfill Jesus' command to deny self and follow Him. Our own nature pulls incessantly at our gaze, but in perpetual communion with God, we keep our eyes not on ourselves, but on Him.

Day 251

ANGRY BURGERS

Give thanks in all circumstances; for this is the will of God.

1 THESSALONIANS 5:18

I'm not much of a cook, but grilling is my domain. As I was making the burgers recently, my wife asked me if I would make them smaller, which I did—with a poor attitude. When she asked a second time if I could make hers even smaller, I had the opportunity for a sweet response. *I love you and I'd be happy to make your burger whatever size you want.* That's not what I said, though. My temper was short, and I snapped something really mature. *Why don't you make the burgers next time?* I went on to make some angry burgers, smashing all the patties into a smaller size.

At the time, in my mind, I was completely justified. Focused only on myself and my preferences, I was easily irritated when I had to adapt when things didn't go exactly as I thought they should. Only after some time had passed was I able to see my profound immaturity and ugliness.

In my focus on self I don't care about right and wrong; and I don't care about kindness or love. I care only about how I think the world should be. Then, when I don't get my way, I lash out like a child, smashing things.

Paul, in today's passage, provided the answer to this problem. It's only in turning my gaze from self to God in all things, that I'm able to act right. "Rejoice always, pray without ceasing, give thanks in all circumstances" (verses 16–18).

When making the burgers, if I had been of the right mindset, I would have thanked God for my wonderful wife, for our food, and for the family for whom I was fixing dinner. In turning my gaze from self to God, I maintain the perspective that allows me to respond right. In obsessing with self, I act like an angry child, making angry burgers.

Day 252

WHEN I SHRINK GOD

| *Do not quench the Spirit.* |
1 THESSALONIANS 5:19

My late father-in-law was a pastor. He frequently said that if I wanted to know God, I had to first understand that He was a person. As such, God can know me and be known to me personally. Because I have a relationship with Him through Christ, I can come to know God a little or a lot. As with any person, I can grow or shrink our relationship.

Paul, in today's passage, said that I must not quench or shrink God. There are those who will chafe at the idea that I can either increase or diminish God, as He is immoveable and unchangeable and cannot be affected by us.

Of course, I'd be a fool to think that my behavior can actually grow or shrink God, but I'd be a greater fool if I didn't realize that I can very much grow or shrink my relationship with Him. If I set out to sow the seeds of me, I will produce a different result than if I purposefully engage in activities that point me to God. I may not notice a dramatic difference in just one day, but an accumulated lifetime of days pointed at either self or at God will make for two very different lives.

I can either grow self, diminishing God in me, or I can grow God in me, diminishing self. I can't grow both at the same time, and there is no third option. I quench me or I quench God. I grow me or I grow God. Christ has freed me to do one or the other, but He doesn't force me to choose.

If we find ourselves harvesting a destructive crop today, we have no further to look than the seeds that we planted yesterday. If we want to know God, we must daily do whatever it takes to abandon ourselves and grow our relationship with Him.

Day 253

ENABLER

Keep away from any brother who is walking in idleness. . . .
If anyone is not willing to work, let him not eat.

2 THESSALONIANS 3:6, 10

It's not uncommon to hear from someone who is greatly distressed by an alcoholic family member—only to find that the person telling me about the alcoholic is the one buying the alcohol. Though the enabling is obvious to anyone else, to the one doing it, it's not so easy to see.

Paul said in today's passage that those close to the one with a defective behavior bear some responsibility not to support that behavior. Idleness was apparently a problem in Thessalonica, where some slothful church members were taking advantage of Christian generosity. Though the church was supposed to provide financial assistance to the poor, those who were able to work were expected to do so. In the church's effort to help the poor, they had contributed to the defect of laziness. Paul insisted that it must stop.

As a Christian, I must first act right myself. Enabling, itself a defect, can become a behavior that's as destructive to me as it is to the one I am enabling. If I'm buying alcohol for an alcoholic, I must stop. If I'm bailing a loved one out of consequences, I need to quit doing so. Enabling a destructive behavior imparts a burden of guilt for that destructive behavior to me. Make no mistake, when I aid someone in a defective behavior, I become an accomplice in that behavior. My responsibility is to avoid participating in the defective behavior myself, whether or not the other person ever changes.

We must maintain boundaries between such destructive behavior and ourselves. We may need to allow those engaging in such behavior to reap the consequences they have sown.

This may seem cold and un-Christian to us, which is why some choose to enable. We think we are doing good by helping, but there's a vast difference between loving and enabling. The most loving thing we can do sometimes is to quit contributing to a destructive behavior.

Day 254
KNOW-IT-ALL

Certain persons . . . have wandered away into vain discussion . . .
without understanding either what they are saying or the
things about which they make confident assertions.

1 TIMOTHY 1:6-7

In medical school, I learned the phrase *often wrong, never in doubt,* used to describe the incompetent person who is, paradoxically, supremely confident. Though this person often errs in his (or her) performance, he maintains complete confidence in his ability. Maddening to work with, this individual's ego is shielded by false self-assurance, as he has zero insight into his own defects and failures.

This seems to be the type of person Paul was describing in today's passage. There were apparently those in Timothy's church who were leading Christians astray with meaningless "myths" and "vain discussions" (1 Timothy 1:4, 6). They wanted to be seen as the religious elite, but they had no idea what they were talking about, as they were not living in faith. Lacking spiritual maturity, they saw knowledge as a route to achieving the status they desired.

I've done this with equally poor results. *Studying* Christianity and *living* the Christian life are two very different things. Reading book after book in an attempt to build a library of knowledge didn't make me more like Christ. It just made me more argumentative and arrogant—and not any smarter.

Knowledge and right doctrine are necessary steps in knowing God, but they're not the end goal. Knowledge doesn't automatically lead to right behavior or faith. We can know right and still do wrong. Knowing right is only step one in faith. Step two is acting in a manner consistent with our beliefs.

It's in our pride that we gather knowledge and consider it to be spiritual growth. It doesn't take a genius IQ or a doctrinal degree to be a disciple. It takes a child-like faith to say *I believe and I will follow.*

Day 255

I AM THE WORST

The grace of our Lord overflowed for me. . . . Christ Jesus came into the world to save sinners, of whom I am the foremost.

1 TIMOTHY 1:14–15

Working with addicts and inmates, it's easy to be frustrated by recurrent destructive behavior. *Why do you keep making the same mistakes over and over?* Of course, it wasn't that long ago that I was repeating my own mistakes with drugs. Worse, I still struggle with destructive thoughts and behaviors today. When I'm tempted to criticize others, I need only to look at my own condition to realize that I have no moral high ground. I am not *better than.*

Paul, in today's passage, provides the cure for my arrogance. He said that Jesus came to save sinners—of whom he was the worst. He realized that, as he had required so much grace from God, he could hardly look down on anyone else. Paul was not trying to impress his readers with how bad he had been. He was simply reminding himself of how much forgiveness he had required from God.

When I'm tempted to look down on the destructive behavior of others, I must remind myself of what God has done for me. Jesus came to save sinners, of which I feel as if I'm the worst . . . because I know all my own evil thoughts and deeds.

I'm not referring to self-loathing or low self-esteem. This is simply recognizing that I'm not better than anyone else before God.

If we're not humbled by what Jesus has done for us, then we've never understood exactly what He has done for us. If we stand in condescending judgment of those around us, we don't understand our own poverty. To condescend is to live in profound dishonesty and blindness to who we are before God.

Day 256

I WANT YOU TO WANT ME

This is good, and it is pleasing in the sight of God
our Savior, who desires all people to be saved and
to come to the knowledge of the truth.

1 TIMOTHY 2:3–4

When I first met my wife and fell in love, I wanted what was best for her, but I also longed to be loved back. This is the nature of love.

In today's passage, Paul describes the heart of God who *desires all people to be saved*. Does God get what God wants? From my perspective, He does not. There are billions who live and die without ever knowing Him. What does this mean? How can God want a thing and not get it?

I don't wish to diminish God's love by comparing it to my 18-year-old heart, but the answer lies in the nature of love. God loves me and longs for me to love Him back. He has gone to great lengths, sacrificing of Himself to draw me close. He desires that I love Him of my own will. God wants me, and He wants me to want Him.

God has done the necessary work of paving the road to Himself; now we must walk it. The road is narrow, though, and few find it (Matthew 7:13–14). In His love, He pursues us, providing salvation, but He does not force it upon us.

God saved us from something . . . for something. We were saved *from* ourselves, saved from separation from Him. We were saved *for* a profoundly real relationship with Him. This should be the most important thing in our lives, and it's our right response to treat it that way.

Our first responsibility every day, is to do whatever it takes to love and follow God. God wants us. If we want Him, we need to live like it.

Day 257

PROSTITUTES AND PRIDE

*The sins of some are obvious, reaching the place of judgment
ahead of them; the sins of others trail behind them.*

1 TIMOTHY 5:24, NIV

When my son was four or five years old, I doubt that he caught much of the Sunday morning sermon. During the service when the pastor read about a *prostitute*, however, I got a question . . . loudly. "Dad, what's a prostitute?" I cringed.

It's difficult not to look down upon certain sins. One good thing about living on earth is that there will always be those whom I find to be more defective than I am. If I can look down on someone else, I feel better about myself. I may even ignore my own defects if I can focus enough on the faults of others. The more destructive the sins of everyone else, the better I feel about myself.

In today's passage, Paul acknowledged that the consequences of some sins are obvious, while the destruction of others is hidden. There's always a price to pay, though—even if it's not immediately obvious. Different sins have different costs, but all sins lead to destruction. Even if that destruction is only to injure our relationship with God, that's no small thing. We may think we've escaped consequences if we don't get caught, but there are worse things than getting caught.

Resentment, lust, pornography, jealousy, and hatred can all exist in secrecy, giving a false sense of security, as the sinner suffers no immediate or obvious repercussions. Other sins hide in plain site because they seem to be more acceptable somehow. Though a prostitute may be shunned in church—pride, greed, and gossip may be quite welcome among believers. Paul said, however, that sin always injures our spiritual life, distancing us from God. There's always a price to pay for following ourselves instead of God.

Day 258

A ROOT OF MUCH EVIL

| *The love of money is a root of all kinds of evils.* |
1 TIMOTHY 6:10

In my drug addiction, the problem did not lie in the pills. Likewise, donuts aren't evil in themselves. It's my relationship with them that causes me harm. I can have a healthy or caustic relationship with either medication or food.

Paul, in today's passage, said that money is similar. Like many other morally neutral things in this world, it's our inappropriate love of money (not the money itself) that causes us injury. "Those who desire to be rich fall into temptation, into a snare, into many senseless and harmful desires that plunge people into ruin and destruction" (1 Timothy 6:9).

How do I know if I have an unhealthy relationship with money? The measure can't be whether or not I have a lot of money. After all, a poor man can pursue riches above all while a rich man can love God more than his wealth.

The destruction lies in my attitude toward money. *Do I pursue money above God?* I may insist that I don't, but I must examine myself. *Do I spend my time and thoughts on money or God? When I work, is it only to bring home a paycheck—or do I do my job for God, with His will in mind?*

Where do I find my purpose and security? If I'm honest, I sometimes find those things in money, not God. I like to think I hold my money loosely, but I think I would feel much different if I lost it all tomorrow.

As with any other addiction, it takes brutal honesty to check a greedy attitude about money. We may tell ourselves that we're not greedy, but we must test ourselves to see if our faith is in God—or our bank account. "We brought nothing into the world, and we cannot take anything out of the world" (1 Timothy 6:7).

Day 259

THE FIGHT OF MY LIFE

> *Fight the good fight of the faith. Take hold of the*
> *eternal life to which you were called.*

1 TIMOTHY 6:12

During medical school, a buddy and I ran our first marathon after only a month of training. Looking back, I have no idea what we were thinking. Our longest training run before the race was 11 miles short of the full marathon distance, and it was miserable. To say the marathon was unpleasant would be an understatement. It was awful. I couldn't walk for days afterward. I'm not sure why we thought we could do it, but we showed up on race day and paid for our arrogance and ignorance.

I'd like to say that I've become wiser with age, but I've done the same thing with my faith as a middle-aged adult. Though I know life is a battle, I've spent years at a time sitting around, doing nothing to prepare for it. Dusting off my Bible once a week, I considered a church service on Sunday to be my *God-time.* As in the marathon, I've paid for my lack of preparation.

I bought into a lazy faith. *Let go and let God. Since I'm saved by faith, not by works, I can't sanctify myself. I'll just sit back and let God do it.* But Paul said this isn't how it works. Life is anything but a spectator sport. If I want true life, I must *take hold* of it. I must *fight* the fight of the faith, *fleeing* destruction and *pursuing* godliness. These are anything but passive instructions.

This is the fight of—and for—our lives, and if we're not actively engaging in it, we're surrendering and losing. As long as we are in this flesh, the gravity of self will pull us toward destruction and seduce our gaze from God. We must daily work at abandoning ourselves to pursue God, or by default we'll follow ourselves away from Him.

Day 260

WET-MATCH DAYS

| *Fan into flame the gift of God, which is in you.* |
2 TIMOTHY 1:6

Sitting in treatment, it was easy to promise myself that, when I got out, I would passionately pursue God every day for the rest of my life. I knew that God's flame would burn hot in me, never growing cold. Many days are like that. I do often awaken with fire and joy at the thought of another day with God.

And then there are the other days. The days when I feel as if I'm trying to start the fire with wet matches and damp wood. And brother, it's starting to rain. As the dark clouds gather, the temptation is just to give up, forgetting the work of a fire. *I'm not feeling it. I guess I'll just get on with the day.*

Whether it's a tempting thought or unwelcome, obsessive ideas assaulting my mind, my nature is to give in to the darkness, allowing the flame of God in me to flicker and fade. Unfortunately, indulging in my nature does not satiate it. Rather, the darkness grows as I abandon the fire.

When the spark is most difficult to fan into a flame—that's when I must demand of myself the effort to do it, for that's when I need it the most. When I don't feel like turning my gaze to God, when I don't feel like chasing away the dark, that's precisely when I must do so. God doesn't leave me alone in my struggle, but it's absolutely my responsibility to feed the flame, fanning it into a roaring fire.

When I sit in my chair at 5:00 a.m. and struggle to turn my thoughts to God for a few minutes of prayer, that's when I must be most desperate to wrestle those distracting thoughts to the ground. That's when I must read, pray, and meditate until I regain focus. Those wet-match days are the days when I must not leave my chair until I turn my mind and life to God.

Day 261

ACT LIKE IT

> *If anyone cleanses himself from what is dishonorable, he*
> *will be a vessel for honorable use, set apart as holy, useful*
> *to the master of the house, ready for every good work.*
>
> **2 TIMOTHY 2:21**

The first time I was on call as a medical resident, I was terrified. Feelings of inadequacy, incompetence, and terror all combined to create an unnerving experience. I wanted to be known as a physician, but I wasn't so sure about the responsibility. I had some knowledge in my head, and I was a doctor *on paper* . . . but if I ever wanted to be a doctor *in practice*, I had to start acting like it.

This is akin to what Paul said in today's passage. He spoke of a great house in which there were many vessels, "some for honorable use, some for dishonorable" (2 Timothy 2:20). He said we are all vessels, and we get to choose how we'll be used. As Christians, when we fill ourselves with the dishonorable, that's what will flow out of us. If we desire to be honorable, to be used "for every good work," then we must start acting honorably.

I can't fill myself with donuts and expect to be fit. I can't fill my mind with smut and expect to be pure. I can't indulge in my anger and expect to know peace. If I want to be honorable, then I must engage in honorable behavior. When I fill myself with the dishonorable, that is exactly what I become. Being a Christian doesn't mean that I can consume garbage and expect that God will magically transform it into treasure.

We must continually examine ourselves, turning from the dishonorable to the honorable. As with gardening, we don't weed just once and quit. If we want a productive garden, we must continually act like gardeners. If we want to be disciples, we must act like it.

Day 262

PASSIONS, DREAMS, AND INSTANT GRATIFICATION

So flee youthful passions and pursue righteousness, faith, love, and peace, along with those who call on the Lord from a pure heart.

2 TIMOTHY 2:22

When my will is at the center of my decision making, I can justify almost anything. *I must follow my dreams. I must be true to myself.* I'm sure there are those who can follow their dreams to something productive; but as for me, following my desires has been profoundly destructive.

The problem, as Paul pointed out in today's passage, is that my passions are often opposed to what is right. If I follow my dreams above all, what do I do when my dreams take me down a dark path? Not all my desires are necessarily wrong; but when I follow what Scott wants, I will—sooner rather than later—find that immediate gratification leads to painful consequences.

I must keep reminding myself of this lesson. While I might not struggle with pills today, I still have other defects that promise pleasure now with no payment later.

This is the seductive lie of pursuing our own desires. We think we can have instant gratification with no price to pay. We fool ourselves, insisting that we can indulge in just a *little bit* of bad behavior without causing any harm. *Just one more time . . . I'll change tomorrow . . . Never again . . .*

God doesn't want to kill our joy and pleasure. Rather, He longs for us to have lasting, authentic joy. Paul likewise insisted that we forgo immediate gratification to pursue lasting purpose and satisfaction in *righteousness, faith, love, and peace.* How do we do this? We daily choose not to pursue self and instead choose to pursue *God in us.*

This isn't natural. It's our nature to be selfish, greedy, angry, and anxious. We don't need to live this way, though. We don't have to follow our base instincts to pain and shame. We can instead know joy and pleasure. We need only to daily pursue *faith, love, and peace, along with those who call on the Lord from a pure heart.*

Day 263

FAKE CHRISTIANS

> *People will be lovers of self, lovers of money, proud, arrogant,*
> *abusive . . . without self-control . . . lovers of pleasure rather*
> *than lovers of God, having the appearance of godliness.*
>
> **2 TIMOTHY 3:2–5**

I despise fake. It drives me nuts. In treatment I knew a guy . . .

When I read today's passage, I immediately thought of several people to whom it pertained. I had multiple stories ready about *other people* who lived lives of hypocrisy, claiming faith while pursuing self above all. I even got a little angry as I started to type out one such story.

You see, I'm profoundly intolerant of phoniness. In other people. But apparently I've been quite comfortable with it in myself. Though I'm deeply offended when someone else makes a sham of following God, I've had no problem doing it myself. I've been there. I've spoken the words, confessed the faith . . . and kept on following self. If I'm going to be honest, I still do it sometimes.

Paul's words, then, were a warning to me. When he speaks of those who have "the appearance of godliness," I must look in the mirror. If the Word of God is sharper than a double-edged sword (Hebrews 4:12), then the first and deepest cut must be to my own soul and spirit. If I use this passage as a weapon—only to point at others—then I've indulged in the exact hypocrisy that Paul exposed here.

So I need to ask myself a question. *Am I a lover of self, or a lover of God?* Am I prideful, angry, without self-control, or greedy? Honesty and introspection are always difficult and painful, but I must always aim the Word of God at myself first. *What do I need to work on? How am I being fake?* If I read lists like this and see only the defects of others, then I am the prideful, fake Christian whom Paul described.

Day 264
GOD IS ALWAYS SPEAKING

All Scripture is breathed out by God and profitable for teaching, for reproof, for correction, and for training in righteousness, that the man of God may be complete, equipped for every good work.

2 TIMOTHY 3:16–17

I'd long looked on those who claim that God talks to them with significant skepticism. *Hmm . . . You might be a nut.* I've come to know the truth, though; God is constantly speaking to us.

We were created for an intensely personal relationship with Him, and He speaks through His Spirit, other people, books, nature, and perhaps most obviously—through His Word.

Paul, in today's passage, said that God's Word, when ingested, will grow me into what He wants me to be. The opposite is true as well. When I turn a deaf ear to His Word, I court disaster. This isn't just my drug addiction of years gone by. This is who I am anytime I refuse to listen to God. I may not be abusing pills, but I still wallow in my self-centered, deceitful, addictive behavior when I don't follow His voice.

It is, unfortunately, often only in my disaster that I actually stop to listen. When I turn a deaf ear to God, He sometimes uses pain to capture my attention. In my pain, I tune back in to God's Word and begin listening again. When I purposefully listen to God, He draws near, growing life in me. When I refuse to listen, I distance myself from Him, breeding destruction.

When I find that God is silent, it's usually because I have chosen deafness. I can't expect to hear Him when I've indulged in the ear plugs of my own flesh. I must daily choose to read, pray, and listen to God's Word if I want the effect of His voice in my life.

So—God talks to me. Does that make me a nut? If the choice is between the destruction of listening to myself or the life of listening to God, then I'm okay with being a nut.

Day 265
I STILL NEED A SPONSOR

*Preach the word; be ready in season and out of
season. . . . For the time is coming when people will not endure
sound teaching, but having itching ears they will accumulate
for themselves teachers to suit their own passions.*

2 TIMOTHY 4:2–3

I used to think this passage meant that Christians must always have a sermon ready to fire off at a moment's notice. I'm starting to see, however, that being ready is more about the condition of my faith.

Giving a sermon (perhaps like writing a book) gives the impression that the one speaking has it all together. The temptation to the one preaching (or writing the book) is to deceive himself into thinking that he does indeed have it all together. In this condition, the preacher (or the writer) no longer requires instruction from others and thus, embraces deadly pride.

If I'm going to be ready to share God's Word, though, I must first work at living it myself. I don't do this perfectly. Sometimes I do it terribly. I still fail and I still struggle. I'm finding that one of the things I do when I struggle is exactly what Paul warned against in this passage: When I want to justify a destructive behavior, I simply avoid voices of truth.

We all do this. We all have blind spots, and we all—even preachers— need mature Christians around us who are willing to speak truth into our lives. However, our tendency, as Paul said, is to accumulate those who will suit our own passions.

In AA, they call it a sponsor. In church, they call it an accountability partner. Whatever we call it, we must be honest with someone who won't just tell us what we want to hear, but what we *need* to hear. Then we must live out that truth. Only when we work at living out God's Word can we be ready to share it.

Day 266
LIFE LESSONS FROM THE DOG

| *Always be sober-minded.* |
2 TIMOTHY 4:5

I must give some credit to my dog, Finnick, as he has provided significant inspiration for my faith and writing. So it was one day when I was out for a run—dog on leash—pondering today's passage. We were doing fine, running along, until the dog saw a squirrel. He's usually quite obedient, but in his squirrel-possessed state of mind, I don't think he was even capable of hearing me.

Though the dog was not drunk on any chemical, he was absolutely intoxicated by that squirrel. Under the influence, he pulled at his leash to the point of choking himself on his collar. Though his breaths became ragged, he wouldn't stop—or couldn't.

Most of us have been there. Most of us have allowed our minds to become so warped by the pursuit of a thing, that we behave as one intoxicated. It may be a chemical, but we also succumb to the influence of sex, money, anger, affirmation, or any defect of our flesh.

Those in recovery insist that just one indulgence changes the way we think. *One is too many and a thousand is never enough.* Though we may fool ourselves into thinking we can indulge in one little taste, such thinking reveals that our intellect is already clouded. Once we indulge just a little in any defect, it starts to work its deadly effect on our minds, controlling, seducing, and intoxicating.

In today's passage, Paul warned that we must be of sober mind. This is profoundly difficult when we're under the influence of something. Those who are drunk often deny it. To be sober-minded is to be alert to those things that tempt us to intoxication.

The fool thinks he can have just a taste of destruction—and walk away unscathed. Personally, I'd put my money on my dog walking away from the squirrel.

Day 267
MAGICAL THINKING

*I have fought the good fight, I have finished
the race, I have kept the faith.*

2 TIMOTHY 4:7

This verse takes me back 30 years to a hot summer day of mowing our church's cemetery. As I mowed, I read inscriptions on the tombstones. Out of hundreds, I remember only the one with today's passage. I remember thinking that I wanted this verse to be true about my life.

I've known some of whom this could be said, and I've looked at them with some envy. When I got out of treatment, I met some who had 20 years of sobriety. I wanted to be able to say that about myself. My addictive behavior, though in the past, was painful—and I wanted it to be something that had happened *long* ago. *Someday I'll be able to look back with satisfaction at how I lived my life . . .*

This is the same sentiment I felt as a child when I watched any sports movie about the underdog who overcame impossible odds. Inspired, I planned to start training . . . the next day. When that day came, my passion failed.

We all do this to some extent. We watch a marathon. *I should do that.* But then we sit on the couch. We see someone else lose weight. *I'll start dieting tomorrow.* We observe someone's growth. *If only I could change.* We engage in magical thinking, which is really the same thing as doing nothing.

What we must accept is that 20 years of sobriety is made only one day at a time—and one moment at a time. That time starts now. If we want a thing to be true tomorrow, we must do what it takes to get there today. Magical thinking gets us nowhere.

Today and every day, we must keep our eyes on God, making our feet follow.

Day 268

MY FIRST LIE

| *They profess to know God, but they deny him by their works.* |

TITUS 1:16

Several years ago we added dormers to our roof as an architectural feature. Though I liked the way they looked, I felt they were inherently dishonest, as we had no upstairs. Like a comb-over, the dormers were false advertising, claiming something on the outside that wasn't true on the inside. This bothered me.

This is the same situation Paul spoke of in today's passage. Describing hypocrites who claim to be one thing but act as another, he said such people were "detestable . . . unfit for any good work" (Titus 1:16). Claiming faith but living for self, they were spiritually paralyzed by the double life.

I've been there. My faith has sometimes been like a comb-over. The facade has been painfully obvious as my actions betrayed me; but still, I've tried to pull off the charade.

We all do this at times. We claim faith, but then live how we want to. It's not that we're maliciously duplicitous. It's just that we *want* to follow Christ in theory, but in practice we follow *self*. As a result, we must build a web of lies and half-truths to shield a guilty conscience.

In such a condition, the first lie is always to myself. I couldn't live with myself if I truly saw what I was doing; so I justify, rationalize, and lie to myself. *God wants me to be happy, right? I deserve it. Just one taste. I'm not hurting anyone. God will forgive . . .*

Like our dormers, I claim one reality while living another. I'm painfully aware that while I was offended by the duplicity of those dormers, I was living a secret life of addiction. I had built a literal and figurative house of lies.

We must continually ask ourselves if there's a discrepancy between what we claim to believe and our behavior. If we truly want God and life, then we must be honest with ourselves and do whatever it takes to make our behavior match our beliefs.

Day 269
THE NEXT RIGHT CHOICE

*Be sober-minded, dignified, self-controlled, sound
in faith, in love, and in steadfastness.*

TITUS 2:2

Some days I find myself despairing over the discrepancy between what I am and what I want to be. I read a list like this and sigh. *That doesn't sound like me at all. When will I get there?* I feel as if my personality traits are in opposition to this passage. I'm impulsive when I should display self-control. I'm full of self and resentment when I should be full of God and His love.

Then I realize I'm in a process of *becoming*—as we all are. I'm not there yet, and it's necessary for me to be comfortable with that reality. Realizing this is the beginning of growth. I must accept this truth, or I'll forever be stuck in a state of arrested spiritual development.

Denying this truth paralyzes me as, in my pride, I convince myself that I've arrived and don't require change. Some days it bothers me that I still require growth, but then I realize the reality that Paul taught. I can be better than who I am.

If I want to live the life I'm supposed to live, it's as close—or as far away—as my next right choice. It's in despair and futility that I imagine living right with God as some far-off fantasy. Paul insisted that living right is something I must do here and now. I need only to make the next right choice. This often requires me to acknowledge that my natural or first impulse is wrong. *First thought, wrong thought.* I learned in treatment that this describes the impulsive thinking of the addict.

We must accept that we're not there yet, and that we don't have to stay where we are. We can choose the next right choice and daily grow in our faith.

Day 270

GUESS WHO RELAPSED?

> Older men are to be sober-minded, dignified, self-controlled, sound
> in faith, in love, and in steadfastness. Older women likewise are to
> be reverent in behavior, not slanderers or slaves to much wine.

TITUS 2:2–3

If I confessed that I once went to church while high, it may not surprise you, but it might offend you. If I told you that I relapsed while writing this book (I didn't), you would probably be even more alarmed. However, if I told you a salacious story about a mutual friend struggling with addiction, you may be concerned, but you would still be interested. *Addiction is bad, but gossip is no big deal.* Slander and gossip are unfortunately all too common Sunday morning behaviors.

I'm not suggesting that all sins are the same in their practical outcomes. Various sins have varying effects. If I say untrue things about a coworker, it has very different consequences from my use of drugs. In today's passage, though, Paul included slander in the same sentence as addiction—"slaves to much wine"—in reference to destructive behaviors. Why?

Sin, by definition, turns us away from God, which is the most significant consequence—even if no one notices. We measure sin, though, by its obvious, practical effects. If it doesn't cause us any immediate, discernable harm, it can't be a big deal, right?

From the outside, some sins look fairly innocent. Thus, particular sins such as pride and vanity may be ignored in church, while others may even be encouraged under the guise of religiosity. Some share *prayer requests* with little intent of ever praying. Speaking poorly of others is often simply an indulgence in a destructive appetite to make ourselves feel better. Make no mistake, though; slander and gossip can be as addictive as any drug, turning us from God just the same.

If I told a you a scandalous story about someone we both know, *guess who relapsed?* Then we would both be participating in malicious gossip—or even slander if it turns out not to be true. Paul said this is sinful and destructive, mentioning it in the same breath as addiction itself.

Day 271

WHAT IS SELF-CONTROL AND HOW DO I GET IT? PART 1

> *Train the young women . . . to be self-controlled. . . .*
> *Likewise, urge the younger men to be self-controlled.*

TITUS 2:4–6

God, give me self-control! I was 14 or 15 years old, praying this desperate prayer repeatedly, wondering why God didn't answer. My testosterone-soaked mind was frustrated by impulsive thoughts that seemed beyond my control.

I didn't really understand what I was asking God at the time. Twenty-five years later, I still misunderstood and continued to pray the same desperate, frustrated prayer. *God, take this addiction from me. Why will you not answer?*

I was frustrated because I misunderstood self-control, my flesh nature, and God. At age 14, I was asking God to magically take testosterone—or at least its effects—from my flesh. I wanted my desire to be supernaturally removed. I was actually asking God to emasculate me, which thankfully, He didn't do.

I have often prayed this way. I don't tend to go to God, asking what I need to change. I go to God asking for Him to change only what I want changed. *I want to be skinny. Make me hate pizza and love broccoli. I want to be sober. Make me hate drugs.* Taken to this extreme, it's easy to see my folly; but still, I pray this way sometimes.

When we change nothing, nothing changes. Being a Christian doesn't mean we get to circumvent this reality. We don't get to do nothing, then claim the name of Christ, and miraculously avoid the destructive pursuits of our flesh.

When Paul talked about self-control, he used action words like *train*, *press on*, and *put on*, insisting that this is something we must choose to work at if we want it to happen. This isn't *God-control*, where He makes us automatons. This is *self-control*, where we learn the discipline to deny self and pursue Him.

Day 272

WHAT IS SELF-CONTROL AND HOW DO I GET IT? PART 2

> Train the young women . . . to be self-controlled. . . .
> Likewise, urge the younger men to be self-controlled.

TITUS 2:4–6

The irony of an addict writing on self-control isn't lost on me. If you want to know how to lose weight, though, you will not likely learn from someone who has never known the struggle. My drug addiction may be foreign to you, but we all know some struggle with self-control, whether it involves anxiety, gluttony, anger, lust, or greed.

Paul urged, in today's passage, to learn self-control. How then, do I do this? How do I stop a destructive behavior? This practice of self-control is no different from the practice of being a disciple. It's the same two-step process that Jesus commanded, "If anyone would come after me, let him deny himself and take up his cross daily and follow me" (Luke 9:23).

Step one, denial of self, isn't a passive process of *Just Stop It*. It's doing whatever it takes to kill the destructive behavior. If I'm struggling with drugs, I may need treatment. If I'm struggling with internet porn, my computer may need to go. I don't achieve the crucifixion of my old nature with mere positive thinking. I must act and obey. God works in my obedience, not in my indolence.

As for step two, taking up my cross to follow Him, I need to see God above all else—reading, praying, and meditating. I don't find God—and self-control—by giving Him five minutes a day plus an hour on Sunday.

God doesn't leave me alone in this. He meets me when I pursue Him, and He does change my desires, but this is often not the instant process I wish it to be. In my obedience, He transforms me day by day. I have not arrived. I still fail often, but I do press on, daily choosing to deny self and follow Christ.

Day 273

I'M A JERK ONLY BECAUSE I'M A CHRISTIAN

> *Avoid foolish controversies, genealogies, dissensions, and quarrels about the law, for they are unprofitable and worthless.*
>
> **TITUS 3:9**

I must admit, I've engaged in bitter, angry arguments over things like the age of the earth. In my perceived defense of God's truth, I've been condescending and rude in disagreeing with others. Arrogantly believing that I understood God's sense of time in the creation of the universe, I found it something worth fighting over. Perhaps my belief in the age of the earth is important to God, but I doubt very much that I was actually defending Him in such disputes.

This is the lie that Paul must have encountered in today's passage. This lie is the one in which I tell myself that I'm fighting for God when I am actually just fighting for my own ego. I would be arrogant if I weren't a Christian, but once I become convinced that I have a righteous, God-given truth, I become something worse altogether. I transform into a self-righteous monster because I cannot be wrong. *God told me I'm right!*

When I encounter someone who doesn't understand God as I do, I envision myself to be God's valiant warrior who must defend His name. It is, of course, not God's offense that I feel. It's mine. It's my own need to be right that's injured when confronted with an opposing opinion. However, because I believe myself to be fighting for righteousness, I can't admit my pride problem, so I blame God. *God wants me to fight!*

It's not that I shouldn't stand up for what I believe. In love, I can tell of God's truth. I should share with others what Christ has done for me. That's vastly different, though, from being arrogant and argumentative "for Christ." God may want me to stand for truth, but He has yet to ask me to sin for Him.

Day 274

THE DONUT IN MY EYE

> *The heavens are the work of your hands; they*
> *will perish, but you remain.*
>
> **HEBREWS 1:10-11**

As I sat down to write this devotion, it was the week before Christmas, thus I had piles of candy and other sweets sitting around. Though I wanted to wake up January first and step on the scale not having eaten any of it, what I really wanted was to eat it all.

This is my life problem. Though I want to live with my gaze on what is good and right in the long run, I can't see past my next snack. My appetite for the immediate continually obstructs my vision. I want to love God and neighbor, but right now I just want to sit on the couch and stuff myself. I have a donut stuck in my eye.

The eternal language of today's passage challenges me to attempt a perspective that looks beyond my immediate appetites. In it, the author draws a contrast between the temporary and the everlasting. The world and all its stuff will one day mean nothing to me. What will remain? What truly matters?

My appetite insists that what I want at any given moment matters— more than anything. God, however, insists that money, stuff, and donuts don't bring authentic meaning to my existence. It's not that I can't find pleasure in those things. It's just that the temporary isn't the purpose of my life.

Right now, I can participate in that which will last an eternity—or I can pursue everything-me and my appetites.

This isn't just about candy or donuts. This is about anything that I pursue to the detriment of my relationship with God. If I want to participate in that which truly matters, I must daily have the discipline to engage in activities that turn my gaze from self to God. I must daily choose to remove the donut from my eye.

Day 275
USING MY STRUGGLE

*Because he himself has suffered when tempted, he
is able to help those who are being tempted.*

HEBREWS 2:18

I used to feel like a fraud when teaching in church. I believed what I was saying, I just wasn't living it very well. It wasn't until after my own life disaster of addiction that I found some authenticity in my own voice when telling others of what Jesus had done in my life.

Hidden in today's beautiful passage is this principle: *Those who have suffered are uniquely qualified to help others who are going through the same thing.* Just as Christ is qualified to aid us because He suffered temptation, we can use our defects to help those who struggle as we have.

If I want to quit smoking or lose weight, I'll be better served by someone who has known the struggle and has had some success with it. No one is qualified to help me like the one who has known some victory over my defect.

In my shame, I have preferred to suffer alone, but this isn't productive. Thus, I seek to find others with whom I can share my burden; and in sharing, I can help and be helped.

When I visit our local jail, I don't go as one who understands being incarcerated. But I do go as one who understands addiction. This makes an instant connection, as most of the inmates are jailed because of some addiction. I use my own mess to tell what Christ has done in my life. When I honestly repent and obey, God can use my failures to help my neighbor.

If you've experienced this, you know how comforting it is to hear a friend say, *I've been there. I have fought this fight. I am still fighting it. Let us carry each other. You don't have to struggle alone. I'm here and I know what it's like.*

As Christ uses His suffering to help us, so we must use ours to help each other.

Day 276
SICK OF MYSELF

> To whom did he swear that they would not enter his
> rest, but to those who were disobedient? So we see that
> they were unable to enter because of unbelief.

HEBREWS 3:18–19

I broke a bike chain last summer. I didn't know how to fix it, but the guy on the internet video made it look annoyingly easy. So . . . I bought a five-dollar kit and set out to fix it. An hour later—covered in grease—I was angry, agitated, and frustrated. I watched the video and tried again to fix it—with no success. Only after I took the bike to the bike shop did I learn that I was never going to fix the chain on my own, as I had purchased the wrong-size parts.

The bike chain experience was a microcosm of my addiction. In my addiction, I knew only agitation and angst. Constantly fearful of discovery, withdrawal, and consequences, yet never being able to stop, I knew only unrest and anxiety. I needed sobriety but thought I could find it without actually changing my behavior. Only when I was forced to get help did I see that I would never get clean without radical obedience. Insisting on my own way had led to nothing good.

In my turmoil, I begged God for His peace but couldn't find it as long as I continued in my addiction. In today's passage, Paul explained how God's peace comes only with obedience. As I remained unwilling to do anything to change, I could never know God's rest. Not until I was willing to confess, go to treatment, and endure the pain of transformation was I able to experience the peace of God.

I believed in God and wanted His comfort, but I was unwilling to obey and follow Him. In this state, I was—as with my bike chain—attempting the impossible. I would never find the peace of God until I changed directions and obeyed Him.

Day 277

MY OWN SWORD

The word of God is living and active, sharper than any two-edged sword, piercing to the division of soul and of spirit.

HEBREWS 4:12

It's not uncommon in Christian circles to hear mournful stories about the secularization of society. At Christmas, we object to the change from *Merry Christmas* to *Happy Holidays*. Our country was founded in faith, and we grieve the drift away from God. The world has always been hostile to our faith, though. Our Messiah was crucified on a cross, after all.

The temptation for me in response to today's passage is to see it as a call to arms, asking me to pick up the Word of God as a sword—to be pointed at those around me. When my faith is challenged, I want to lash out in defense of it, using the Bible as a weapon.

I envision myself to be a Christian culture warrior, swinging my blade at those who offend my faith. I can recall a time 20 years ago when I had a strong political faith, while my personal relationship with God was a bit of a desert. The advantage of this kind of faith was that I could conveniently ignore all my little sins . . . because the world was so much worse than I was. The disadvantage, of course, was that this isn't what it means to be a disciple of Christ.

When I use the Word of God only to point at others, I avoid its deadly effect on my own flesh life. His Word must first be pointed at self. As Christ commanded me to crucify myself daily, Paul insists I must fall on my own sword daily. "I die every day!" (1 Corinthians 15:31). Christ's message of self-denial and obedience is the sword that must pierce my flesh continually.

How does this passage apply to me? What's God asking that I crucify? How does He want me to follow? When I read the Bible and think only of everyone else's needs, I become blind to my own need for the sword.

Day 278

THE STUFF I CLING TO

> *Let us then with confidence draw near to the throne of*
> *grace, that we may receive mercy and find grace.*
>
> **HEBREWS 4:16**

My family recently attended a professional sporting event, where we were required to pass through security before entering. Purses were not allowed into the venue; so at the gate there were trash cans full of purses. Anyone with a purse had the choice to keep it and remain outside—or discard it and enter. Most, it seemed, wanted to enter more than they wanted to keep their purses.

Thankfully, we don't have to rid ourselves of our baggage and we don't have to become perfect before God accepts us. Because of Christ's sacrificial death at the cross, we can enter into a right relationship with God. This is the beautiful message of the gospel. He loves us, and nothing we do changes that. When we come to faith, we are forgiven for all time.

However, to know God's intimate presence in a practical sense while in the confines of this flesh is somewhat different. The author of Hebrews, in today's passage, insisted that we must make the choice to boldly enter and live in the manifest presence of God. Though we are forgiven and restored to God in position, in practice we can come to know Him a little—or a lot.

Here is where we must discard our baggage and draw near to Him, or we'll hang on to whatever keeps us from Him. I may be forgiven for all time, but the practical reality is that I can't willfully defy God while enjoying the wonder of His intimate presence. I don't get to indulge in pills, porn, greed, anger, resentments, or selfishness while simultaneously enjoying intimacy with God.

If I desire to enter into God's very real presence, I simply must be willing to discard that which keeps me out. I cannot defiantly cling to my purse *and* enter. I must choose one or the other.

Day 279

ARRESTED DEVELOPMENT

| *You need milk, not solid food. . . . Solid food is for the mature.* |

HEBREWS 5:12, 14

With my kids in high school, I'm frequently reminded that their time under my roof is drawing short. Though this saddens me, I'm happy they will someday leave, not because I want them gone, but because I want to see them grow. As much as I love them, I don't want them to be children forever. It would be heartbreaking if they suddenly stopped developing.

The author of Hebrews echoed this same sentiment in today's passage as he chastised his spiritual children for remaining in a state of infancy. They had been given the nourishment required for growth, but they didn't ingest it and thus remained in a state of arrested development.

I imagine God has often felt the same about me. Just as I must continually take in physical nourishment, I must continually take in spiritual nourishment to grow in my faith. I have for years, though, existed in a state of spiritual starvation, taking in little or no sustenance. Then I wondered why I was still a spiritual infant, enslaved to my appetites, wallowing in my own filth.

I rarely miss a meal. It would do me well to adopt this same attitude about my faith. I must discipline myself to get up every morning and fill myself with God, or—by default—I'll starve myself spiritually.

What is it that stunts our growth? Why do we not continually fill ourselves with God? It's because we try to satisfy ourselves with the immediate gratification found in the flesh nature. Instead of pursuing joy, purpose, and meaning in God, we attempt to take the shortcut to pleasure with food, entertainment, money, and affirmation from others.

If we want to grow spiritually, we must continually fill ourselves with God. We can't fill ourselves with the world and expect to grow our faith.

Day 280

I'M SORRY. I'M JUST NOT GOING TO CHANGE.

*For it is impossible, in the case of those who
. . . have shared in the Holy Spirit, . . . and then have
fallen away, to restore them again to repentance.*

HEBREWS 6:4, 6

I think most of us can identify with saying *sorry*, only to quickly repeat the offensive behavior. We swear that we will never do it again. *I'll never yell again. I'll never overeat again. I'll never look at pornography again.* Then, as sure as the sun rises, we're back at it shortly after.

We often say *I'm sorry* impulsively without any actual change in behavior. In this context, *sorry* is simply acknowledging that we feel bad. I may have good intentions, but if that's not followed by action, I'm not actually repenting. If I apologize daily to my family for being harsh with them but I continue to yell, they'll find my apologies insincere. They'll find it hard to forgive when I apologize for the hundredth time.

This is the position many of us find ourselves in before God. We ask forgiveness repeatedly, only to return to our destructive behavior. Then, we read passages like today's—and we're terrified. *What if my sin means I've fallen away from God?*

We should take comfort that this passage doesn't mean that there's a finite number of times we can fail after which God casts us away. God forgives us when we repent, no matter how many times we fail. We should, however, also recognize that repenting means changing behavior. Saying *I'm sorry*, with no change in behavior, is not actually repentance. It's just a hollow recognition of bad behavior.

If we have a behavior that's hurting our family or our relationship with God, we need to ask forgiveness and then do *whatever it takes* to stop the behavior. We may need help. We may have to give up our internet access. We may need to radically change behavior. This will be uncomfortable . . . but this is repentance.

Day 281

DRINK THE RAIN

*Land that has drunk the rain that often falls on it,
and produces a crop useful to those for whose sake
it is cultivated, receives a blessing from God.*

HEBREWS 6:7

A man once told me that he had been trying too hard to grow spiritually—and was failing. He realized that he couldn't do it on his own; so he was going to switch gears, sit back, and let God do the work. His recurrent failures stood as evidence that he had been going about spiritual growth the wrong way. He was going to stop trying. *Let go and let God.*

That didn't seem quite right, but I didn't challenge him, as he spoke with authority and sounded pretty smart. The writer of Hebrews, though, would beg to differ about my part in the process of growth. In this agricultural analogy, he said that God pours the rain on the land, but the land is responsible to drink deeply of it. In drinking, the land produces a useful crop. If, on the other hand, the land *refuses* to drink the rain, "it bears thorns and thistles" (Hebrews 6:8).

The problem is that I want instant results. I eat healthy for three days and expect to be skinny. Growth is rarely that immediate. Spiritual growth is a lifelong process, and I must daily drink deeply of God to see growth. In my addict's mind, if I don't see instant results, I want to give up.

I must continually do my part to consume God. He will always do His part. I must do mine. What does that look like? I can only tell you my experience. Every morning I must get up early, spending time reading, praying, and journaling. I must continually choose to drink of God. The fact that I still struggle and still have defects is no reason to quit. It just means I still have a lot of room to grow.

Day 282

NOT READY FOR A JESUS FISH

> For land that has drunk the rain that often falls on it,
> and produces a crop useful to those for whose sake it is
> cultivated, receives a blessing from God. But if it bears thorns
> and thistles, it is worthless and near to being cursed.
>
> **HEBREWS 6:7–8**

On my way to my Saturday morning Bible study recently, I found myself tailgating a slow driver in the passing lane. I was fuming, yelling. *Get out of my way, I've got a Bible study to get to!* It only took a few minutes for the absurdity of my actions to hit me. I'm not ready for a Jesus fish on my car. I don't want people to associate my driving with my faith.

The verses above beg the question. *For what fruit am I known?* As God has given to me, am I producing a crop that's useful to those around me—or am I producing thorns and thistles? Am I sharing the love and grace that God has shown me—or am I cursing the slow drivers who dare inconvenience me?

What would others say about our lives and our fruit? Often as Christians, we identify our faith by what we *don't* do. *I don't smoke, drink, or cuss, so I'm doing pretty well.* Jesus, however, said that we are to feed those who are hungry, clothe those who are naked, and visit those in prison (Matthew 25:35–36). We are to do for others as God has done for us.

This assumes that we've allowed God to do something for us. We can display His love and transforming power only after we've experienced it ourselves. It's when we deny self, focus on God, and allow His love to flow out of us that we produce the crop He desires.

Day 283
THE PAIN OF MEMORY

| *I will remember their sins and their lawless deeds no more.* |
HEBREWS 10:17

A random memory popped up recently that was particularly condemning. The shame of my past suddenly came rushing back. The weight of my memory sometimes seems to crush the breath out of me. I've never had a panic attack, but I imagine it feels similar.

To those of us who have evil memories, God offers the most comforting words in Scripture, that He will remember our lawless deeds no more. The God who created the universe offers me complete forgiveness when I place my faith in Jesus.

That we often return to our old ways is testament to the fact that we don't realize the significance of this gift. We are forgiven and set free so we can spend the rest of our lives pursuing the God-life we were meant to have.

Not all memories are evil, of course. Sometimes I need to remember where I've been. There's a godly grief that leads to repentance (2 Corinthians 7:10). In treatment I've met those who, on day two, decide that they have no life regrets, as they have been forgiven. In their exuberance, they feel that the world should see them as God does. *God's forgiven me! Why can't you?*

God's forgiveness, to be sure, doesn't set me free from earthly consequences. If I rob a bank today and turn to God tomorrow, He may forgive; but the judge will not be impressed by my rebirth.

It's in looking to God that we may discern how to handle our memories. When our past condemns us, we can be comforted by today's verse while simultaneously grieving over the pain we've caused. We can use that grief to produce a hunger for repentance (2 Corinthians 7:11). Our grief can remind us that we want to be more than we have been.

Day 284

THE MOST TERRIFYING PASSAGE IN THE BIBLE

> *For if we go on sinning deliberately after receiving the knowledge of the truth, there no longer remains a sacrifice for sins, but a fearful expectation of judgment.*
>
> **HEBREWS 10:26–27**

I've never liked today's passage. I prefer to address verses of comfort, but today's passage is anything but comforting. This passage is a terror in the night.

In treatment I met a young man who, on his eighth treatment, asked a painful question. *How can I be a Christian and keep failing?* I wanted to comfort him, but his question . . . was *my* question. Today's passage echoed in our ears. "If we go on sinning deliberately . . ."

We've all been there. We know right but we do wrong. Sure, we feel bad and say we're sorry, but then we do it again. And again. Then, we come across this passage of fear, fire, and judgment—and we're terrified.

I believe this is the whole point of the passage. When we profane the name of God and trample the mercy of Christ by doing whatever we want, we *should* be terrified.

If I say that I believe in God but I never actually change, do I have an authentic faith? Am I a Christian—or an impostor? True faith should have an impact on how I live; and if it doesn't, then I'm fooling myself.

When I was abusing God's grace, I needed a painful, terrifying wake-up call. It was that dread that drove me to answer those tough questions. I desperately needed to stop following self and to start following God. I still do. I do still fail, but I find God infinitely graceful when I honestly try to follow Him.

It's in turning away from God and pursuing self that we should feel the terror in the night.

Day 285

LIVING THE DREAM

> *For you had compassion on those in prison, and you joyfully accepted the plundering of your property, since you knew that you yourselves had a better possession.*

HEBREWS 10:34

Early Christians were odd folk. They were happy in their suffering and they joyfully accepted persecution, not fighting back when others stole their stuff. They were *thankful* for their trials. Like I said, odd.

I'm generally not thankful for trials. I'm thankful for stuff. I thank God for my car, my house, and my boat. When I encounter trials, I don't thank God for them, I ask Him to fix them.

It's the American dream to live the good life. Then Jesus came along with an uncomfortable message. "Blessed are you who are poor, for yours is the kingdom of God" (Luke 6:20). Why would He say this? Was He not on board with the American dream?

When I hear people thanking God for all the blessings we have in this country, I chime in. I like it here. I do, however, have deep suspicions that my success and self-sufficiency have not always been the blessings I thought they were. What if the pursuit of stuff is actually the pursuit of self, masquerading as good while distracting me from God?

The early Christians considered their relationship with God as their greatest possession. They had such a spiritual mindset that they didn't worry about stuff. They identified with those in prison, because in knowing God, they were richer than any king.

These disciples had a bizarre view of their worldly possessions—a view we should emulate. It's not that we should invite people to steal our stuff. We should, however, hold our stuff loosely. We're not to be addicted to our things. Our relationship with God is to be our greatest treasure. Life is about the pursuit of God, not stuff.

Day 286

I THINK I CAN, I THINK I CAN

> *Without faith it is impossible to please him, for whoever*
> *would draw near to God must believe that he exists*
> *and that he rewards those who seek him.*

HEBREWS 11:6

What is faith? This question has vexed me since childhood. I vividly remember standing on the peak of my roof, wanting to fly, whispering, *"If you have faith, nothing will be impossible for you."* Faith was a mental exercise of believing in a thing hard enough. I'm fortunate that I survived my misunderstanding of "faith."

I'll insist that faith isn't simply positive thinking. It's not convincing myself that God will work life out to my specifications if I believe hard enough. That is magical thinking, focused on the desires of self.

The story of Peter walking on the water (Matthew 14) is my favorite picture of faith. To exercise faith, Peter *believed* in Jesus, *obeyed* Jesus, and then *kept his eyes on* Jesus. Then, in a dramatic illustration of not-faith, Peter—distracted by the wind and waves—took his eyes off Christ and started to sink. From Peter's example, I've taken my definition of faith: *Faith is doing whatever it takes to keep my eyes on Christ and walk accordingly*.

Faith doesn't mean that I believe *really hard* that God will give me what I want. Eleven of the twelve disciples died violent deaths—not because they were faithless, but because they were consumed with God's will. Unconcerned about the wind and waves, they kept eyes on Christ and followed Him above all.

The wind and waves that distracted Peter's gaze still distract us. The desires of our flesh are constantly seducing our gaze from God. Faith, then, is the constant discipline of learning to walk on the waters of life while orienting our eyes toward the living God.

Day 287

WHEN I THINK GOD FAILS

| *These all died in faith, not having received the things promised.* |

HEBREWS 11:13

Have you ever felt that God failed you? In my addiction, I prayed for God to change me, but He didn't. Did God fail? Philippians 4:19 says that "God will supply every need of yours," but I know from experience that God doesn't always provide what I think I need.

Christians throughout history have been tortured and killed for their faith. Did God's promise not apply to them? In today's passage, the writer of Hebrews listed heroes of the faith and the promises that God made to them, which they received only in the afterlife. From our perspective this may seem to be a cosmic rip-off, but that response only exposes our shortsightedness.

God *always* provides what we need—even when we can't see it. We see this world as our definitive reality, but it's not. In 100 years, we'll be dead. In 1,000 years, you and I will realize that our *spiritual life* has always been the greater reality. This should radically change our understanding of *need*.

We may think that our greatest need is a certain job, car, or house. God sees that our greatest need is far beyond the things of this world. We may think that God has failed us, but that's just a failure of perspective. When confronted with the idea that either God is faulty or Scott is faulty, it's always me. God never fails.

Faith is to keep our eyes on God, following Him, even when it seems that our needs are going unmet. God sees our ultimate needs and never fails to deliver, even when we can't see it.

When we feel God has failed, we must ask Him to give us perspective. We must ask for faith in what we can't yet see. It's in turning our gaze to God that our defective sight is corrected.

Day 288

I SWEAR, I'LL NEVER DO THAT AGAIN

In your struggle against sin you have not yet resisted to the point of shedding your blood.

HEBREWS 12:4

I'll never do that again. If you're like me, you've said this a thousand times about some behavior. It may be overeating, drinking, lust, or anger. Whatever it is, we all struggle with some behavior that we *try really hard* to stop doing. But there's a problem here. *I'll never do that again* isn't a plan. It's the battle cry of those doomed to failure.

We don't need to be drug addicts to understand this. We all do it. We have no plan and we do nothing to change our behavior, but we expect that next time will be different because *we will just say no.* Positive thinking isn't a plan. It's preparation for failure.

I once met a man who told me he would do anything to be free of his addiction. I told him that I would get him into treatment that day. *Oh, I won't do that.* He claimed he would do anything . . . but what he *meant* was that he would do nothing except to wish that things were different.

A participant in our jail Bible study said something profound recently, "We must pursue the new life with as much energy as we pursued the old life. I once would have fought to the death to protect my turf. Now I need to work that hard at the new life."

Many feel that, since we are saved by faith, we don't need to work at our new spirit life. The writer of Hebrews, however, says that we must do whatever it takes to *lay aside every weight and sin* (Hebrews 12:1).

Are we willing to do what it takes to leave ourselves behind to pursue God? Are we willing to go to treatment? Are we willing to give up our phone or Facebook? *Oh, I can't do that. I'll just never do it again.*

Day 289

MAKE IT STOP!

For the moment all discipline seems painful rather than pleasant, but later it yields the peaceful fruit of righteousness to those who have been trained by it.

HEBREWS 12:11

When I encounter pain, I ask God to stop it. The author of Hebrews, though, explained that my pain is an opportunity for God to work in my life. He uses my discomfort to grow me.

I know this to be true experientially. I've grown the most during the worst times of my life, as that is when I've been the most desperate for God.

This begs the question: *Is all pain discipline?* When I cause my own destruction, it's easy to see God's hand of discipline. It's much more difficult to know how to comprehend those trials that are apparently disconnected from any bad behavior. When a child gets cancer, is God *causing* that cancer to *teach someone a lesson?*

I certainly don't have the answer to *why* God allows pain. My focus here is not *why*, but rather, *what my response should be.*

From that perspective, I'm not sure it makes any difference if my pain is connected to my behavior or not. My response to pain must be the same either way. I must look to God, asking what He wants from me. Instead of first praying for the pain to be removed, I must pray for His will to be done.

This isn't easy, and it's not natural. In a difficult situation, it's our nature to beg God for deliverance—or to be angry with Him. As with all else in life, it's a constant challenge to keep our eyes off ourselves and focused on God. In our pain, we must ask for His will to be done. This is sometimes a difficult prayer, but it's always the right one.

Day 290

ANXIETY AND THE UNSHAKABLE

> *Therefore let us be grateful for receiving a kingdom that cannot be shaken.*
>
> **HEBREWS 12:28**

My anxiety has admittedly been mostly self-inflicted. I have, in my drug addiction, caused drastic, life-altering situations during which my family, career, and future were all up in the air. In the worst of my destruction, every day brought more bad news that weighed heavier and heavier on me, threatening to crush what little hope I had left.

It was in this helpless and hopeless state that I began to see the depth of my need for God. This reality is paradoxical to us. It's only in our profound weakness and need that we learn to rely on God. Our lives can be shaken, and we can be wrecked to the core. God, however, cannot be shaken and cannot be moved. Our eternal attachment to Him is the one thing about us that the world can't touch.

In my destruction I imagined the worst things that could possibly happen, and I realized even those losses could not take away the most important thing in my life. In my utter helplessness, I came to rely on the One who I was meant to cling to all along.

I have a friend who, while going through horrible, painful trials, refers to those trials as opportunities to *lean into God*. He has figured out that the most anxiety-inducing events are the ones that cause us to rely on our immovable God the most.

Anxiety is the focus of our mind's eye on ourselves. *What if the world doesn't turn out the way I want it to?* Faith is the focus of our mind's eye on the immovable One. No matter what happens, the world cannot touch the eternal, unshakable reality of our relationship with God.

Day 291
LOVE IS SCARY

Let brotherly love continue. Do not neglect to show hospitality to strangers, for thereby some have entertained angels unawares. Remember those who are in prison.

HEBREWS 13:1–3

There's no way around it. As Christians, we must love others. Today's passage says we must love even *strangers*. This is unnatural to us. We may not mind giving money to a good charity, but if you ask us to brush elbows with those whom the charity serves, we're a little busy.

Strangers can be scary people, but Jesus didn't say our love was to be limited only to Christian, heterosexual, wealthy, attractive people who share our culture. If we're really going to get involved in the lives of those around us, it may disrupt our comfort.

In Matthew 25, Jesus told his followers that when they fed the hungry, clothed the naked, and visited those in prison, they had done those things for Jesus Himself. In today's passage, we're told that some strangers are actually angels in disguise. We connect with God when we do for others.

I've found this to be true in my life. One of the best remedies for my selfishness is to reach out to another. I can pray for change, but authentic transformation requires obedience. We can and should pray—but if we never obey, then we're not following Christ.

Every Sunday morning, I visit the local jail for a Bible study. The first time . . . I was terrified. *Jail is scary.* However, I've come to love jail church, as it's where I meet with others who, like me, are desperate for God. Though I started this venture to help *those people*, they have radically affected me. When I obey, God works wonders.

Though our faith is first about relationship with God, it was never meant to isolate us from our neighbors. If we have faith, we will be obedient, loving others—even when it's uncomfortable.

Day 292

MIND CONTROL

Count it all joy, my brothers, when you meet trials of various kinds,
for you know that the testing of your faith produces steadfastness.

JAMES 1:2–3

As I was meditating on today's passage, God used a phone call from a man who was under the impression that I had been prank-calling his phone. As he chewed me out in angry, profane language, I remained calm, politely informing him that he had the wrong number.

I then spent the next half-hour seething about what a jerk he was. It took fully 30 minutes for me to realize that I had just given this man control of my mind.

James said that when I face trials, it's my responsibility to choose my attitude. Instead, I often give that control away. *It's your fault I'm angry!* Most of us have impulsive responses to trials, but the fact that a specific response is our natural one still doesn't make it right. We could justify any behavior by insisting it's simply our natural response. Our nature is broken, and we can choose to control it—or we can allow it to control us.

I can either focus on self, becoming angry, resentful, and bitter; or I can turn my gaze to God. I can't change the fact that I'm going to encounter pain in this life. I can, however, choose what I do with it. When I give a trial control over me, I allow my broken nature to rule.

If we don't want to be slaves to our own nature, and if we don't want to give control to other people or situations, then we must maintain our focus on God. This is a choice that we must make again with every new trial. Some trials will challenge us to the core, and in them we'll have to choose a thousand times to turn to God.

Day 293
WHAT IF I'M BLIND?

If any of you lacks wisdom, let him ask God. . . . But let him
ask in faith, with no doubting, for the one who doubts is like
a wave of the sea that is driven and tossed by the wind.

JAMES 1:5–6

I've made enough mistakes in life that I must remain suspicious of my own thinking. We all know those who think themselves wise but who, in reality, are fools. The problem, of course, is that foolishness is blind to its own presence. Thus, I fear that I'm blind to my own folly.

Wisdom involves looking to God instead of my natural preferences. My perspective, however, is so spoiled by my own fallen flesh nature that I think it's probably best to question all of my own thinking. I often find myself asking a question of God. *What would a wise person do in this situation?*

I may go to God asking if I should buy this house or that house. God responds, *"I'm not that concerned with the roof over your head. Stop following the desires of your own flesh. Abandon your lust, greed, pride, and self. Love me and love your neighbor."*

Therein lies the problem. I often go to God asking for wisdom, when what I really want is confirmation of my preference. To truly go to God, asking for wisdom means being open to the possibility that my best thinking is absolute foolishness.

James said we must not be distracted by the same wind and waves that caused Peter to begin sinking. We must ask God for wisdom and then keep our eyes on Him. The wind and waves of this world will constantly seduce our gaze from God. In looking to self, we'll remain blind to our own foolishness. Wisdom, like faith, keeps eyes on God.

Day 294

BORN THIS WAY

> Let no one say when he is tempted, "I am being tempted
> by God," for God cannot be tempted with evil, and
> he himself tempts no one. But each person is tempted
> when he is lured and enticed by his own desire.
>
> **JAMES 1:13–14**

I have, in a display of my self-centered thinking, blamed God for my disasters in life. *You did this. You made me this way. If you are in control, then you can't blame me.*

At times I've taken it even further. *If God made me this way, then I cannot even be wrong. I was born this way, right?* I can justify anything if I insist that, since God made me this way, I must be the way He wants me to be.

James must have encountered thinking like mine, as he found it necessary to point out the fallacy of this idea. God is not evil, and God does not tempt us, but He has allowed us to be born into a flesh nature with corrupt desires.

I'm not responsible for the hand I was dealt in life, but only I am responsible for how I play that hand. I may inherit a predisposition for anxiety, depression, or pride—or an appetite for sex, drugs, and alcohol. I'm not to blame for my defects. I am, however, responsible for how I respond to those flaws.

When we follow our desires to destruction, we're following ourselves, not God. God is not our enemy. He is the answer to our defects. He may have allowed us to be born with a corrupt nature, just so our need would turn us to Him. God is not cheering for our failure. He desires that we turn to Him in our struggles.

Day 295
APPETITE FOR DESTRUCTION

> *Each person is tempted when he is lured and enticed by his own desire. Then desire when it has conceived gives birth to sin, and sin when it is fully grown brings forth death.*
>
> **JAMES 1:14–15**

In my fascination with our flesh nature, I don't have it all figured out. However, I've come to understand that, while not all of our desires are destructive, we do all have corrupt desires that lead to destruction.

When we indulge in our faulty appetites, we do get some reward, but it often leads to addiction. Addiction is engaging in some harmful behavior repeatedly, despite suffering consequences. James called these consequences *death*, not necessarily meaning a literal death, but rather, a living death, in which we suffer physical, mental, and spiritual injury.

I don't have to be a drug addict to know this to be true. When I yell at my loved ones, I hurt them and damage our relationship. When I eat donuts instead of training for that race coming up in two weeks, I get fatter instead of faster.

When I allow my will to run unchecked, I cause a thousand little deaths a day. Compounding the problem is my refusal to acknowledge that my preferences can be destructive. Then I blame the world, other people, or even God. This may allow me to avoid feeling guilty (at least temporarily), but it's completely useless in preventing the recurring deaths.

It's only in humbly accepting that I have defective desires that I can begin to understand what to do about them. Alcoholics Anonymous speaks of how honesty is a prerequisite for recovery. This truth transcends alcoholism or drug addiction.

If we want to turn from that which causes us death, we must accept that we cause our own biggest life problems. We must learn to continually turn from our will to follow Christ's.

Day 296

INTOXICATED WITH ANGER

Let every person be quick to hear, slow to speak, slow to anger; for the anger of man does not produce the righteousness of God.

JAMES 1:19–20

Under the influence of chemicals, my thinking was twisted. Not only did I inappropriately justify my toxic behavior, but my self-awareness was perverted as well. I wasn't the one with the problem . . . everyone else was wrong. I wasn't irritable . . . others were irritating me. Only later, in recovery, could I see how my thoughts had been warped by my intoxication.

Anger is not that dissimilar in this regard. When I indulge in anger, my thinking becomes delusional. I imagine myself to be always right and everyone else to be always wrong. In our house we have a running joke in saying, *I always . . . you never . . .* In my anger, though, it's no joke. I indulge the fantasy that I'm the victim. *I always do all the work. I always act professional. You're the problem here.*

This kind of thinking isn't constructive, as it's perverted by the intoxicating influence of my anger. In my anger, it's simply impossible to see or think clearly. I can see only how my will is frustrated—and how nothing is my fault. Then I lash out and say horrible things that I later regret. Later is too late, though, as the words cannot be taken back.

In today's passage, James said that I must choose to keep my anger in check because it leads not to righteousness, but to destruction. My first impulse is wrong often enough that I must learn to control it.

In my anger, it's tempting to claim that I am angry for God. While that may be possible, blaming God for my anger is usually like suggesting that God wanted me to use drugs. It's just another intoxicated lie I tell myself to justify my bad behavior.

Day 297

APPETITE FOR POISON

Therefore put away all filthiness and rampant wickedness and receive with meekness the implanted word, which is able to save your souls.

JAMES 1:21

When I was a child, I drank strawberry shampoo because it *smelled so good*. I got a couple gulps down before I realized the horrible taste. Ingesting shampoo hasn't been my worst choice in life, though. I may not drink everything that smells good, but I sometimes still consume that which promises pleasure and delivers poison.

James' words remind me that we are what we eat. As followers of God, we must fill ourselves with His Word. We cannot eat a diet of donuts and expect to be trim and fit. We can't drink poison and expect to be healthy.

In my worst destruction, I was able to look back and see that I had been living on a diet of self for 10 years. I consumed poison and suffered the consequences. In those consequences, I realized that if I want to be somewhere tomorrow, I must take the steps to get there today.

God doesn't instruct me to avoid filth because He wants my life to be boring. He, like a loving parent, wants me to avoid destruction. I don't want my son to start looking at pornography, and I don't want my daughter to become obsessed with self-image or popularity. I want them to pursue what is healthy and productive—not because I'm a fun killer, but because I want what is best for them.

Filth and wickedness, like the strawberry shampoo, promise pleasure but deliver poison. I simply cannot pursue God while using drugs, looking at pornography, lashing out in anger, or obsessing with self.

We must *put away* the evil that destroys, and we must fill ourselves with the things of God, which produce life.

Day 298

JUST A HEARER?

| *Be doers of the word, and not hearers only, deceiving yourselves.* |
JAMES 1:22

I've heard thousands of sermons and forgotten most of them—not because they were unworthy of memory, but because I have mostly been simply a *hearer*. James said, though, that I must not be just a hearer. If I'm a Christian, I must be a *doer*. My greatest destruction in life has come to pass, not because I was ignorant of the truth, but because I failed to obey it.

There are those who believe that if we simply hear and know the truth, our behavior will automatically follow. They believe that action is an automatic byproduct of knowledge; so they teach the truth in the hope that everyone will learn it and bad behavior will end.

James knew us better than that. He knew that *hearing* the truth, while necessary, is just a stepping-stone. He knew that without the second step of *doing*, the first step is just useless knowledge.

When I choose to do wrong, it's rarely out of ignorance. When I over-eat, indulge in pride, get angry, or gossip, it's not because I don't know what's right. I just want wrong more. My problem isn't lack of knowledge. It is a lack of obedience.

How do I move from being a hearer of Christianity to being a doer? I have often read the Bible for five minutes in the morning, only to walk away and live the rest of my day according to what I want. The challenge is to *hear* the word and then *do* it. I must take it with me, meditating on it, choosing to do something about it today.

James said the one who hears only is like one who looks in a mirror and then immediately forgets what he looks like. When we learn God's Word but fail to act on it, we live as though we forgot what we just saw. If we truly embrace God's Word, we won't just be hearers of it. We will be doers.

Day 299

THIS ONE IS TOTALLY ABOUT YOU

*If anyone thinks he is religious and does not bridle his tongue
but deceives his heart, this person's religion is worthless.*

JAMES 1:26

It's not uncommon for someone to ask if one of my blog posts is meant for him or her. It never is. I always write about lessons meant for myself. I would, however, like to deviate from that pattern and point this devotion at someone else. Anyone else. I'd like to say that James' convicting words today are about anyone but me. But they are meant for me, and they make me squirm.

James said that if I claim to belong to God, but my words indicate the opposite, then my *religion is worthless*. If I say that I have God in me, but I am known for vicious, angry, vile, and bitter language, then I'm a hypocrite. He said that whatever comes out of my mouth exposes the reality of what's truly inside me.

What is the kind of speech for which I am known? Am I known as a loving, gracious person—or am I known as a bitter, angry complainer who is hypercritical of others? How do my coworkers know me? Would they testify that I love God, or would they know by my sharp tongue that I am self-absorbed? What does my family think of my faith? Do my words prove to my wife that I live in humility before God—or do they betray the fact that I'm still a selfish, immature, and petty man?

What if everything I said in private ended up on these pages? What if it ended up on social media? I would need to get a muzzle. My speech reveals that I'm still in desperate need of God's grace and forgiveness.

The problem, of course, is not simply our tongues. Our tongues just reveal what's inside us. Our primary need, as always, is to focus the gaze of our souls on God instead of ourselves. Then what comes out of our mouths will reflect the goodness of the Holy Spirit inside us.

Day 300

PURE AND UNDEFILED RELIGION

> *Religion that is pure and undefiled before God the Father
> is this: to visit orphans and widows in their affliction,
> and to keep oneself unstained from the world.*

JAMES 1:27

Though the book of James is among my favorites, it's not an easy book. Like a mirror, reflecting the truth that I don't want to face, James described what my life should look like if I have an authentic relationship with God.

The ever-pragmatic James must have been writing to Christians who wanted a feel-good religion. They must have wanted a faith consisting only of knowledge that left their daily lives alone. He must have been writing to Christians who had more interest in the pleasures and cares of the world than they did for their neighbors in need. He must have been writing to me.

James said that if we have a *pure and undefiled* relationship with God, our lives will focus on loving those around us. James never said that we earn our relationship with God by doing these things. He simply insisted that a true relationship with God would lead to these things.

How does my religion compare? *Well, I'm mostly just interested in what I want.* Widows and orphans? *That's a lot of work. I have a job and a family to think about.* Unstained by the world? *I'd rather not answer that one.*

Thankfully, I don't have to rely on my deeds to save me. James didn't say that I'm damned if I don't do enough. He did, however, insist that if I truly have a relationship with God, it will have a radical effect on my behavior. It's a hollow religion that consists only of empty words and knowledge.

James, like his brother Jesus, demanded that if we claim to be disciples, we must deny ourselves, take up our crosses daily, and follow Christ (Luke 9:23). This is what pure and undefiled religion looks like.

Day 301

ZOMBIE FAITH

> *What good is it, my brothers, if someone says he has faith*
> *but does not have works? Can that faith save him? . . .*
> *Faith by itself, if it does not have works, is dead.*
>
> **JAMES 2:14, 17**

I grew up knowing that I am saved, not by what I do but rather by my faith. I have, though, in my defective interpretation, understood faith as a simple knowledge of a thing. *I believe in God; therefore, I'm saved by my faith. I don't have to do anything because I'm not saved by doing.* This kind of faith is synonymous with *doing nothing.*

James gave such thinking a satirical pat on the back. "You believe that God is one; you do well. Even the demons believe—and shudder!" (James 2:19). He said faith without works is dead. Though we claim faith, without doing, we're just spiritual zombies.

Faith, if it is real, must impact my behavior. If it doesn't, it's not alive. I've lived in this corpse-like state, insisting I believed, while my behavior revealed that I followed self, not God.

Many of us have prayed a sinner's prayer but have never made it much further than that. We remain addicted to our flesh nature and thus cannot really follow God. We're still living enslaved to our pride, lust, anger, beauty, or chemical—and thus cannot exercise a living faith. James called this a living death (James 2:26).

What can I do about this condition? If I want to know a living faith, I must make my behavior follow my belief. I don't earn my salvation, but God breathes life into my relationship with Him only when I follow Him with my actions.

We have this daily choice to follow God or self. If we continue to claim faith but follow ourselves, we are as walking corpses. If, however, we do *whatever it takes* to deny self and follow God, He animates us, breathing His life into us.

Day 302

YOU'RE NOT ALONE

| *We all stumble in many ways.* |

JAMES 3:2

When the consequences of my addiction erupted, I felt as if I were the worst person in the world. Eventually, I sought out a refuge where I could meet with other addicts. I found comfort in knowing I wasn't alone.

The fact that "we all stumble in many ways" should comfort us. We're all in this together. Our failures may not all have the same consequences, but we all have flawed traits that in some way enslave us. We all have things that we don't want to do . . . that we still do. The consolation lies not in denying our flaws, but in realizing that we are all flawed.

I should find comfort in meeting with those who struggle as I do, but I should also be compassionate about those who struggle differently. The temptation is to look down on others' struggles simply because I don't struggle in the same way.

I should, in my own imperfections, find grace and mercy for the imperfections of others. Being able to hide my own flaws is very different from actually having none of them to hide. The secret addiction of pornography or pride is no less destructive than a food or drug addiction.

Drug addiction may be my most glaring failure, but it's hardly my only life problem. I may have some success at recovery—only to find myself embracing pride. Then I might work on humility . . . only to find myself being judgmental about those whom I find prideful. I'm not going to run out of flaws in this life.

This shouldn't cause us to despair. We can comfort each other, knowing that we're not alone in our struggles—and we can actually use them to help each other. This will require painful honesty; but if we want help from God and others, honesty is a prerequisite. *We all stumble in many ways*, but we can use our failures to help each other and turn toward God.

Day 303

THE GIFT OF CRITICISM

The wisdom from above is first pure, then peaceable, gentle, open to reason, full of mercy and good fruits, impartial and sincere.

JAMES 3:17

When it comes to wisdom, I have two conflicting desires. I want the wisdom that James described, but I also want *to be known* for being wise. James says, however, that I can't pursue both heavenly wisdom and self-promotion.

James insisted that true wisdom does good works out of humility and doesn't seek the accolades of the world. True wisdom exists for and pursues the good of others. It's peaceable, gentle, and full of mercy. True wisdom cares little if it's recognized by the world.

In contrast, human wisdom seems to be all about promotion of self and criticism of others. *What good is wisdom if no one recognizes me for it? I have great vision, and I need to make sure that everyone knows it. I must use my gift of discernment to point out all the flaws of everyone else.*

Many of us do have some discernment, but with the focus on ourselves instead of God, we've developed the gift of *criticism.* Seeking to elevate ourselves, we focus on the defects of others. *But I'm able to see what others cannot! I have a gift and I need to use it!* We wield our *wisdom* like a sword, cutting others down to elevate ourselves.

We all know people who need to read this passage. They may seem wise, but when we get close, we see that they're more about self-promotion than God-promotion. Then, in our own defectiveness, we want to expose their hypocrisy for all to see. *I must show the world your true colors, revealing how wise I am. Oh wait. Now I'm doing it.*

Our concern should be to focus on God instead of the praise of man. We must love our neighbors, not cut them down. We are to pursue true wisdom, not the "gift" of criticism.

Day 304

I'M THE PROBLEM?

> *What causes quarrels and what causes fights among you? Is it not this, that your passions are at war within you? You desire and do not have, so you murder. You covet and cannot obtain, so you fight and quarrel.*

JAMES 4:1–2

When I'm in conflict with another, it's never my fault. It's always due to some defect on the part of the other person, right? In my self-centeredness, I always have the moral high ground.

James didn't sympathize with this view. He pointed his finger directly at me, insisting that when I have conflict . . . it's due to my own broken desires. I can imagine James saying, *"There is something wrong with your passions. It's your own pride, selfishness, and ego that cause conflict. You are the problem."*

James didn't suggest that others don't act selfishly. He just insisted that my part in a conflict is my responsibility. I can't change how another person acts. Yes, if we all acted selflessly, we would all get along better, but I can't change another's behavior. If I'd give up my own pride and my need to be right, most of my conflict would evaporate immediately.

I can be irritated for days about some unfortunate interaction with a coworker, an acquaintance, or my spouse; but James insisted that my joy, peace, and attitude are my responsibility alone. I surrender control of my joy and attitude when I rely on another's behavior for those things.

We must always find our joy and meaning in God first. As long as we depend on other people or things to fill the space that God alone was meant to fill, we'll live in a state of frustration.

If, however, we keep our eyes on God and—in humility—realize that our joy comes from Him, then we can properly enjoy our relationships with others. When our eyes are on God, everything else falls into its proper place.

Day 305

GIVE ME WHAT I WANT

You do not have, because you do not ask. You ask and do not receive, because you ask wrongly, to spend it on your passions.

JAMES 4:2–3

God has abandoned me. In my addiction, I prayed and prayed that God would change me, but I received no answer. I began questioning whether God even existed. If He did, then why did He not answer my prayer? I eventually had to accept the fact that God was not lacking . . . the deficit was in me.

I came to realize James' meaning in today's passage. Our prayers are often frustrated because we are like children demanding a new toy, asking for all the wrong reasons. *How could I be wrong in asking? I just want to be sober!* In my addiction, I wasn't willing to change anything about my life, I just wanted a magical fix. James said God doesn't work like this. He's no genie in the lamp.

"You want to get better? Obey me. Confess your sin. Go to treatment."

I wasn't willing to do any of those things. I just wanted God to snap his giant fingers and get me out of my mess. *God, if you get me out of this, I'll be a missionary in Africa.* Africa, apparently, didn't need an addict at that moment. He didn't take me up on the offer.

I then had the audacity to blame God for my behavior. *If you won't help me, then this is your fault.* James said, though, that we're frustrated because we ask wrong. We must go to God, asking Him what it is that we need to do . . . and then we must do it.

If we could follow our own desires to destruction and then go to God for a magical clean up, what would we learn? We'd learn that we can do whatever we want with no consequences. God will not be mocked. We reap what we sow. If we pursue destruction, we find it. If, however, we pursue God, we'll find life in Him.

Day 306

WHY ARE WE MISERABLE?

> *Whoever wishes to be a friend of the world*
> *makes himself an enemy of God.*

JAMES 4:4

Have you ever looked around and wondered how you got where you are? I'm not speaking of geography. I'm talking about looking down at my life—and gasping in horror. I'm talking about looking at my existence and asking, *What happened? This isn't how I planned my life. Why am I so miserable?*

I've been there. In my addiction, I had to accept that I got where I was by walking in one direction for years. When I pursued drugs I found addiction, not God. I had to realize that I can't walk toward God and toward self at the same time.

I still try sometimes, though. Daily I try to straddle the two paths, and daily I find that I can't do it. I start out the day following God, and ten minutes later . . . I'm following the path of pride, anger, and selfishness.

Do you want to know why you live in misery? It's because you try to straddle the two paths. You are living torn in half because you think you can have all the world has to offer—and know God at the same time.

James said that no matter what my life problems appear to be, my primary need is always to stay on God's path. I may have health problems, money problems, or relationship problems. I may think I *need* a thousand different things, but what I always need at this moment is to turn to God. Only when I follow Him does all the chaos fall into its proper place.

We can walk a thousand miles from God, and if we will but turn around, we'll find Him right there. We can return to our right relationship with God if we will only turn from the path of ourselves to follow Him. This is always our primary need, to keep our eyes on God, following only His path.

Day 307

PRIDING MYSELF ON MY HUMILITY

God opposes the proud but gives grace to the humble.

JAMES 4:6

James insists in today's passage that God's grace is granted only to the humble. Faith keeps its eyes on God and acts accordingly. Pride says, *I believe in God, but I do what I want. I know best.*

My failures in life, big and small, haven't come from disbelief, but rather from following self above all. When I chose to follow myself . . . that was pride, not doubt. Pride is ever the faith killer because pride convinces me that *I've got this. I'm in control.*

The problem with pride, of course, is that it's blind to itself. We dare not miss this. The most prideful among us will convince ourselves that we don't struggle with pride. *Actually, I find myself quite humble. I pride myself on my humility.*

It's when I find myself thinking that I don't struggle much with pride that I'm surely blinded by it. When I find myself looking down on those sinners beneath me, I'm in trouble. If I pray, *God, I thank you that I am not like other men* (Luke 18:11), then I've surely become profoundly ignorant of—and blind to—my own pride.

James said that my pride actually puts me in opposition to God. This is a fight I cannot win, and it can lead only to destruction. If, however, I humble myself before God, bowing to His will and following Him in faith, He shows me grace. When I pray, *God, be merciful to me, a sinner* (Luke 18:13), then I am in right position before Him and can bask in His grace, love, and mercy.

In my pride I can look down on others, refusing to accept my own profound need for God; or I can live in humility before Him. I can then enjoy God's grace instead of struggling in miserable opposition to Him.

Day 308

WHERE HEAVEN MEETS EARTH

| *Draw near to God, and he will draw near to you.* |

JAMES 4:8

In my drug addiction, I became passionately interested in how God changes me. Where do heaven and earth meet? Do I just sit back—let go and let God—or does God make me do all the work? The ever-pragmatic James, brother of Jesus, provided the perfect response to my question. "Draw near to God, and he will draw near to you."

James said that if I want God, I must pursue Him. If I seek God a little, I will find little. If I feel that God is distant, the defect is with my effort, not God's.

Some will chafe at the idea that we can move God, but James insisted that this is how it works. We must radically pursue God if we want Him.

This is why so many of us, for so long, have had so little of God. We *sort-of want God* when we give him only an hour on Sunday. Why do we seek so little? It's always the distraction of self that stands in the way. We don't have to be perfect to know God, but we don't get to enjoy intimacy with Him while pursuing something above Him.

Whatever appetite I pursue above God, whether it is money, drugs, sexuality, pride, food, status, or beauty . . . that appetite becomes my god and prevents me from pursuing *the* God. If I am distant from Him, it isn't because He is failing. It's because He insists on being my only God. God doesn't play second fiddle.

God doesn't leave us alone in this process. He has given radically to draw us to Himself. Practically, it's our job to do whatever it takes to leave behind the pursuit of ourselves to pursue Him. When we draw near to God, He keeps His promise and He draws near to us. This is where earth and heaven meet.

Day 309

GUILT AND SHAME

Cleanse your hands, you sinners. . . . Be wretched and mourn and weep. . . . Humble yourselves before the Lord, and he will exalt you.

JAMES 4:8–10

When I went to treatment, I had a tremendous amount of guilt. I was encouraged repeatedly to *forgive myself.* I was told that feeling wretched over what I had done was self-destructive. God had forgiven me, so I needed to forgive myself and stop mourning my sin.

James, however, said that it's necessary to mourn for one's sin. When I come to repentance, I should mourn my sin.

While it is a blessed truth—God has forgiven me—forgiveness doesn't free me from earthly consequences. God will not be mocked. I reap what I sow. If I lose my job, go to jail, and leave my family homeless, it does little good to tell them of my forgiven state.

When those around me suffer the consequences of my actions, it's disingenuous to claim that I'm happy and free. James said when I sin, I should weep over my failure. God uses that pain and misery to change me. If I dismiss the guilt and shame, I remove the impetus to change.

There is, of course, a shame that leads to more death. If I insist that I'm too far gone to be forgiven, then I'll throw my hands up in defeat, which leads only to more destruction. I must rejoice in God's forgiveness if I want to grow and change.

It's not wrong, however, to mourn the destruction we've caused. If we sin boldly and then hold our heads up proudly when we fail, we won't change. Our sin grieves God and thus humility and mourning are right responses to our sin. It's in humbling ourselves before God that He lifts us up.

Day 310

PLAYING GOD

> *Do not speak evil against one another. . . .*
> *Who are you to judge your neighbor?*
>
> **JAMES 4:11–12**

In treatment we all witnessed two guys being hauled out by police for using drugs. Thirty of us, in treatment ourselves, suddenly became very critical of those two. *What idiots! Can you believe how stupid they are to use drugs in treatment?*

I had two thoughts simultaneously. First, if a group of addicts thinks you are dumb, you have sunk to a new low. Second, how did any of us think that we had any right to be critical of these two? Had we suddenly forgotten why we were in treatment? I realized how silly it was to be judgmental. *The idiots are the ones being judgmental. Oh, I'm doing it again.*

James said that when I judge, I make myself out to be God. I can't speak harshly of others without assuming His role. I make a miserable god.

This presents a predicament for Christians because we see ourselves as standard-bearers of the truth. How do we stand for truth without casting judgment? I am to love my neighbors, but when I love them, they think that I approve of all they do. If I let it be known that I find their addiction to be destructive, then I'm seen as a hateful judge.

One of the hardest things to do is to love others and to be truthful with them. It's so easy to choose one or the other. I either err in love and abandon truth, or I whack them over the head with the truth, forgetting love. Love without truth is anarchy and chaos. Truth without love is cold legalism.

The challenge for us is to maintain our commitment to what we believe is right—without playing God. Here's the key: We'll find it difficult to judge others when we're on our own knees in humility before God. When we keep our eyes off ourselves and on Him, it's impossible to play God.

Day 311

THE HARDEST PRAYER

> *Come now, you who say, "Today or tomorrow we will go*
> *into such and such a town and spend a year there and*
> *trade and make a profit." . . . Instead you ought to say,*
> *"If the Lord wills, we will live and do this or that."*
>
> **JAMES 4:13–15**

When I was a kid, I went through a phase when I thought it would be pretty cool to have diabetes. In my short-sighted self-interest, I actually hoped for sickness. I give thanks now that I did not get what I thought I wanted.

This must be how God views my self-centered scheming even now. James said, "You do not know what tomorrow will bring" (James 4:14), yet I often follow my own route. I'm still that child hoping for diabetes, ignorant of what I am actually pursuing. *God, please save me from my own stupidity.*

When I pray, I usually go to God asking for my will to be done. James said, however, that the right prayer is always to ask for God's will. This is the hardest prayer; *God, not my will but yours* (Luke 22:42).

I may be willing to do this in one area of life. *Thank you, God, for freeing me from drug addiction, but I would prefer to manage my career, thank you very much.* I think God smiles at me as if I'm still that child wishing for diabetes.

James said I must follow God in every area of life, seeking His will in all things. This isn't easy. Sometimes it seems that we need to remind God of what's going on down here. *Do you not see the pain you are allowing? Fix this!*

When we follow God, though, we follow the One who can see not only tomorrow . . . but all the tomorrows. He holds the world in His hands, and His is the only will we should follow. Our will is as seductive as it is short-sighted, and thus, we must constantly pray—not for our will but for God's. This is the hardest prayer, but it's always the right prayer.

Day 312

DO THE NEXT RIGHT THING

*So whoever knows the right thing to do and
fails to do it, for him it is sin.*

JAMES 4:17

I picked up this phrase—do the next right thing—in recovery when I came to realize that my first instinct is usually wrong. As James' words imply, mine is not a *knowledge* problem. It's a *doing* problem.

I must purposefully make the right choice in every situation. I tend to think that I need to follow God only on the big decisions; but as I've learned, if I don't do right on the little decisions, I'll fail the big tests.

When the inmates I visit in jail tell me their stories, they report that they never just start out dealing drugs. They start out with some small but poor choices. *It was just some friends who I knew were bad for me. Then I had a drink. Then a drug. Then I started selling. Then the police showed up.*

I ask those same guys in jail what they're doing now to break this cycle. Most say the same thing. *It'll be different when I get out.* I ask what they are doing *now* to break the cycle. *I can't do anything. I'm in jail.* I ask if they're reading the Bible, praying, and living out their faith. *I'll do that stuff when I get out.*

The problem? When I fail to follow God in a little thing, it exerts some destructive influence on my next decision. I can't ask God to help me with that one big problem and yet completely ignore Him in every other area of my life.

Thankfully, when we choose to *do the next right thing*, something fantastic happens. God retrains our brains. Our impulses begin to change, and we learn to live right. If we pursue God in the little things, life grows in us, inevitably affecting everything else. If we want to pass the big tests, we must work on following God and do the next right thing.

Day 313

RUSTPROOF

> *Your riches have rotted and your garments are moth-eaten. Your gold and silver have corroded.*
>
> **JAMES 5:2–3**

In perhaps his most blistering words, James plays the grand auditor, sifting through the eternal worth of my life, searching for anything of permanent value. What will he find in me that will truly stand the test of time? Is my life a sum of the temporal wealth I've accumulated, or have I stored up treasures that cannot rust?

James asks me to look to the future, for a day is coming when my riches have rotted and my garments are moth-eaten. We each have a finite amount of time and energy. James insists that I interrogate myself to see where my heart lies. Am I slaving away for money and possessions that will all decay with time? Or do I have an eternal perspective that uses my time and effort to pursue what can never fade, even in death?

When I pursue my own appetite for temporal toys and wealth, James says I'm pursuing my own destruction. "Your gold and silver have corroded, and their corrosion will be evidence against you and will eat your flesh like fire" (James 5:3). He could just nicely point out that *you can't take it with you*, but that wouldn't be James' style. He hammers the point home, insisting that I'm actually fattening myself up for the day of my own slaughter (verse 5).

When we pursue God, however, we pursue a timeless relationship. When we love those around us and together we pursue the eternal, we store up treasures that do not corrode and decay with time. James says we can own the world, but in the end it will all burn and fade, doing us no ultimate good. In a thousand years, it won't matter one bit if we had nice stuff. If, however, we invest our efforts in God and in those around us, then we can build an estate of the eternal.

Day 314

GIVE ME PATIENCE. NOW.

> *Be patient, therefore, brothers, until the coming of the Lord. . . . You have seen the purpose of the Lord, how the Lord is compassionate and merciful.*
>
> **JAMES 5:7, 11**

I'm not a patient person. I want what I want—immediately. When I got out of treatment, I knew I was a changed man. Thirty days had undone years of pursuing self (in my mind), and I was ready to show my new self to everyone. It took a little time for the world to catch up, as my life was still a bit of a disaster. It was more than a bit frustrating that I could not effect this immediate change.

It had taken years to get where I was. I had to realize that, though I was forgiven, I still had consequences to deal with. James said my life is like a seed. "See how the farmer waits for the precious fruit of the earth, being patient about it" (James 5:7). I was like a farmer, but skipping straight to the harvest to avoid the work of preparation. I just wanted the reward without the hard work.

I still do this often. When I feel discomfort, I ask God for immediate deliverance, demanding instant freedom from defect and pain. God's transforming work in me, however, is rarely one that teaches impatience by skipping the hard work. I have mistakenly seen God as a magician who provides an easy route to transformation. He didn't make the world this way, however. A blade of grass grows a day's growth in a day's time.

I want all the growth without all the toil and pain. I want to be delivered from my storm immediately, but James says this isn't what I need. What I need is to wait patiently on God, keeping my eyes on Him. In doing so, I can be delivered into God's presence, which is, of course, always my most important need.

Day 315

WILL GOD HEAL ME?

*Is anyone among you sick? . . . The prayer of
faith will save the one who is sick.*

JAMES 5:14–15

In today's passage, it seems James taught that all I have to do is perform a specific ritual (call the church elders, anoint with oil, pray) and healing will be guaranteed. This, however, opposes the reality that we know: Everyone dies. This passage cannot mean, then, that everyone who follows these instructions will always be healed.

"It is appointed for man to die once" (Hebrews 9:27). We'll all get sick and we'll all eventually die, which is almost always painful for someone. James' words do not guarantee the opposite. God's miraculous intervention seems to be the exception, but that doesn't mean He's absent in our sickness and death.

Some receive miraculous healing, which is a mystery to us. We do know, however, that God always spiritually heals those who repent. "If we confess our sins, he is faithful and just to forgive us our sins" (1 John 1:9). God always meets our greatest need, even when we don't see it that way. Our bodies won't last an eternity, but our spirits will.

Praying in faith for healing means looking to God's will, not only my own. Faith is not simply positive thinking. Faith means that our hope is in God and eternity, not in our own temporal existence.

Death will eventually catch us all. No amount of good diet, exercise, chemotherapy, drugs, or positive thinking can hold back the inevitable. God doesn't plan that we will all be healed from our physical decay. Rather, He plans that our spirits will eventually be set free from these bodies of death. He does, however, desire that we bring Him our pain . . . and in Him find the peace and comfort that we truly need.

God wills that we keep our eyes on Him in faith. This may mean miraculous healing, but more often it means spiritual healing, which, in the grand scheme of things, is vastly more important.

Day 316

ACCOUNTABILITY

My brothers, if anyone among you wanders from the truth
and someone brings him back, let him know that whoever
brings back a sinner from his wandering will save his
soul from death and will cover a multitude of sins.

JAMES 5:19–20

James previously warned me not to judge others, but this doesn't mean that I ignore my brother's destructive behavior. Here, in his final words, James described accountability, the antithesis of being judgmental.

In a courtroom, the judge is seated above the defendant, looking down at him. This isn't how it works with my brother, whom I lovingly come alongside when he wanders. He should do the same for me.

When I tell someone that he's a sinner and needs God, the reception is cool. When I share my own struggles instead, explaining what God means to me, doors open. This will always be more effective than playing the part of the condescending judge.

When we keep our failures a secret, we falsely elevate ourselves. It's when we're totally honest that others see us as caring and sincere. I'm not saying we should paint PORNOGRAPHY STRUGGLER or DRUG ADDICT on our t-shirts, but it's important that if we do struggle with lust, drugs, or anything else, we find those with whom we can be open.

Honesty and openness do not automatically eradicate addictions; but if we want to work on our destructive behaviors, honesty and openness are prerequisites. If we want to help others, we can and should openly share our own struggles. It's much easier to shine the light on a brother's wandering when we're honest about our own tendency to wander. James said that in this mutual accountability, we'll save each other "from death and will cover a multitude of sins."

Day 317
FINDING JOY

Though you do not now see him, you believe in him and rejoice with joy that is inexpressible and filled with glory, obtaining the outcome of your faith, the salvation of your souls.

1 PETER 1:8–9

It would seem at times that God really doesn't care about whether I am happy or not. He uses trials and pain to shape me. He asks me to abandon the desires of my flesh, and He insists that I *take up my cross daily* to follow Him. If happiness is my goal, Christianity can look a little grim.

To this, Peter would object. Today's passage paints a picture of anything but a cold, joyless faith. He said that, although we cannot see God, when we keep our focus on Him, we receive an *inexpressible joy, filled with glory.* This is no somber, miserable life.

Peter insisted that our joy should not be a product of our circumstances. If we allow the trials of this life to make us miserable, then we are doing faith wrong. When we believe in Christ and find our confidence in Him, joy will follow. This doesn't mean that we're insulated from pain and suffering. Joy isn't the absence of sadness or pain. Joy is an experience that transcends what this world can do to us.

I know joy in measure with my faith. It's in my focus on self that I'm the most miserable, and it's in my focus on God that I'm the most joyful. Peter says this isn't some far-off promise, but rather something I can know here and now. I tend to think of eternal life as something I'll experience only when I die, but Peter spoke of a joyful life that I can know here on earth.

God is not disinterested in our joy. He is, in fact, intensely interested, and He desires that we find it the way we were made to find it. If we want to know true joy, we must find it in God.

Day 318

DEATH, DECAY, AND ETERNITY

All flesh is like grass and all its glory like the flower of grass. The grass withers, and the flower falls, but the word of the Lord remains forever.

1 PETER 1:24–25

I recently learned of a fellow struggler's death by overdose. I'm ashamed to admit it, but my first thought was to question his salvation. *Christians do not die of drug overdoses, do they? My second thought? How dare I? Was he in any way worse than I am? Have I forgotten my own repeated failures? He knew Christ. He was born again, "not of perishable seed but of imperishable"* (1 Peter 1:23). He failed horribly, but even his failure couldn't rob him of that which does not decay.

The truth is, we all fail. Addicts probably don't fail any more often than others, it's just that when we do, it's usually unfortunately spectacular. If you and I were told we would die the next time we were prideful, had an evil thought, or yelled at our kids, how long would we last?

Still, it's not wrong to be saddened by how this man died. Let's not pretend otherwise—an addict's death by overdose is a painful culmination of a lifetime of destructive behaviors.

The reality, however, is that his struggle is my struggle . . . and his ultimate fate is my fate. I may not find death by the same route; but, as Peter promised, this flesh, like the grass, will fade and it's only the Word of God in me that stands forever. In the end it's not the manner of my death that matters, but whether or not I have Christ in me.

Though I feel sadness and even anger over this death, I do feel a certain joy at knowing that, for him, the struggle is over. Though his life was marred by a miserable battle with addiction, he's now free from the decay of this earthly body and is now made gloriously perfect in Christ.

Day 319

STUFF THAT MUST GO

So put away all malice and all deceit and
hypocrisy and envy and all slander.

1 PETER 2:1

When I was in fifth or sixth grade, I had a favorite shirt that I thought was pretty cool. It wasn't. I probably wore it three out of five days a week and when it finally disintegrated, it was long past time to retire it. I couldn't see it at the time, but I needed to take off that shirt long before I finally did.

Peter said that we have behaviors that, like that shirt, need to go. Daily we must make this choice to take off the old rags, and daily we must put on something new. This two-step process is the same that Jesus prescribed when He commanded that we leave behind the old to follow Him (Luke 9:23).

Though I am living in recovery from my drug addiction, I find that a hundred other flaws still exist. Peter said I must continually recognize this . . . and do something about it. If I don't choose to work on a flaw, I continue in it. If I do not choose to stop eating donuts, talking harshly to my wife, speaking evil of others, or looking at pornography, then I have already chosen to continue those things.

Though I may always live in the gravity of certain struggles, that doesn't mean I'm destined to continue in destructive behavior. Peter commanded that I must discover and eradicate these behaviors. I can indulge in my flaws, or I can use them to continually turn me to God. I may not be responsible for a predisposition to lust or using drugs, but only I am responsible for doing whatever it takes daily to take off the old and put on the new.

Day 320

I AM WHAT I EAT

> *Like newborn infants, long for the pure spiritual milk, that by it you may grow up into salvation—if indeed you have tasted that the Lord is good.*
>
> **1 PETER 2:2–3**

I once joked with a pregnant friend that she had it easy, as she had to carry the extra weight only for a few months—I had to carry it for years. She was too kind to say it, but I could see the look in her eyes. *You don't have to carry it. You have chosen to. You are what you eat, and you eat too much.*

The reality that struck me in that moment involved more than just my dietary choices. I am what I consume—in my belly and in my life. If I feed on a steady diet of whatever my flesh desires, I can't be surprised when I'm a creature of the flesh.

Peter says I must live on God as a baby lives on milk. I must consume Him daily, as my spiritual life depends on it. Just as an infant will die without milk, we experience destruction when we don't fill ourselves with God. When we feast on a steady diet of drugs, porn, pride, anger, bitterness, and self-obsession, we reap the consequences. We are what we eat—and when we consume destruction, we experience the weight of it.

All of our destruction can be traced back to *little* indulgences—things we choose, things we tolerate. It can be something that seems harmless, like watching television. We may not end up in jail from watching soap operas, but we must learn to ask a key question about all things: *Does this draw me closer to God—or closer to self?*

Daily we must feed on God instead of our own desires. We must read, pray, and meditate on His Word. If we want to leave behind the destruction of our flesh nature, we need to stop feeding our flesh nature. We need to consume the things of God as a baby consumes milk.

Day 321

WHAT AM I?

> But you are a chosen . . . people for his own possession, that
> you may proclaim the excellencies of him who called you
> out of darkness into his marvelous light. Once you were
> not a people, but now you are God's people; once you had
> not received mercy, but now you have received mercy.

1 PETER 2:9–10

In Alcoholics Anonymous, the alcoholic is encouraged to identify himself as an alcoholic. Many chafe at this, insisting that identifying oneself by a defect is self-defeating. *If you insist you are an alcoholic, you will drink.*

Conversely, many well-meaning Christians insist that, since we are born again into a new life, we must identify ourselves only by that new life. Therefore, I can't say that I still have addictions. Rather, I must identify myself by my new life. *My name is Scott and I am now made perfect.*

Insisting that I'm made perfect, though, is only a half-truth. In my spiritual rebirth, I've been made righteous before God. The other truth, however, is that I still live in the flesh—and I still struggle.

I'm profoundly grateful that God sees me as righteous in my spirit life. Still, I require mercy, as I still fail in my flesh life. Jesus commanded that I take up my cross daily (Luke 9:23) to crucify the old in me. If I were made perfect in my flesh, Jesus would not have commanded me to continually abandon it.

It's necessary to remain aware of our struggles so we can keep working on them. Ignoring the truth and insisting that we're perfect in our flesh life (as I am in my spirit life) isn't helpful. Ignoring that we have a flesh life doesn't make it go away, it just makes us more likely to fail. It's only by acknowledging both our flesh reality (we still struggle) and our spiritual reality (God has saved us) that we understand who we are.

Day 322

THE ESCALATOR WAR

> *Beloved, I urge you as sojourners and exiles to abstain from the passions of the flesh, which wage war against your soul.*
>
> **2 PETER 2:11**

We're caught in the middle of an ongoing war between our spirit lives and our flesh lives; and at any given time, we pursue one or the other. When we indulge our flesh lives, we cause destruction. When we follow God, we grow in the Spirit. The outcome of the entire war is predetermined. Through Jesus we are forgiven; and when our flesh finally surrenders, we'll know perfection. For now, though, we live in a perpetual state of conflict.

This ongoing war is like an escalator with the spirit life at the top and the flesh life at the bottom. As the escalator is naturally descending, I must continually and purposefully take steps toward the top. I'll never be perfect in this life, but I can and should know the peace and joy of walking in the Spirit.

Unfortunately, we often dwell at the bottom of the escalator, mired in our flesh lives. Many of us have found ourselves there. We know God, but we've pursued our own desires enough that we feel chained to the bottom where addiction to drugs, porn, pride, anger, bitterness, envy, malice, self-image, or food becomes overwhelming and paralyzing.

Why am I not freed from the gravity of this flesh? I asked God many times to deliver me forever from my flesh nature, but I heard no answer. In the spirit life, He has delivered me from the eternal consequences of my destruction, but it's only in death that I'll finally be free of the battle.

We can, however, be delivered daily when we pursue Christ daily. It's in doing whatever it takes to ascend the escalator that we walk in the Spirit, free from slavery to the flesh. The mistake we often make is this: In our success we get lazy, and in our apathy we naturally descend. Today, then, we must walk in the Spirit.

Day 323

LIVE FREE

*Live as people who are free, not using your freedom as
a cover-up for evil, but living as servants of God.*

1 PETER 2:16

In my defective thinking, because God has forgiven me, I'm now free to do whatever I want. Living in God's grace means no consequences, so I'm free to do as I please, right? *It is my God-given right to follow my heart.*

The irony, of course, is that it has been the pursuit of my own desires that has led me into the worst destruction of my life. I've thought that when I pursue self, I'm living free. The reality, however, is that when I pursue the desires of my flesh, I become enslaved to them.

The paradox of the Christian life is this: If we truly want to be free, we must surrender our will to God. The blessed news? God never enslaves. Our will and our flesh nature always enslave. God longs to set us free from ourselves so that we can know freedom in Him.

When I do whatever I want, I became enslaved to self and I can't follow God. Even so, I'll always follow *some* god. When I insist on pursuing my desires, I make a god of my own will. I make a terrible, destructive god.

One of Satan's greatest accomplishments is to convince me that I'm fine because *I'm not that bad.* Many of us have lived addicted to some small flesh defect, as it's just not that destructive. *I'm not hurting anyone when I look at pornography. I don't use drugs; I just get a little angry sometimes. I can stop anytime I want. It's not that big a deal.* It's often the subtle, insidious, seemingly insignificant things that enslave us.

If we want to live free, we must daily do whatever it takes to leave behind ourselves to pursue God. It's only in the paradox of abandoning self that we truly become free.

Day 324

TRUE BEAUTY

> *Do not let your adorning be external . . . but let your*
> *adorning be the hidden person of the heart with the*
> *imperishable beauty of a gentle and quiet spirit . . .*
>
> **1 PETER 3:3–4**

Today's passage is specifically written for women—wives in partic-ular—so it really has no application for me, right? *I'm never superficial. I fell in love with my wife only because of her quiet, gentle spirit. I didn't even notice how beautiful she was when I first met her. I'm never superficial.*

A friend once suggested that I look like a certain movie star. Before my ego could swell, someone else muttered, "Maybe 40 pounds ago." The fact that this memory has stayed with me reveals that I'm guilty of the super-ficiality that Peter warns of in today's passage. I'd like to think that I'm not shallow; but the truth is, when I met my wife, I was profoundly affected by her physical beauty. I still am.

I spend a fair amount of time exercising every week. I tell myself that it's because exercise helps with my mental health (it does) and that it's my meditation time (it is), but I know that a part of me just wants to look more like that movie star—without the 40 pounds.

It's not wrong to exercise, dress nice, or comb my hair . . . but it is destructive to derive my self-worth from others. This kind of affirmation can become an addiction in itself. There's a fine line between caring for God's temple and being enslaved to affirmation.

What would our condition be if we spent as much time on our knees as we did at the gym? What if we put as much effort into our spirit life as we do into our flesh life? We must continually acknowledge our tendency toward superficiality. Then we must invest in what truly matters.

Day 325

THE ANGRIEST MAN

Husbands, live with your wives in an understanding way, showing honor to the woman . . . so that your prayers may not be hindered.

1 PETER 3:7

I realized one morning that my shampoo was missing. For some reason, I was sure that my wife had moved it—and I wasn't happy. She denied moving it, but I knew it had to be her. I realize now how stupid this sounds, but I was angry. *Now I am going to have to use hers and smell like a girl.* I threw a fit. She then gently reminded me that I had used the guest shower the previous day and probably left my shampoo in there. *Sigh. I'm a jerk.*

How is it that I can be infinitely patient and kind at work . . . but then go home and be the hardest on the ones I love the most? Peter says it ought not be this way. I should not be the angriest, most difficult man my wife knows. I'm to treasure and honor her. Instead, she gets the brunt of my frustrations.

Peter says that how we act at home matters. He must have known men who acted one way in church and then another way at home. Many of us can be pleasant in public while miserable at home. The ones we love the most suffer the most.

Peter says that this behavior is spiritually destructive, actually hindering our prayers. As in the rest of life, if we indulge in our flesh nature, we sow seeds of destruction—and we reap the consequences. How I treat my spouse affects my relationship with God.

I find that when I'm frustrated and angry, it's almost always because I've turned my gaze to self—again. It's hard for me to be angry about shampoo when my eyes are focused on God. It's only then that I treat my wife the way I should. If I want to be the most loving person she knows, I must act like it.

Day 326

I AM OFFENDED

> *Do not repay evil for evil or reviling for reviling, but on the contrary, bless, for to this you were called, that you may obtain a blessing.*

1 PETER 3:9

I sometimes find myself in that hypercritical place where I feel it's my job to call out all evil in the world. *Everyone else is an idiot.* When confronted with the very real darkness in this world, I often start thinking and saying evil things myself.

It's not that I'm wrong to identify evil. My error is in my *response.* This is a lesson I have to learn over and over. *I can be completely right and still act very wrong.* Being on the right side of an issue doesn't guarantee that I will act right. Being right doesn't justify an evil response.

How do I return evil for evil? When someone irritates me at work, I say wicked things to my coworkers about him. When I see someone struggle in a way that I don't, I judge and condemn her. When I disagree with others, I get angry at them.

Our offense is usually a result of keeping our eyes on ourselves. *I am right, and I am offended. I have the right to say so.* We may even try to blame God. *This offends God, so I too am offended!* This is nothing but pride, evil in itself. When we fabricate evil in response to evil, we're not doing the will of God. He never asks us to sin for Him.

If, however, we bless instead of curse, Peter said we will obtain a blessing in our own lives. This doesn't mean that we can't identify evil. It means that we can't respond with evil. When offended, we must respond with kindness and love. *But that will only enable and encourage the evil!* It's true that our kindness may not change the evil, but we are responsible only for our own behavior. We want our right behavior to change the world . . . but often, our right behavior changes us.

Day 327

LIFE AND DEATH

Whoever desires to love life and see good days, . . . let him turn away from evil and do good. . . . For the eyes of the Lord are on the righteous. . . . But the face of the Lord is against those who do evil.

1 PETER 3:10–12

I've met many who, in their recovery from addiction, find forgiveness in Christ, only to find that the world is not as kind. They had been told that all was forgiven, only to find that judges, parole officers, and even spouses were not as merciful. I too have tended to think that, because I'm God's child, He has freed me from the laws of this world. The truth is, knowing God doesn't shield me from the consequences of my destructive actions. I reap what I sow.

Today's verse is not about a prosperity gospel. It is about the death and destruction that we cause in pursuit of our flesh nature. This is the broken marriages, wrecked relationships, destroyed trust, lost jobs, shame, guilt, and sleepless nights that come from our own evil. When we pursue the desires of our flesh, we sow the seeds of our own destruction.

We can be saved by faith and still struggle with an addiction to food. We can choose to crawl back into our destructive desires and live under the toxic influence of pornography, tobacco, pride, money, self-image, popularity, status, or success.

Or . . . we can *turn away from evil and do good.* In doing good, we don't grow earthly riches, but we do grow the life God desires for us. This wonderful life doesn't happen automatically, though. It's a daily battle.

When we turn from ourselves daily to pursue God, we show our love of life instead of our love of destruction. If we want to know the joy and peace of the life of God, we must choose that life.

Day 328
MY TRUTH HAMMER

Honor Christ the Lord as holy, always being prepared to make a defense to anyone who asks you for a reason for the hope that is in you; yet do it with gentleness and respect.

1 PETER 3:15

When on a high school mission trip to Mexico, I found myself trying to explain to random Mexicans that they were sinners. I was on a mission to tell the truth, so I got out my truth hammer. *You are going to hell. You need Jesus.* I don't know that I made much of an impact, even though I was swinging really hard.

Peter says that, as Christians, we must tell others of the hope that is within us. He says we need to tell this truth with love, in *gentleness and respect.* I've failed miserably at this. I've seen my faith as something I express in truth—or I've seen it as something I express in love . . . but I have a hard time doing both. It's one or the other. *You are terrible, would you like to accept Christ?* Or . . . *Here, let me love you, but I really don't want to talk about Jesus or hell.*

So how do I speak truth without abandoning love? How do I love without abandoning truth? I've found that sharing my faith in love is best done by telling my story to those who know their need. Call me lazy, but I don't spend much time trying to convince anyone of need. "Those who are well have no need of a physician, but those who are sick" (Matthew 9:12).

I go to those who know their need and I tell them of my need. I visit the local jail and drug treatment centers. There I don't have to spend time and effort convincing others of their need, as they are already quite aware. Then I can tell my story in love, which seems to be the key to opening the door to the gospel. For me, sharing my faith is just that—telling my story. *Jesus saved me from myself. He can save you from yourself.*

Day 329

JESUS—THE WORST SALESMAN

Since therefore Christ suffered in the flesh, arm yourselves with
the same way of thinking . . . so as to live for the rest of the time in
the flesh no longer for human passions but for the will of God.

1 PETER 4:1–2

We often try to convince people how easy it is to be a Christian. *Just say this prayer.* Jesus came along, however, and said, *"If anyone would come after me, let him deny himself and take up his cross daily and follow me"* (Luke 9:23). He insisted that if we want to live, we must first die. Jesus was a terrible salesman.

Likewise, Peter commanded that I must put my flesh nature through what Christ went through. Jesus' death was not only a sacrifice for my sin, but also an example. I must crucify my flesh nature to follow Him.

Who would want this? Only those who are desperate to leave the destruction of the old nature will find Christ's offering attractive. Those who recognize no need will find Jesus' plan ridiculous. For those of us who hate the decay of our flesh, though, His offering is a sweet salvation.

How does this work? The New Testament writers were insistent that we *crucify the flesh*, a phrase that may not mean much to us. Though the process may look different for all of us, we all must do whatever it takes— different actions for different issues—to crucify self and follow Christ.

Our willingness to commit to self-crucifixion is dependent on our perceived need for Christ. If we don't see our need, then we'll not likely be willing to do much to change. If, however, we're desperately sick of our own destruction, then we'll be willing to do whatever we must do to abandon self and follow Christ.

In whatever we do, we must remember that Christ is asking us to pursue Him above all. The death of my flesh nature is necessary to get there, but it's not the goal. We die to ourselves so we can live for Christ.

Day 330
NSFW

> *For the time that is past suffices for . . . living in sensuality, passions,*
> *drunkenness, orgies, drinking parties, and lawless idolatry.*
>
> **1 PETER 4:3**

Not Safe For Work—NSFW—is a warning for internet links that are highly sexual in content. I write what I know, and I know testosterone. Women, read on if you want, but consider yourself warned. This is for men and it may be uncomfortable.

On one of my first days in treatment, another addict asked if I engaged in sexual fantasies. As I turned to run, he quickly explained that God had convicted him—if he wanted sobriety, he had to give up his promiscuous lifestyle. This included pornography and fantasy. God wanted *all* of him, even his thoughts. He had learned this profound truth: All destructive behavior starts in the mind.

I alone am responsible for my mind's focus. When our faith is anemic, we must ask ourselves what is distracting us. We can't pursue God while fantasizing about destructive relationships. Pornography can be as spiritually destructive and addictive as any drug.

Viewing pornography or lusting after another woman is the spiritual equivalent of being unfaithful to my wife. The external consequences may not be the same, but I can't pursue Christ while indulging in lust.

How to change? That's a question each man will have to answer for himself. If you can't stop looking at porn on your computer, your computer must go—right along with any other electronic devices. *But I need my computer for work!* Go ahead. Keep it. And keep your porn addiction.

For me, I don't allow myself access; and I work hard at what I do—and don't—put in my mind. I avoid porn and I daily consume God's Word. Daily meditation on a Bible passage has completely revolutionized my thought life.

If we want to live in the Spirit, we must be willing to rid ourselves of everything that enslaves and distracts us.

Day 331

WHAT IF I AM GOD'S PLAN?

Above all, keep loving one another earnestly,
since love covers a multitude of sins.

1 PETER 4:8

I've never found God's plan to use people as his hands and feet here on earth to be a particularly good one. Frankly, the thought that He is relying on me . . . is terrifying. *God, I'm a mess. I'm not your guy. I just was in treatment not that long ago.*

Well, good. The guy I want you to talk to is an addict, and he's in jail.

Fine, I'll go.

Perhaps it would be a good plan if, when we came to know God, He made us all robots, incapable of defect or disobedience. God doesn't do this, though. The people I meet in church—including me—are still defective and still need Jesus as much as the guys I meet in jail. Though we're spiritually reborn, God doesn't make us perfect in this life.

He's done something better, though. He has filled us with His *love*. It was God's love that compelled Him to the cross, and it's that same love that flows through us, back to Him, and into those around us. When I choose to feed those who are hungry, clothe those who are naked, and visit those in jail, I share His love with those who need it most.

If you asked me what I would like to be known for, my pride would insist that I be known for my intelligence, writing ability, or being a good physician. When I keep my eyes on God, however, I want to be known only for His love.

As Christ's hands and feet, we certainly must strive for truth and right knowledge. However, Peter says that above all we must be known for our love. Without love, we're just clanging cymbals (1 Corinthians 13:1). We may be profoundly imperfect, but God doesn't require perfection. He requires obedience. When we share His love, we participate in His perfect plan.

Day 332

ASSETS AND LIABILITIES

As each has received a gift, use it to serve one another,
as good stewards of God's varied grace.

1 PETER 4:10–11

I think if I were reading my own writing for the first time, I would be struck—or annoyed—by how often I refer to my defects. Admittedly, I am a little passionate about understanding what most distracts me from God. It's possible, though, that I occasionally over-emphasize my flaws.

Sometimes I've been so sick of my failures that I've errantly thought that there's nothing salvageable in me. Before you get too teary-eyed at my low self-esteem, I must remind you that I'm as inconsistent as I am prideful. I can switch from utter humility to glaring pride in a heartbeat, especially if someone praises me. Still, at times, I'm tempted to think that there's nothing good in me.

This is, of course, ridiculous. We're not all flaw. Just as our physical flesh has both assets and liabilities, our flesh nature has the same. We all have unique personalities that make us special and beautiful to God.

Many of us dread following God, fearing that we'll lose ourselves in the process. We worry that God will reduce us to mindless, identical automatons. God doesn't want to destroy who we are. He simply wants to peel back the layers of dirt and grime so that our gifts can shine through. Then we become who we were always meant to be.

Just as we daily have the choice to pursue ourselves or God, we daily have the choice to pursue our own defects or our own gifts. If we want to know who we were meant to be, we must use our gifts to fulfill the purposes for which He created us.

Day 333

JESUS FREAK

Do not be surprised at the fiery trial when it comes upon you. . . . But rejoice. . . . If you are insulted for the name of Christ, you are blessed.

1 PETER 4:12–14

In treatment for chemical dependency, I told God that I would do anything to change. He promised that if I followed Him daily, I would never have to go back to treatment. I'm ashamed to admit it, but I told God that I didn't want to be a Jesus freak. *I have a reputation to maintain.* He asked me if I would rather be known as a drug addict. The choice was suddenly a little easier.

Why do we worry so much about what others think? Why are we concerned more with our own popularity, image, and appearance than we are with our faith? We say that God is the most important thing about us, but then we're ashamed to speak His name in public.

For me, this is just another manifestation of my pride. As much as I hate to admit it, I still derive some affirmation from others. I'd rather be popular than be a religious nut in others' eyes. My desire for affirmation distracts me from God more than I ever thought possible.

In today's passage, Peter said that if we are doing faith right, at some point we will take some heat for following Christ. We're going to be called Jesus freaks if we insist on talking about what He has done for us. Peter said that we shouldn't be surprised by this. Rather, we should embrace it. We must remain more focused on God's opinion than we are on man's opinion. If man mocks us for following God, then we should rejoice that we're doing something right.

We must daily work at abandoning our need for worldly affirmation, and we should be happy when the world sees us as freaks for Christ. We must keep our eyes on God and find our meaning and value only in Him.

Day 334

GOD WANTS ME TO MEDDLE

*But let none of you suffer as a murderer or a
thief or an evildoer or as a meddler.*

1 PETER 4:15

I'm fantastic at identifying those who inappropriately insert
themselves into a situation. When I see this it irritates me, as I know it's
just another defect, disguising itself as right behavior. When I recognize
it, I want to let the meddlers know how wrong they are. I'm the kid at the
dinner table who keeps his eyes open . . . just to make sure no one else
does. Apparently, I'm a meddler too.

Meddling is one of those defects that our faith seems to promote. It's
easy to use my *rightness* as grounds to indulge in my defective desire to
see the world run my way. *I know what is right, and you are wrong! I must
involve myself!* As Christians we may consider ourselves to be keepers of
the truth, and as such, we feel that it's our obligation to point out others'
wrongs. Couple this righteous conviction with a busybody personality,
and you get a perfect storm of meddling.

It's telling that Peter included meddlers in his list of sinners—alongside
thieves and murderers. Meddling seems to me to be a trivial behavior;
so why would Peter be so harsh with busybodies? I think it's because it
offends God when I use Him as an excuse for my destructive behavior.
When I meddle and insist that God wants me to, I blame my sin on Him.

As in all things, we must examine our desire to involve ourselves in
another's life. We must admit when our eyes aren't on God. The problem,
of course, is that we so easily lie to ourselves, insisting that we are God's
special meddlers.

God never asks us to sin for Him, though. When we truly keep our eyes
on God, we'll find it difficult to meddle.

Day 335

FAITH KILLER

Clothe yourselves, all of you, with humility toward one another,
for "God opposes the proud but gives grace to the humble."

1 PETER 5:5

I imagine that if you know me only from my writing, you may think me to be humble. I speak of my past addictive behavior freely, giving the impression of humility. If you bring up the mistakes I made just yesterday, however, I may react very differently. I embrace humility . . . as long as it refers to the distant past. *Look at how well I've recovered.* My pride can turn anything into a reason to focus on myself.

Pride is a faith killer. It's in my pride that I turn my back on God. Peter said that when I do this, I'm choosing hostility toward God. God hates my pride because it causes me to follow myself as a god. The one true God doesn't take it lightly when I usurp His throne.

When we tell God that we're going to do it our own way, we displace Him from His proper position, and we suffer the consequences. Open rebellion to Him isn't something we just walk away from, unscathed. Fire may not rain down from heaven, but there's always a cost when we oppose God.

Humility in all things is a prayer that I must whisper to myself over and over every day. It seems that, even though I desire to keep my eyes on God, my pride constantly seduces my gaze. When I encounter any conflict, my first reaction is to be irritated by how it affects my will—not God's. When tempted, my first instinct is to think of what I want—not what God wants. *I, me, my, mine.* It's easy to pass this off as normal; and in a sense it is, but that doesn't make it right.

If we don't want to live in a state of opposition to God, we must continually embrace humility, keeping our eyes off ourselves and on Him. Pride is a faith killer.

Day 336

REAL CHRISTIANS AREN'T ANXIOUS, RIGHT?

Humble yourselves, therefore, under the mighty hand of God . . .
casting all your anxieties on him, because he cares for you.

1 PETER 5:6–7

There are those who would use passages like today's to suggest that, as Christians, we should never be anxious. I will insist, however, that anxiety is just one of the many frustrations of the flesh nature from which we all suffer. Like our other flaws—though we do not choose it—anxiety causes us tremendous misery and can lead to self-destructive behavior.

Anxiety is a predisposition to an unhelpful way of thinking about—and interacting with—the world. Like any of our unhealthy appetites and flaws, we are not responsible for the personality trait, but we are absolutely responsible for the behavior that stems from it. We are not accountable for the hand we are dealt, but we are certainly responsible for how we play it.

We could, in our anxiety, find comfort in alcohol, which would compound our problems. Conversely, we could seek counseling, learning to deal constructively with our anxiety. Just as the diabetic may not be responsible for his disease, he can surely make decisions that either worsen or improve his condition.

Peter didn't say it was wrong to have anxiety. He simply insisted that we deal with it constructively, taking it to God, seeking His will. This, in fact, may be exactly why God allows us to struggle, so that we turn to Him in our need. Seen in this light, we can embrace our weaknesses, as they keep us dependent on God.

Christ, the Great Healer, insisted that to live the life we were made for, we must daily deny ourselves and follow Him (Luke 9:23). If we daily suffer from anxiety, then our daily job is to turn from it, giving it up to God.

It's not wrong to have a struggle. That's just life. Everyone has something. We are, however, responsible for how we respond to that *something*. We can experience peace in Christ as we daily practice giving our anxieties to Him.

Day 337

LIAR, LIAR

*Your adversary the devil prowls around like a
roaring lion, seeking someone to devour.*

1 PETER 5:8

I realized, when working on this passage, I give little thought to the Devil, as I feel that I'm very capable of my own destruction. My flesh nature is enough of a distraction from God that I don't give much thought to some outside force trying to deceive me. That he's not real—or he's not influencing me—may be exactly what the *Father of Lies* wants me to believe.

In Genesis, we find Satan's first recorded lie. In the garden, he convinced Eve that she could indulge in her appetite without consequence, even after God had warned Eve that she would die if she ate of the fruit. *"Enjoy. Eat. Your eyes will be opened. No consequences."*

This sounds so similar to the lies I've whispered to myself. *Just one time. It's not that bad. I deserve it. I'm not hurting anyone.*

I don't want to attribute too much of my failure to Satan. It's uncanny, however, that both Satan and my flesh nature whisper the same lies. I really don't know if it's important to differentiate where the lies originate, but I do know the Devil uses my past failures and struggles against me. I know that he appears beautiful and he appeals to my flesh nature. I know that both he and my flesh nature are opposed to *God in me*. Satan wants to destroy me, and my flesh nature appears to be his weapon of choice.

I must embrace rigorous honesty if I am to recognize the voice of deceit. *No one will know. I'll change tomorrow.* When that voice comes calling, I need to understand that it's the voice of destruction—and I must resist it with everything in me. I must deny self and turn to God. When I recognize and resist the lies of my flesh nature, I disarm Satan, the enemy of my soul.

Day 338

BLAMING GOD

> *His divine power has granted to us all things that pertain to life and godliness . . . so that through them you may become partakers of the divine nature, having escaped from the corruption that is in the world because of sinful desire.*

2 PETER 1:3–4

I once met a man who, in his self-inflicted destruction, decided that God had just not chosen him. He believed God's failure to remove his destructive desires was evidence that God had rejected him. He concluded that he should just continue on his path, blaming God all the while.

I still do it sometimes. I ask God to change me and when He doesn't, I object. *God, just take away my appetite for donuts.* He may tell me to learn self-control. *That's not what I want. I just want you to take away the desire.* It sounds ridiculous with donuts, but I think we all do this with pride, anxiety, depression, lust, anger, greed, and selfishness.

Peter said that God has given me the tools I need to live the godly life. I now have this choice to live either in the divine nature or in the corruption of myself. So, when I find myself in the misery of my own flesh, I have to ask, is this God's fault or mine?

In my worst destruction, I came to the obvious realization that, when faced with the possibility of whether it is God or me who is defective, the answer is never God. God never fails to pull His weight in this relationship. When faced with the likelihood of who is causing the misery of my flesh . . . I am always at fault.

God gives us this daily choice of pursuing Him—or pursuing ourselves. He has given us the tools we need to pursue Him. We already know how to pursue sorrow and death. When we find ourselves in the misery of our own flesh, we must leave it behind and follow Christ.

Day 339

JUST FOLLOW YOUR DREAMS

There will be false teachers among you, who will secretly bring in destructive heresies. . . . And many will follow their sensuality, and because of them the way of truth will be blasphemed.

2 PETER 2:1–2

Not long ago, when speaking with another about recovery from addiction, I was given this advice: *You just have to follow your dreams.* I responded that I was pretty sure following my dreams and desires was what got me into trouble in the first place.

Peter warned us in today's passage that what leads us astray from the truth isn't necessarily wrong doctrine, but wrong desires. He revealed the reality that we often don't follow the truth, but rather, we follow our preferences. This has been painfully true in my life. My greatest failures haven't been a result of ignorance, but of preference. I knew what was right. I just wanted what was wrong more.

It's not that all my dreams are bad. I aspire to do good things too. I write a blog. I enjoy helping others in recovery. The idea that all my dreams are to be followed blindly, however, is disastrous. My desires need a filter, and that filter has to be the truth. I must use the head to rein in the heart. If a desire leads to destruction, I shouldn't indulge in it. If it leads to life, then I can and should pursue it.

We can convince ourselves of anything when pursuing our own appetites. *How can my desires be wrong? God gave them to me. I only live once.* When our eyes are on God, though, we gain the wisdom to know which dreams lead to life and which will lead to death. When our eyes are on God, He guides and shapes our dreams to pursue life in Him.

Day 340
SLAVE TO MYSELF

They promise them freedom, but they themselves are slaves of corruption. For whatever overcomes a person, to that he is enslaved.

2 PETER 2:19

Most of us know from experience that when we choose to do something destructive, though it may initially irritate the conscience, it becomes easier the second time—and the third. Any inhibition we feel fades with repetition. Soon, the only struggle is when we try to stop. The freedom to pursue our appetites is a trap that leads to slavery.

When I indulge in pride, lust, food, drugs, anger, greed, and selfishness, those things overcome me and make me their slave. There are those who teach that once we come to Christ, we're *delivered* from the flesh nature and thus cannot be enslaved to it. *Christians cannot be addicted.*

If this were true, it would mean that we never have to worry about any destructive desires of the flesh simply because we're Christians. It would mean that we could never find ourselves addicted to any defect of the flesh. *If you do struggle and you are addicted to pornography, then you are not a Christian. You have an anger problem? Then you are not a Christian.* This, of course, is ridiculous. Peter debunked this kind of thinking by warning Christians that we must not become enslaved to the flesh.

The beautiful reality is that in our spirit lives, we are forgiven and seen as righteous by God. In this temporal reality, however, we have a daily choice to pursue our spirit life or our flesh life. The pursuit of our flesh life leads to destruction and slavery. The voluntary surrender of our freedom to pursue the spirit life paradoxically leads to true freedom from our flesh. In His divine wisdom, God desires that we choose to love and pursue Him, but He never enslaves us.

If we want to know authentic freedom from our flesh, we must daily deny self and follow God.

Day 341

ON DOGS, VOMIT, AND HUMAN NATURE

What the true proverb says has happened to them: "The dog returns to its own vomit."

2 PETER 2:22

Our dog gets carsick. If he doesn't throw up in the car, he throws up as soon as he gets out. Then, in a grotesque act, he tries to consume again that which his body has just expelled. As we are above such behavior, we look down on him in disgust. We would never do something so vile, right?

As repulsive as I see my dog's behavior, how revolting must God find my behavior when I repeatedly return to my own destructive ways? Peter says that I'm like my dog, returning to my own vomit, when I make the same mistakes over and over.

If this disgusts us, it should. It's revolting, but my dog is just obeying its animal instincts. We humans have been made in God's image and should know and act better. We descend to become like a dog, however, when we follow our flesh, refusing the Spirit that God has given us.

This would not be so painful if it pertained only to the past. I can look back at my addiction with distorted thinking. *I'm glad I'm not a sinner anymore.* This admonition from Peter, however, is applicable to those destructive behaviors that I still embrace today. When I follow my lust, pride, anger, jealously, selfishness, and greed, I'm still like my dog eating his own vomit. I must continually ask myself, *What destructive, repulsive behavior am I tolerating today?*

If we want to follow God, we must be willing to be honest with ourselves about our own offensive behavior, and we must be willing to abandon that behavior. We then must keep our eyes on Christ and follow Him.

Day 342

THE LONG GAME

> *The Lord is not slow to fulfill his promise as some count*
> *slowness, but is patient toward you, not wishing that any*
> *should perish, but that all should reach repentance.*
>
> **2 PETER 3:9**

I am not patient. I want what I want now. When I don't get my way, I can throw the adult equivalent of a tantrum. Those close to me know this is slightly less fun than when a three-year-old does it at the grocery store. I sometimes find myself doing this with God when He doesn't work on my timetable.

Peter insisted, however, that God's timing is not my timing. When I focus on myself and my own preferences, I expect God to work when and how I see fit. God plays a much longer game than I can see, though.

I must admit, when I indulge the most in my pride, I'll look on a man who's failing and wish destruction upon him. This person may be profoundly arrogant, condescending, difficult, angry, hurtful, self-obsessed, or addicted to some destructive behavior. Whatever it is, it bothers me, and I want God to intervene—immediately. It's at those times that I must remember how patient God has been with me. I've often been that person whom others wished God would smite.

At other times, my frustration is simply with myself. *God, why do I still struggle? Why have you not fixed me yet?* In those times, I must accept that God is still working on me and that I won't be free of my flesh nature until I am free of my flesh.

Since it's our need that keeps us dependent on God, we may embrace that need, continually allowing it to drive us to Him. Our job isn't to worry about God's schedule. Our job is to keep our eyes on Christ. We'll never obtain God's perspective, but when our gaze is on Him, we can at least surrender to His will—and His timing.

Day 343

DO I STILL NEED FORGIVENESS?

If we say we have no sin, we deceive ourselves, and the truth is not in us. If we confess our sins, he is faithful and just to forgive us our sins and to cleanse us from all unrighteousness.

1 JOHN 1:8–9

We all love the story of the one who used to sin but then came to Christ and sinned no more. We may not teach it on purpose, but we all have this idea in our heads that coming to Christ should end our sin problem. We know "if anyone is in Christ, he is a new creation" (2 Corinthians 5:17). We look at our lives, however, and we do not feel like new creations.

Why do I still fail? Am I forgiven for all time? Why must I still ask forgiveness? If I die before I repent, am I in trouble? I have wrestled with all of these questions, as I think many of us have. In my addiction, I became desperate for an answer.

When I came to know Christ, I was born again and made new in my spirit life. I was saved for all eternity, and if I sin tomorrow and then die, I am not lost. God, in His timelessness, sees me as eternally righteous and pure in my spirit life through Jesus' death on the cross.

In my flesh life, however, I'm still attracted to the destructive. I still fail. Does this failure separate me from God? Not in the sense that I lose my salvation . . . but I do injure my temporal relationship with Him, which is why I must continue to confess my sins when I do fail.

John insisted that, because we continue to sin, we must continue to repent. Though God has forgiven us once and for all, we must continue to ask for forgiveness, as we continue to sin.

We may love the story of the one who sins no more, but this isn't reality. We all continue to fail, but the beautiful message of the gospel is that God sees us as righteous and continues to forgive us.

Day 344

HYPOCRITE

> *Whoever says "I know him" but does not keep his commandments is a liar and the truth is not in him.*
>
> **1 JOHN 2:4**

My biggest failure in life has not been any one particular dark deed. My biggest failure in life has been knowing of God while failing to follow Him. I have been a hypocrite. I've proclaimed faith in God while my actions exposed my servitude to myself. To be honest, I still, at times, follow myself instead of God.

Don't be so hard on yourself, Scott. Show yourself some grace. This is the kind of thinking that tolerates destructive behavior, destroys relationships, ends marriages, and decimates faith. This abuse of grace is what led to my addiction.

John insists that my walk must match my talk. If I claim to know Christ but do not follow Him, I'm a liar and hypocrite. In my hypocrisy, I find faith simply to be *knowledge* of a thing. I know God exists, so I have faith, right? *I'm forgiven, so I can now do whatever I want.* Not so fast. John says this isn't faith. It's dishonesty, and with it I deceive myself.

There is, of course, a danger in clinging to deeds to prove my faith. This is a trap for many of us who harbor secret sins. *I don't drink, smoke, or chase women so I'm a good Christian.* Faith becomes defined by what I don't do . . . instead of being defined by following Christ. In the meanwhile, I can be tremendously prideful, condescending, hateful, and judgmental. This is still a pursuit of self that is cleverly disguised by a false faith.

John said we're liars if we claim to follow Christ but continue to follow ourselves. We must be continuously and rigorously introspective, asking if we are truly following Him. Faith is following Christ. If we say that we have faith, but we don't follow Him, we're just hypocrites. It's when we obey that we truly know Christ.

Day 345
STUFF GOD

Do not love the world or the things in the world. If anyone loves the world, the love of the Father is not in him. For all that is in the world—the desires of the flesh and the desires of the eyes and pride of life—is not from the Father but is from the world.

1 JOHN 2:15–16

Whenever I read this passage, I put myself in the shoes of the rich man whom Jesus asked to sell all his possessions (Matthew 19). He went away sad because even though he wanted God, he wanted his stuff more. His god was his stuff.

Jesus' point to the young man was the same as John's here. I can't love the stuff of the world and God equally. One or the other will rule in my life. The thing I won't give up is the thing that becomes my god. If that thing is money, stuff, desires of the flesh, or my pride, then *the love of the Father is not in me.*

So how do I know if I love stuff more than God? Jesus hasn't yet asked me to give away everything I own, so I can still tell myself that I would do it if He did.

For me, it's all about how I hold my things and how I use them. Do I use my job as an opportunity to love others? Or is my job just a paycheck so I can buy more stuff? Do I use my stuff for the kingdom . . . or do I just entertain myself with it?

Like everything else, I must continually work on this. Stuff has a way of growing on me. I daily must turn my gaze from *the desires of the eyes and pride of life.* I don't want stuff to be my god. I want God to be my God, so I will daily turn my gaze to Him. "The world is passing away along with its desires, but whoever does the will of God abides forever" (1 John 2:17).

Day 346

HIDING FROM GOD

> *Abide in him, so that when he appears we may have confidence*
> *and not shrink from him in shame at his coming.*

1 JOHN 2:28

In my drug addiction, I identified very well with Adam and Eve, who tried—in their guilt—to hide from God. In my self-reproach, I didn't want to hear His awful voice or look into His piercing eyes. His face was an excruciating mirror that reflected my shame. Like Adam and Eve, I hid, disgraced and naked—hoping that God couldn't find me.

Some will insist that, as I am eternally forgiven, I'm unable to injure my relationship with God. While I don't believe that I lose my relationship with Him when I fail I can absolutely distance myself from Him in my sin. As John pointed out in today's passage, I can abide—or not abide—in Him. When I choose to abide in Him, I find comfort in that relationship. When I follow myself, I fear and loathe His presence.

As miserable as it is to hide from God, there's a worse condition in which many of us have found ourselves. When we become numb to God's absence, we're truly in a desperate position. We can hide for so long that we simply become accustomed to separation from God.

We grow comfortable with our own lies, anesthetizing ourselves to the absence of God. *I'm not that bad. I sin only a little. I'm not hurting anyone.* We all have our own lies that we use to cover our shame, but like Adam and Eve's fig leaves, they don't address the problem. They only help us avoid it.

John insisted that the only solution to our condition is to abide in Christ. This means that we do whatever it takes to abandon our secret sins, spending as much time and energy pursuing Christ as we did pursuing those destructive desires. It's only in following God that we come to enjoy His presence instead of fearing it.

Day 347

WHEN I WANT TO CUT OUT PART OF MY BIBLE

> *No one who abides in him keeps on sinning. . . . Whoever*
> *makes a practice of sinning is of the devil . . . No one*
> *born of God makes a practice of sinning.*
>
> **1 JOHN 3:6, 8–9**

Since I began this book, I have dreaded the approach of today's passage. I've often wished I could just take my scissors to these verses. I sleep easily with grace and forgiveness, but today's passage is the bed of nails on which I find no comfort.

Who can withstand the crushing burden of today's passage, insisting they never struggle with any recurrent sin? What was John saying? Did he really mean that anyone who still sins is of the Devil?

When I examine this passage, it's necessary for me to look at what John wrote previously. He already said that we all sin (1 John 1:8); and when we sin, God forgives us (1 John 1:9, 2:1–2). With that, John couldn't have meant that a Christian cannot struggle.

It's important, however, not to minimize the gravity of John's words. John insisted that the life of Christ is completely incompatible with the life of the flesh. If my life is defined by habitual, recurrent sin, I am, by definition, not abiding in Christ.

When I was living enslaved to pills, I was right to read these words and fear. My behavior wasn't compatible with abiding in Christ. Did that mean I had lost my status as God's child? Looking back, I don't think so . . . but at the time I was right to be terrified. Dread is the appropriate response to this passage while one is enslaved to sin.

When we come to a terrifying passage, we must never take the scissors to the passage—but to our own behavior instead. What deeds and thoughts do we tolerate in ourselves that are incompatible with abiding in Christ? We must ruthlessly cut out whatever distracts us from following Him.

Day 348

VOICES IN MY HEAD

Beloved, do not believe every spirit, but test the
spirits to see whether they are from God.

1 JOHN 4:1

As I was meditating on this passage, I wrestled with distracting thoughts of discontent. Incidentally, I was also wrestling with working unusually long hours, which leads to resentment of my job. As I was attempting to meditate, my resentment kept interrupting my thoughts.

What did John mean about testing every spirit? There I was, wrestling with distracting thoughts of resentment, not understanding that this passage is all about filtering out distracting voices.

When I find myself anxious, agitated, or distracted, I must test the voices I've been allowing to speak into my mind. I alone am the gatekeeper of my mind. I may not be able to prevent the arrival of some thoughts, but I'm the only one who can test and assassinate evil thoughts. Only I can decide what I allow in my brain.

When a thought enters my mind, I must ask a question: *Does this thing spur me on to Christ, or does it distract me from Christ?* I tend to think of my job as a distraction; but with discipline, I find that I can do my job while keeping my mind on God. In fact, it's when I keep eyes on God that I'm able to use my occupation for His will.

There are voices, though, that produce thoughts and behaviors that are completely incompatible with pursuing Christ. These are not *of Jesus*, but rather are *of the world*. I can't claim naivete. I know what motivates me toward destruction and what motivates me toward Christ.

We must constantly test those voices we allow into our minds. Sometimes we must shut off the TV, close the computer, open the Bible, go for a run, meditate, talk to a friend, or just talk to God. It's our responsibility to test the voices to which we listen.

Day 349

TWO-FACED GOD

| *God is love.* |

1 JOHN 4:16

I tend to think in black and white. It's my first impulse to embrace a simple view of everything. When I read that *God is love*, I run with it. This is a concrete statement that I can cling to. *God is love, end of story.* I tend to reduce God to one attribute that I like and comprehend.

Many of my errors in understanding God have been a product of this narrow viewpoint. When I read today's passage, I thought of God as all love, grace, and mercy. I embraced His forgiveness, and I used this perspective of God as a license to live however I wanted. *Love means no consequences, right?* This view of God is, of course, as unbalanced as it is blind to His holiness, justice, and discipline.

In other passages, I read, "You shall be holy, for I am holy" (1 Peter 1:16). This verse seemed (to me) to be at odds with the "God is love" passage. Could God be less soft and fuzzy than I have thought? I read about God striking Ananias and Sapphira dead for their deceit (Acts 5), and I felt a cold sweat. Suddenly, I was fearful of God. *I thought I was forgiven.*

God is a perfect balance of both love and holiness. He's not too much one or the other. He always knows exactly how to deal with me in my destructive pursuits. He looks into the depths of my being. *Scott, I love you and I forgive you for all that you have done. Right now, though, you must turn from your path of destruction. You are my child. Start acting like it.*

This may not be what I want to hear. I may *want* to hear that *God is love*. What God gives me, though, is always what I *need*. I need to hear that He loves me and also expects that I follow Him. God is love . . . and holiness. It's in seeing both faces of God that I begin to know Him.

Day 350

FEARLESS

> *There is no fear in love, but perfect love casts out fear. For fear has to do with punishment, and whoever fears has not been perfected in love.*

1 JOHN 4:18

In my addiction, I lived in constant fear. Fear of daylight. Fear of discovery. I lost hours of sleep to the terror of the inevitable consequences. I was embracing destruction, and thus, I couldn't look at God. I knew the road back to God, but it was too painful and I was too cowardly to face it. So, I lived in constant fear.

John said in today's passage that God's perfect love casts out fear. It's only in knowing God's perfect love that I stop fearing consequences. Some will rightly point out that God loved me just as much in my addiction as He does today. The difference is in my disposition toward Him. When I walk in the Spirit, following Him, I don't earn more love . . . but I come to truly understand His love for me. When I walk in the flesh, though, I distance myself from God and I fail to experience His love.

God's love gives me confidence that the most important thing in the universe cannot be taken from me. This life can bring horrific trials, but God's love gives me the assurance that no matter what happens, in the end I still have God. Nothing can separate me from His love (Romans 8:39).

If I find myself living in fear, I must do whatever it takes to leave behind my destructive pursuits and draw near to my Father. I must abandon myself to follow God.

I sleep like a baby now—not because I live perfectly, but because I no longer live in constant fear of my own self-destruction. I know the peace and love of God because I'm making a genuine effort to pursue Him daily. I now experience God's love, knowing that though this world will bring trials, nothing can separate me from Him. In His love, I can be fearless.

Day 351

MORE THAN A FEELING

For this is the love of God, that we keep his commandments.

1 JOHN 5:3

When I claim with my words to follow God, but then fail to follow through with my behavior, I am a hypocrite. My hypocrisy is often most apparent to me in church worship. In church, I enjoy the music, feel the emotion, say the words . . . and can leave it at that. In the moment, I can feel that I love God without ever changing my behavior.

John insisted that love isn't just a feeling, though. It's a way of life. If I say I love my wife, then certain behaviors are expected of me. If I live in a manner that's inconsistent with being in love with her, then it will be apparent to all that my love is false. It doesn't matter what emotion I feel. If my behavior does not align with my words, then my words are hollow.

Unfortunately, I've often done this with God.

At one point, this discrepancy stemmed from the fact that I had not yet allowed God to do anything for me. If you had asked me several years ago what God had done for me, I would simply have told you that He had saved me from hell. He may have done such a thing, but still, I didn't have a vibrant relationship with Him. Though I felt some emotional attachment, I really didn't love God, as I really hadn't yet allowed Him to transform me.

Though I'm not thankful for the destruction I caused in my addiction, I've become very thankful for the work God did through it. Because He saved me from myself, I now have a vibrant, tangible relationship with Him. I still fail, but I daily turn to Him to save me from myself.

In our love for God, we must abandon ourselves to follow Him. If we simply have a feeling for God, but it never leads to action or change—then we don't truly have love. We just have empty words.

Day 352

THE BROKEN WORLD AND MY RED PEN

| *For everyone who has been born of God overcomes the world.* |

1 JOHN 5:4

I once lost my red pen while grading tests for a college class I was teaching. I had it one second but the next, it was gone. My computer had died earlier in the week. I had more stuff to do than I had time to do it—and then I lost my pen. I'm ashamed to admit it now, but I threw a little tantrum, blaming God—as He is obviously sovereign over my red pen. *Seriously God, first my computer and now my pen?*

A few hours later, I ran into a friend whose family had just lost a loved one in a horrible accident. I had two thoughts simultaneously: I am a terminal whiner, and the world doesn't make any sense. I complain and carry on at the smallest inconvenience, while others endure unspeakable pain. The world is broken, and I don't understand it.

John said that the only way the world makes sense is if we take the eternal view that anyone who is born of God is eternally invincible. We all eventually leave this world, but like John, we can have the view that in a thousand years, the sorrows of this life will mean little. The world cannot touch our ultimate reality, no matter what it may do to our temporary existence.

I find comfort in the eternal perspective, but eternity still seems far away. Jesus said, however, that eternal life is to know God (John 17:3). Eternal life is not some far-off promise. God saves me from myself in this reality. If I'm sick of the wreck of myself, then God provides me with the only answer to my deepest needs.

It's only in God that I truly overcome the brokenness of this life. God in me is the only way I get to the point where the world can do nothing to me. From lost pens to lost loved ones, this world is broken. In God, though, I can have eternal life now.

Day 353

PRAYER AND MY RED PEN

> *If we ask anything according to his will he hears us. . . . We know that we have the requests that we have asked of him.*
>
> **1 JOHN 5:14–15**

As I was looking for my red pen (again) recently, I found myself contemplating today's passage and prayer. I don't generally pray to find pens. Should I? I tried praying but didn't find it. Why not?

John said that motive is important in prayer. Honestly, most of my prayers are about myself and my will. John said, however, that it's only when I ask in God's will that He answers. This seems to be another way of saying that God is going to do what God wants to do—whether or not I ask for it. So . . . why pray?

I found the answer to that question in my most desperate prayer. When life fell apart in my addiction, I begged God for protection from consequences. *Get me out of this, God.*

This is the kind of self-serving prayer to which God turns a deaf ear. When I finally went to treatment, I stopped praying for God to fix my situation and I started asking Him to fix me instead. He started answering. From my perspective, my prayer absolutely had an effect on how God worked in my life.

Is it selfish or wrong to pray to find my red pen? No. I can and should take my desires to God. I must always seek His will, though. Through prayer, I become more aligned with that will. Still, there are many examples in the Bible where God appears to change plans in response to prayer.

John said *pray*. He said *ask of God*. If what I ask is in line with what God wants, He'll bring it to pass. In the context of my desperate prayer to fix myself, God started working with me when I prayed for His will. That is the hardest prayer—that God's will be done. It is, of course, always the right prayer. I eventually found my pen.

Day 354

CANDY CIGARETTES

| *Beloved, do not imitate evil but imitate good.* |
3 JOHN 1:11

When I was a child, my father and I were downtown one day when I talked him into buying me candy cigarettes. Being a father now myself, I imagine that he thought it would be amusing to see what Mom would say. She was not amused when she came home to find me puffing sugar-smoke clouds. I thought it was grand, though. It felt good to be bad.

Why is it that I desire destructive things? Why do I want donuts instead of broccoli, the couch instead of the gym, and the flesh instead of the Spirit? Why do I crave instant gratification when I know I'll pay for it later? It doesn't need to be more complicated than this: It's simply the nature of my flesh. Since the fall, humans have had an appetite for the forbidden fruit. I'm no different. I have a voracious appetite for the destructive.

The problem is that I pay now—or I pay later. Anyone who has worked hard for anything will attest to the reality that pursuing good requires hard work up front. With instant gratification, however, the price is paid later. The darker and greater the pleasure, the greater and more destructive the price. I can lie to myself, insisting that I can engage in drugs, pornography, greed, gluttony, pride, anger, and bitterness—without paying any price . . . but I won't escape forever. I'll eventually pay.

John said we don't have to live this way. Because of Christ, we're not base creatures of instinct, destined to wallow in our evil appetites. We are free, daily, to choose to do good. It's the harder choice, but it's always the right one. If we're tired of our destruction, then we must choose good. If we want to reap life instead of decay, then we must pursue God instead of the pleasure found in being bad.

Day 355

A WASTED LIFE

These are . . . waterless clouds, swept along by winds; fruitless trees in late autumn, twice dead, uprooted; wild waves of the sea, casting up the foam of their own shame; wandering stars, for whom the gloom of utter darkness has been reserved forever.

JUDE 1:12–13

I may be taking some liberty with today's passage, but when I read it, it speaks to me of a squandered life. I have lived as the waterless clouds, being useless to God, living only for self. I can identify with the barren trees. Even if I live to be 80, I'm now past half of my time on this earth. What have I lived for, if not myself?

I don't want to waste the short years of my life. I long to be able to look back at the end and see a life that was about something other than myself. Living for myself has led to misery. Now that God has graciously allowed me to rebuild my life, I must live for Him.

I sometimes think that I must leave my job and go to some far-off land to live the fruitful life. Then I see those in need around me and realize that I don't need to go anywhere. Every day I meet those who are hurting—right here. Every day, I have the opportunity to help those in need. I don't need to change my geography; I need to change my behavior. I must share the love God has shown me with those He has put into my life.

I am occasionally asked where I find the time to write every day. When asked, I want to point to the wandering years behind me. My urgency is born out of those idle years. If I want my life to be about something important, I must be purposeful about it.

A wasted life is a tragedy. God, however, can turn our tragedies into fruitful lives—when we give those tragedies to Him. That's the beautiful message we need to share with those He has put into our lives.

Day 356

LOOK AT ME!

These are grumblers, malcontents, following their own sinful desires; they are loud-mouthed boasters, showing favoritism to gain advantage.

JUDE 1:16

When Jude speaks of the grumbling malcontent, focused on self, I know exactly whom he is talking about. *I know someone who needs to read this. He is so blind to his own narcissism that he actually finds himself humble. Perhaps I should inform him of his failure.*

In my irritation at his arrogance, I imagine putting this person in his place. I want to see tears, groveling, and humiliation. *I demand misery! This passage is about you, and I'm going to show you how awful you truly are.*

I eventually remember that my meditation time is rarely supposed to be about someone else. I usually have enough of my own issues to deal with that I need not concern myself with others.

To be honest, I can see that my frustration with those obsessed with themselves is born out of my obsession with myself. It's my own pride that bleeds when I see the pride in others. When I'm humble, I don't bear the burden of another's pride. When my eyes are on myself, I find the failures of others to be quite irritating. If I want to follow God, I must keep my eyes on Him, not on those around me.

This doesn't mean it's wrong to recognize destructive behavior in others. It just means that I don't give someone else the power to make me miserable. It's only in humility that I'm able to respond properly to the flaws of others.

When we do turn our attention to our neighbors, it should be to show them the love that God has shown us. It may well be that in love we must address a neighbor's destructive behavior, but it's only in keeping our eyes off of our own pride that we can do so appropriately.

Day 357

GOD IS GOD

Fear not, I am the first and the last, and the living one. I died, and behold I am alive forevermore, and I have the keys of Death and Hades.

REVELATION 1:17–18

I occasionally encounter the atheistic argument that if God exists, we should be able to study Him. *If God exists and if He answers prayer, we should be able to measure the effect of prayer. If God doesn't answer a test prayer, then He's not real.*

Jesus dispelled this stunted view of God by explaining that He dwells in a reality beyond time and space. He is the first . . . and the last. He's beyond the known universe, and, as such, He isn't subject to its laws that we could measure Him on our scales.

Though I know it's futile to try to measure God, I often expect Him to conform to my version of reality, insisting that He behave in a manner that fits my sense of reasoning. *I cannot believe in a God who would allow this. I will accept God only if He makes sense to me.*

As soon as I design my own god, though, I no longer have God. I have a false idol. I can know Him, but to pretend that I can contain God within the confines of my own logic is ludicrous. I know this to be true, but still, I often do this. *If you really are God, you will not allow these horrible things to happen.*

God is not subject to our desires, though, and He's not required to satisfy our sense of justice. We don't dictate terms to Him, and we don't determine what's right and wrong. God is God, and if we want to begin to know Him, we must accept—no matter the paradox—that He is beyond what we can fully comprehend. He will, of course, be God whether we allow it or not. The important thing is whether or not we'll truly come to know Him.

Day 358

LIVING ON PURPOSE

> *You have abandoned the love you had at first. Remember therefore*
> *from where you have fallen; repent, and do the works you did at first.*
>
> **REVELATION 2:4–5**

Have you ever looked at your life and wondered, "How did I get here?" I'm not speaking of the events of life over which we have no control. I'm talking about looking back at the choices you've made. *That is not me. That's not what my life is supposed to be about.*

It's to this life that Jesus says, *"Remember your first love. Remember who you're supposed to be."* Life has a way of redirecting our energies away from what we know to be most important. We cannot just stop living our normal lives to follow God, so we allow everyday life to suffocate our pursuit of Him.

Jesus, however, said that I can learn to live with my eyes on God. Like Peter walking on the water, I can choose to keep my eyes on Christ—or I can be overwhelmed by the wind and waves of the world.

When I walk through life with my eyes on God, everything is in its proper place. It's when I put something or someone in front of God that everything is askew. When I pursue my own desires above all else, disaster ensues.

Even good things can become something they're not meant to be if I don't keep my gaze on God. When I ask people to fill my deepest needs, I put a burden on them that they can't carry. It's only when I'm in right relation with God that I can love others as I am meant to love them.

If we want the life we were made to have, we must purposefully pursue it. The Spirit-filled life doesn't happen automatically. Daily, we must choose to do what it takes to point our lives at God above all else. If we look at our lives and wish for change, we must choose to live differently.

Day 359

LUKEWARM

> *You are neither cold nor hot. Would that you were either*
> *cold or hot! So, because you are lukewarm, and neither*
> *hot nor cold, I will spit you out of my mouth.*
>
> **REVELATION 3:15–16**

I once had the audacity to tell God that, though I wanted him in my life, I didn't want to get too radical. I preferred people to think of me as a competent doctor, loving husband, and good father who happened to be a Christian—not a religious nut. At the time of that statement, I was sitting in treatment for chemical dependency. I was known as an addict.

We often want God in our lives without getting too carried away with Him. We want God *and* a normal life. We want God *and* world, God *and* self, God *and* politics. God doesn't want to be just another merit badge on our chests, though. If our faith in God is worth anything, it's worth everything.

The most dishonest thing I can do is to pursue myself while trying to pursue God. I desire the best of both worlds. I want to pursue the desires of my flesh all week . . . and then give an hour to God on Sunday.

To this type of inconsistency, Jesus takes offense. *"I wish that you were either hot or cold! Make a choice. At least the one who pursues himself is honest. You cannot chase both me and yourself."*

What's my life about? Am I living free from drugs, only to pursue some other defect? Am I willing to do what it takes to abandon all of myself to follow God? I don't want to live the wandering, lukewarm life, and I don't want to pursue my flesh to destruction anymore.

If we truly want life and if we truly want to know God, we must follow Him above all. This isn't a hobby or a part-time job. We receive in measure with our seeking, and if we only sort-of want God, we'll never really find Him. God doesn't want part of us. He wants all of us.

Day 360

THE DANGER OF SUCCESS

> *You say, I am rich, I have prospered, and I need nothing, not realizing that you are wretched, pitiable, poor, blind, and naked.*

REVELATION 3:17

When in life have you pursued God with the most intensity? Was it during good times or bad? I have no doubt that I've pursued God with the most passion when my life was the most chaotic. Success has never motivated me like disaster has. It has been in my desperate need that I've pursued God most desperately.

The truth is, I'm always in need. I just get distracted by success. Prosperity doesn't alleviate my need for God. It just blinds me to it. I always need God.

The *poor in spirit are blessed* because they see their own poverty and their need for God. The difference between apparently successful people and those whose life is a disaster isn't how much they *need* God, it's in how much they *see* their need.

It's not necessary to seek out a new life disaster to find God. My need is as far away as my honesty about my continued defects. No one likes to be in constant need, but as long as I'm in this flesh, I'll have a continual supply of need. With honesty and humility, I can use my flaws to keep me focused on God. When I see my defect as that which drives me to my knees before Him, I can embrace it and be thankful for it. As it turns out, I need my need.

I spend very little time trying to convince others of their flaws. If a man doesn't see a need for God, then he just will not seek Him. I'm not going to try to convince him otherwise. I'll share God's love and healing with those who are desperate for it, though. To do so, I must remain continually aware of my own shortcomings and use them to keep me clinging to God.

Day 361

DOES GOD SPANK?

Those whom I love, I reprove and discipline.

REVELATION 3:19

I prefer to think of God as a kind, grandfatherly figure who would never discipline me. Being forgiven, I like to imagine that the strings between my behavior and the ensuing consequences have been forever severed.

In today's passage, Jesus said otherwise, though. It seems that it's precisely because God loves me that He allows me to suffer the consequences of my destructive behavior. Paul promised that when I sow the seed of my fleshly desires, I will eventually reap a crop of corruption (Galatians 6:7–8). It's an unavoidable principle that, when I pursue my selfish desires, I find some misery.

It's often only in my misery that I become willing to change. When I'm comfortable, I feel no need to undergo the discomfort of transformation. As change is rarely easy, I usually refuse to go through it until the pain becomes too severe.

In my addiction, I acted like a child and required a giant time-out. I got it. In treatment, I had time to think about what I had done. I had behaved like a child and deserved to be treated like one.

I would love to say that I learned my lesson and have followed God perfectly ever since. Like a child, though, I quickly forgot. When life returned to normal, I became distracted by my selfish desires, and once again I pursued myself. Then, I found pain and repeated the cycle of discipline and repentance. Eventually things got back to what I thought was normal.

I don't want normal or natural though. I want supernatural. I want God—in good times and in bad. I want to follow Him because I know my need for Him. I don't want to follow only in times of trial and discipline. Daily, I must choose to deny self and follow Him, not just because He disciplines me, but because He loves me, and I love Him.

Day 362

THE SEEKING GOD

> *Behold, I stand at the door and knock. If anyone*
> *hears my voice and opens the door, I will come in*
> *to him and eat with him, and he with me.*

REVELATION 3:20

Here, in the Bible's final book, Jesus aptly summed up its message. The Creator of all constantly seeks to establish a right relationship with us. From beginning to end, the Bible is a record of God's purpose toward mankind. He made us to live in communion with Him, but He allows us to open the door or leave it closed.

The book of Hosea chronicles the misadventures of the prophet of the same name, who was commanded by God to marry a prostitute. Hosea married the prostitute, only to watch her repeatedly return to destruction. She ended up back in prostitution, at which point God commanded Hosea to buy her back—again.

The point of the painful story is that God, like Hosea, continues to pursue and love us despite our wandering, toxic behavior. God, however, doesn't turn His back on us, even when we turn our backs on Him. He continues to seek and pursue.

God is not needy, groveling, or pathetic. However, He is love, and He desires that we love Him back. He has gone to tremendous work to reach us, and He longs for us to respond. We were made to love God with all our hearts, souls, and minds (Matthew 22:37).

Our only right response to God's seeking is to open the door, allowing Him to invade every aspect of our lives. We may think we've done this once, but if we don't continually respond to God, we automatically close the door, excluding Him from those parts of our lives that we wish to keep to ourselves. If we want to live in right relationship to God, we must daily open our lives to Him.

Day 363

OTHERWORLDLY

And I looked, and behold, a pale horse! And its rider's name was Death, and Hades followed him.

REVELATION 6:8

Revelation reads to me like a hallucination. Most of it is in metaphoric or visionary language that I struggle to understand. John's description of the future reads to me as otherworldly.

This difficulty in understanding should not, however, discourage me from trying to develop my spiritual senses. The Bible teaches that we are spiritual creatures and, as such, can feel and know the spiritual realm.

We're familiar with the natural flesh life, but we also have a spirit life gifted with supernatural senses, which we can grow and develop. We've all likely felt this spiritual sense tugging us heavenward when looking at the stars or staring at the ocean. We've all known the wonder in contemplating the vastness of time and space, sensing something greater.

It's inherent in our spiritual life to long for God. We were made to walk hand-in-hand with Him, and though it may have been suppressed by long years of following self, we all have the capacity to know God. He has gone to great lengths to reveal Himself in a tangible relationship in which we can know Him—as real as anything else in this world.

If we want to know God, though, we must put purposeful effort into developing our spiritual senses. We were made for God, and we are incomplete without Him. When we feel hollow and are hungry for a food that doesn't exist, it's only in God that we find our true satisfaction.

So I meet God, in the early quietness of the day, to talk and listen to Him. I meet Him in the silver moonlight of a late-night run. When I work at it, I can learn to see Him, feel Him and know Him everywhere. Through practice, the spiritual can become real—here and now. So, though I sometimes find Revelation confusing, if it inspires the otherworldly in me, it is not wasted effort.

Day 364
ONE DAY . . .

> *He will wipe away every tear from their eyes, and death shall be no more, neither shall there be mourning, nor crying, nor pain anymore.*
>
> **REVELATION 21:4**

Have you ever longed for the relief that will come when every misery of this life is over? I'm not speaking of depression or suicide. I'm referring to the fact that life in this flesh is inherently painful. From the time we are born, our bodies have already started down the path to the grave. We are born to die.

In today's passage, God also promised that one day every tear will be wiped away—and that death and pain shall be no more. We carry death in our flesh life, but in our spirit life, we carry eternal life. One day all pains will be healed, and all wrongs will be righted.

Though I don't love my defects, I don't wish this life away. I may dislike my addiction, but without my failures I would never have come to know my God as I do. As it turns out, I need my imperfections, because they drive me to God daily. Without my flaws, I would likely remain ignorant of my spirit life, missing out on knowing God now.

Still, I do at times long for the day when I'm free from this flesh. On that day . . . I'll finally know the perfection for which God made me. I'll walk hand-in-hand with Him in the garden, and all will be as it should. I'm in no hurry to die, but I do look forward to that day.

Though we await that day, our lives in this world are not devoid of beauty and joy. In our spirit life, we can know beauty, love, laughter, and joy. One day, all the pain of this world will be erased, and all of those joys and triumphs will be made perfect. One day, *He will wipe away every tear from our eyes, and death shall be no more.*

Day 365

THE DAY OF RECKONING

*Behold, I am coming soon, bringing my recompense with me,
to repay each one for what he has done. I am the Alpha and
the Omega, the first and the last, the beginning and the end.*

REVELATION 22:12–13

Shortly before my father-in-law's death, my brother-in-law asked him if his life had gone by quickly. The answer, relayed by my brother-in-law at the funeral, brought tears to my eyes. He replied simply, "I blinked—and it was over." Time passes . . . and the end comes for us all. We will all face our own day of reckoning.

Jesus, in today's passage, reminds us that just as there was a beginning, there will be an end. He is the Alpha and Omega, and He is the only one before whom we will one day stand.

On that day, what will be the verdict of my life? I know that I'm forgiven and that my eternal destination is heaven. Still, the question I want to be able to answer without shame is, "What was my life about?" Will I look back at a life of addiction, selfishness, pride, resentments, and greed?

Am I destined to struggle continually? I'll always feel the gravity of the flesh, but I'm not doomed to obey its corrupt desires. Paul insisted upon this when he wrestled with the horror of his own behavior. "Wretched man that I am! Who will deliver me from this body of death?" (Romans 7:24). Thankfully, he immediately answered in verse 25: "Jesus Christ our Lord."

Daily we must continue to do whatever it takes to abandon self and follow Christ. This requires effort—and often discomfort. Some behaviors must be removed . . . painfully. It's not always easy, but it's always worth it. In daily following God, we can know that on the day of reckoning, we won't look back on our lives with regret.

NOTES